T0076043

Pro Apache Ant

■ ■ ■

Matthew Moodie

Apress®

Pro Apache Ant

ISBN (pbk): 1-59059-559-9

Printed and bound in the United States of America 9 8 7 6 5 4 3 2 1

Lead Editor: Steve Anglin
Technical Reviewer: Carsten Ziegeler
Editorial Board: Steve Anglin, Dan Appleman, Ewan Buckingham, Gary Cornell, Tony Davis, Jason Gilmore, Jonathan Hassell, Chris Mills, Dominic Shakeshaft, Jim Sumser
Project Manager: Beth Christmas
Copy Edit Manager: Nicole LeClerc
Copy Editor: Kim Wimpsett
Assistant Production Director: Kari Brooks-Copony
Production Editor: Laura Cheu
Compositor: Susan Glinert
Proofreader: Kim Burton
Indexer: Carol Burbo
Artist: Kinetic Publishing Services, LLC
Cover Designer: Kurt Krames
Manufacturing Director: Tom Debolski

Distributed to the book trade worldwide by Springer-Verlag New York, Inc., 233 Spring Street, 6th Floor, New York, NY 10013. Phone 1-800-SPRINGER, fax 201-348-4505, e-mail orders-ny@springer-sbm.com, or visit http://www.springeronline.com.

For information on translations, please contact Apress directly at 2560 Ninth Street, Suite 219, Berkeley, CA 94710. Phone 510-549-5930, fax 510-549-5939, e-mail info@apress.com, or visit http://www.apress.com.

The source code for this book is available to readers at http://www.apress.com in the Source Code section.

To Laura

Contents at a Glance

Contents

About the Author

MATTHEW MOODIE is a native of southwest Scotland and is a graduate of the University of Edinburgh, where he obtained a master's degree in linguistics and artificial intelligence.

Matthew enjoys a life of fun in Glasgow, Scotland. He is a keen novice gardener with a house full of plants.

About the Technical Reviewer

CARSTEN ZIEGELER is a member of the Apache Software Foundation and is involved in various open-source communities such as Cocoon, Excalibur, Portals, Ant, and Maven. In paid life, Carsten is the chief architect of the Open Source Group at S&N AG in Paderborn, Germany. The focus is on middleware functionality such as web frameworks, component and service-based architectures, and portal solutions and technologies. Carsten is a well-known speaker at open-source conferences such as ApacheCon.

Acknowledgments

I would like to thank Laura for her love, friendship and cakes.

Love to Mum, Valla, Alexandra, Harcus, Angus, Uncle Andrew, Granny, Grandpa and Howard. A great big thank you to Andrew, Brian, Katy, Lindsey, Mad, Paul, Sally and Disco Robot Craig for more good times. Life would be pretty grey without you all.

Thanks to Billy, Dave, Pete, Broon, Stuart and Mark for your friendship over all these years. It's been 20 years, give or take, and it's been great.

CHAPTER 1

Introducing Ant

In this first chapter, I will give you an overview of Ant so that even someone who has never come across it before will be up to speed on what Ant is, why it was created, and why it is such a useful tool. To start, I will deal with the history of complex programming projects and the evolution of build tools.

By looking at the history of build tools, it should become clear why the creators of Ant produced a new build tool. Placing the Ant project in context will be a useful exercise.

Organizing Complex Projects

To see why a build tool is necessary in most, if not all, projects, consider a typical project. You begin by writing your code, in whatever language is appropriate, and then you compile it as you proceed. As the project expands, this becomes a much more difficult job, especially if your code depends on many outside libraries. If this is the case, you may find yourself with large search paths for each compilation.

Compiling Simple Projects

The next logical step is to record the location of the code and any outside libraries and use this information in some kind of script. For example, a Java project may have the following javac command:

```
javac -classpath ./dist/antBook.jar;%CATALINA_HOME%\common\lib\➥
mysql-connector-java-3.0.11-stable-bin.jar;➥
%CATALINA_HOME%\common\lib\servlet-api.jar;➥
%CATALINA_HOME%\common\lib\jsp-api.jar org\mwrm\plants\client\*.java
```

While this is not as complicated as some compilations, it is complex enough that you run the risk of omitting or misspelling some of the JAR files in the classpath.

Note I am assuming a blank CLASSPATH variable here because that is, in general, good practice, though adding the JAR files to the classpath would solve this problem in this instance. This kind of fix is pretty unwieldy because either you have to specify the CLASSPATH variable every session, which replicates the problems described, or you have to modify the existing variable when you introduce or change a library, which means you have to start a new command-line session to reflect the update.

The simplest solution is to include the javac command in a script, such as a Windows batch file, a Unix shell script, or a Perl script, and run the script from the command line. This allows you to specify the correct libraries at each invocation of the javac command.

Now you have a script that you can use to compile a single class in the project. You can of course generalize the command to compile a whole package at once. If you have more than one package, then you can add more javac commands as needed, as is the case with commands to package the project. This can quickly build up into a large script that you can reuse for each compilation of the project. You can include any command from your operating system in the script, which can make it a powerful tool when working with a project with multiple packages and libraries.

Compiling Larger Projects

The previous situation is no bad place to be if you are working on a small- to medium-sized project by yourself. You have control over the directory structure and the script, and build times are quick because of the project's size. A point will come in most projects, however, where one of these factors makes a script unworkable.

Using a Common Format

You will undoubtedly have written your automation script in the scripting language of your choice, which may not be the language other people working on the project are using. While this may not be a consideration in some projects, it is amazing how often a small project that scratches a personal itch becomes a major project that scratches a lot of itches. Ant, of course, is one such example, as are Perl and any number of open-source projects. Therefore, you should always assume that someone other than you will want to compile your project at some point.

If everyone is using a different technique for automating their section of the project, this makes it difficult to centralize the compiling and packaging process. Ideally, the lead developer runs a single script that performs all the required tasks before a project is ready to distribute to users or clients.

The project leader may even want to distribute the application as part of this process. If this is the case, the script should employ some automated testing to ensure that the project team releases a working application. The script is getting larger and larger as the project increases in complexity.

As you can appreciate, the larger and more serious a project becomes, the larger the need for an automated process becomes. In many stages of the process, human error can lead to delays or unusable code. Testing is absolutely necessary before a project is released to its users. Leaving the testing to a developer when the pressure is on, a deadline is looming, and a product has to ship will inevitably lead to problems. A common format for the script becomes more necessary to integrate all the stages of development.

Compiling Only New and Changed Files

Large projects have, by definition, a large number of classes, each of which may have dependencies on a number of outside libraries. As a project grows, the compilation time inevitably grows with it, eventually to the stage where a complex Java application can take up to an hour and an operating system, such as Windows 2000, can take eight hours on the most powerful hardware money can buy.

With this in mind, consider what happens when you change the application in some way, for example, by making a bug fix or adding functionality. The changes are unlikely to warrant a recompilation of the entire project, though this is unavoidable when using a script. It is possible to work around this to a certain extent by breaking the compilation into logical, named chunks within the script and calling only the chunk with the changed code.

Problems will still exist if the chunk itself is large or if a large number of chunks contain changed code. This also assumes the person building the project knows which pieces of the application have changed, which is again a problem in a large application written by a number of people where the number of changes could be large.

Controlling the Project

On a small project, you have control of the script and the structure of the project, so you have a good overview of where everything is in the directory hierarchy. This allows you to change the directory structure to suit your development style and the type of scripting you are using.

On larger projects, you will not necessarily have this control, so keeping the script up-to-date and usable becomes increasingly difficult. Large scripts used by many people can easily degenerate into a mess of unmaintainable gibberish.

Reflecting on the Project's Life Cycle

In the preceding sections, I hinted at certain aspects of a project's life cycle to demonstrate some of the deficiencies of scripting. However, it will now be useful to go through a detailed project life cycle to explain the final problem with scripts. The following describes the process of building the example project for this book. You will see the details of this application in later chapters, but these details are not necessary for understanding the project's life cycle.

1. Obtain the source code from the archive or repository.

2. Create a directory structure to hold the source code and the resultant binaries. This typically includes a temporary or scratch directory where you carry out the intermediate stages. You may also want to move any outside libraries into this directory structure for ease of access. The example application uses two libraries that you can download in source form and compile if you want to use the latest version. Otherwise, you can use precompiled binaries.

3. Configure the script to suit your environment. This is necessary here because someone else has written the source code. Their directory hierarchy may not be the same as yours. For instance, third-party libraries could be in different places on each system (`usr/local/java/tomcat5/common/lib/servlet-api.jar` versus `usr/local/java/jakarta-tomcat-5.5.9/common/lib/servlet-api.jar`, for example). In fact, someone else might not have been working on the same operating system. You should make sure any paths are correct and that the script references any outside resources properly. As described, this may be more difficult if the script is in a format with which you are not familiar. You may even find that the script will not run on your operating system because it was written in an incompatible scripting language, so you will have to convert it to one your operating system understands.

4. Compile the source code with your configured script.

5. Package the binary files into libraries for the users. You can distribute the example application as a JAR file for command-line access or a WAR file for use on a servlet container. In this step, you may be adding image and configuration files to the distribution. If your application requires outside libraries to run, you may also be adding them to the package. The web application version of the example application can include the third-party libraries mentioned previously so that it is a discrete package. Alternatively, you can let the administrator of the servlet container place the third-party libraries in an appropriate location.

6. Unit test the application with appropriate criteria. Ideally, you would use a testing framework with predefined test cases. If you are responsible for the code and the project is still at a development stage, then performance testing may be appropriate once unit testing has finished. You should test the application on a test server and not a production server.

7. Create the documentation bundle. This should include `README` files and instructions on how to install and use the application. The documentation could be simple text files or could be sophisticated HTML pages that you have generated using a standard process such as the `javadoc` utility. If you are distributing the documentation as a web application, which is an option with the example application, you should create a WAR file. Another option is an archive that the user can expand in their file system.

8. Package the entire distribution, which includes the packaged binaries and the documentation bundle. At this stage, you have to consider who you will be sending the application to and tailor the package accordingly. This may mean you have to produce more than one package. For example, Windows users prefer a `*.zip` file, and Unix users prefer a `*.tar.gz` or `*.bz2` archive.

9. Provide the application to your users. You can achieve this in a number of ways, including using e-mail, using FTP, copying and pasting onto a web server, or hot deploying onto a running web server.

10. Clean up the directory structure. When you have finished with the scrap directory and the third-party libraries, you may want to remove them from your file system. The scratch directory created in step 2 may no longer be necessary, and you could remove it if this is the case. Should you want to do a clean build every time, you will definitely want to do this. The example application gives you this option.

This is quite a list of actions to perform before an application is ready for your users. You should note that the example application is not a complicated application in any way, and many applications require you to execute more steps or perform more actions within steps.

The serial nature of the previous list belies some of the complicated dependencies and relationships within a build process. For example, you cannot package the application unless you have compiled the code and successfully built the documentation bundle.

The different processes outlined previously are not naturally linear because the build process can follow many paths. Figure 1-1 shows a simplified section of the build process that ignores the various choices for binary packages (JAR, WAR, `*.zip`, `*.tar.gz`, and so on). Path (a) compiles, tests, and documents only the web application. Path (b) compiles, tests, and documents only the client. Path (c) compiles, tests, and documents both versions of the application. The vertical lines delineate the discrete steps mentioned in the previous discussion.

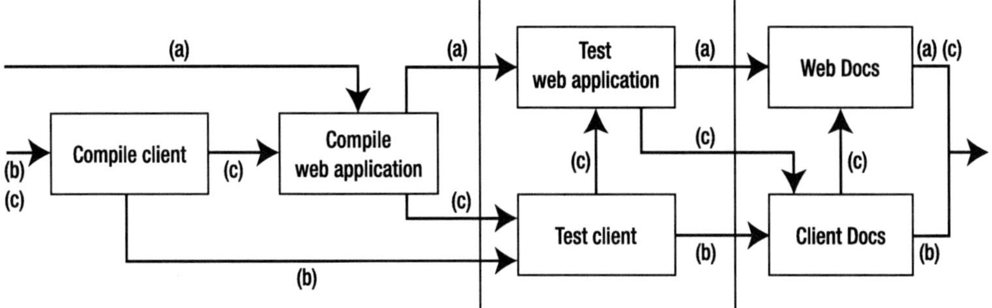

Figure 1-1. *An example build process*

A custom build script cannot adequately describe the complexities within a build process. Describing a build process helps you as the builder and maintainer, helps other people who may be building and maintaining the project in the future, and helps other people who may need an overview of a large project.

Figure 1-1 also shows another reason you may not want to perform every step in a build process every time you run it. Take, for example, an instance where you want to create a new version of only the client for your users. In this case, you would follow path (b) from Figure 1-1 and would not want to perform any of the steps in path (a). A linear script either would force you to do all the steps in a build process every time or would force you to encode the complicated logic of dependencies into the script.

Introducing the Build Tools

Having seen a number of problems inherent in the build process and how scripts can alleviate only some of them, you probably understand why scripts are not really a satisfactory answer. They can become unwieldy, hard to maintain, and unhelpful when you begin to deal with larger, complex projects. It was for this reason that many developers began working with build tools, of which Ant is a fairly recent example.

Build tools rely on build files that describe the project and the dependencies and relationships within it. Each discrete step in the build process has its own entry in the build file so that it plugs into the build process without affecting other steps in the build process. This allows you to change one step in the process without affecting any of the other steps.

Having a common build tool also means people who want to work on and maintain the project can get started straightaway. If a project did not use a build tool, then new contributors could take days to master the build/run process, thus losing valuable development time. Unifying the process makes collaboration much easier.

As a result of using the build file as a description of the build process, a build tool can examine the current state of the build's environment and act accordingly by comparing the two. For example, a build tool will examine the timestamp of a source file that it is about to compile. If that timestamp is later than the timestamp of the compiled version of the file, then the build tool will not compile that file and will move to the next stage in the process. This test is equally applicable to files and directories, where the build tool checks the timestamp of the original version of a file against that of the copied version in the scratch directory of a build area.

The description of the process allows the build tool to determine in what order it should perform tasks and create a running order from the many possible paths through the build process (refer to Figure 1-1). The inherent dependencies built into the description ensure that all the relevant steps take place throughout a build. Listing 1-1 shows a pseudo–build file describing the situation in Figure 1-1.

Listing 1-1. *Pseudocode Showing the Dependencies Described in Figure 1-1*

```
web-compile:
  javac Web.java

client-compile:
  javac Client.java

web-test:
  depends="web-compile"
  web-test01
  web-test02

client-test:
  depends="client-compile"
  client-test01
  client-test02

web-docs:
  depends="web-test"
  javadoc web

client-docs:
  depends="client-test"
  javadoc client

path-a:
  depends="web-docs"
  echo "Path (a) completed"

path-b:
  depends="client-docs"
  echo "Path (b) completed"

path-c:
  depends="web-compile, client-compile, ➥
           web-test, client-test, web-docs, client-docs"
  echo "Path (c) completed"
```

This shows how a build file can define different paths depending on how you want to build the application. Each named section, when called, executes the code it contains and then returns to the main build process. If a section depends on another, the build process must successfully run the named section before it can continue. If you wanted to run only one section, you would supply its name to the build process.

```
> build path-b
Path (b) completed
```

The `path-b` section tells the build process to run the `client-docs` section before executing it. The `client-docs` section in turn tells the build process to run the `client-test` section, and so on. You could of course use the code in Listing 1-2 to simplify the build file.

Listing 1-2. *A Simplified* `path-c` *Section*

```
path-c:
  depends="path-a, path-b"
  echo "Path (c) completed"
```

While this is not the situation you see in Figure 1-1, it is equally valid as a build path. The ease with which you can make this change compared to changing complicated build logic in a script shows the advantage of using a build tool.

Introducing make

`make` is one of the most widely used build tools for software products and is popular in the open-source movement. If you have ever downloaded the source bundle of an open-source project and installed it, you have used a version of `make`.

■ **Note** Java-based projects are the exception to this, as Ant is better suited to Java projects and the developers are likely to be familiar with the way it works.

`make` executes the commands listed in the build file via the operating system's shell. On Unix systems, you can specify the shell you want `make` to use; on Windows, it uses the standard command line. A number of versions of `make` exist, one of which is available from the GNU Project (`www.gnu.org/software/make/`).

While `make` is an excellent tool and many users have no problems with it, it does suffer from a few drawbacks, most of which drove Ant's creator to produce a new build tool.

All versions of `make` should conform to the IEEE standard 1003.2-1992 (POSIX.2). However, many extend this standard, and no two versions of `make` are the same. This means writing portable build files that will work on any system is much harder than it should be, because you are never sure which version of `make` your users will be using. This returns to the problem of different application developers using different scripting styles, as discussed previously. If you are sending the source bundle to your users so they can build it themselves, the problem becomes more acute.

Portability across versions of `make` is an important consideration but so is portability across operating systems. `make` is a standard tool on Unix systems but is unfamiliar to most Windows users. If you are confident all your users will be building the application and they will be building it on a Unix system, then you can assume that `make` will be readily available. However, if some of your users are on Windows, you cannot assume make will be available or that your users will have experience configuring make build files.

The syntax of make's build files, while defined by the 1003.2-1992 standard, is a new syntax to learn, with all the frustrations and idiosyncrasies that implies. For example, each command within a make section must be preceded by a tab, only a tab, and nothing but a tab. If you include a space before or after the tab, the command will not work, and your build process will break. You cannot totally escape this problem with build tools (Ant has its own idiosyncrasies, as you will see), but you can alleviate it in some ways.

Introducing Ant

Ant is a Java-based build tool from the Apache project that was originally bundled with early versions of Tomcat. Its creator had become dissatisfied with make as a way of building Tomcat from source and developed a tool to make his life easier. Ant was designed to fix the problems with make described previously and so mirrored the portability aims of Java.

As is the case with all the best projects, a tool created for a simple, specific fix was generalized and put to use on other problems. In Ant's case, the tool for building Tomcat was acquisitioned by people working on other Jakarta products when they realized how useful it could be. Ant use spread from this group with the official launch of Tomcat, and now Ant is the standard build tool for Apache Java projects, though many non-Apache Java projects also use it.

Ant is written in Java and so requires no further modifications as long as the target operating system has a JVM written for it. As such, you can write an Ant build file with the knowledge that it will function in a similar way, no matter which operating system the user runs Ant on. Therefore, by harnessing Java's portability, Ant overcomes the portability problems that can hamper make and its ilk.

To solve the problem of learning a new format, you write Ant's build files in XML. In this case, XML carries at least two advantages. First, it is a well-known format, so many people are comfortable with using it and can pick up new vocabularies quickly. The syntax of an XML document never changes, and a well-formed Ant build file is easy to write if you have never written one before. Second, XML is a portable, open standard, which means you can be sure that it can be used on every platform on which Ant is available.

For those of you familiar with Tomcat, Ant's build file resembles a Tomcat `server.xml` file in that each XML element represents a Java class and each XML attribute corresponds to an attribute in the underlying Java class. This approach means there is no DTD with which you can validate build files, because an element can have different attributes depending on where it is in a build file; specifically, in Ant this usually means the parent element determines what attributes are permissible in the child element.

Ant does come with a facility you can use to create a partial DTD, though its *caveat emptor* is that the user applies this DTD with the knowledge that it is not a complete or useful DTD.

Introducing Ant Targets and Tasks

Each named section of the build process in Ant is called a *target*, and each target contains a number of *tasks*. These tasks correspond to the command-line calls described in the previous sections and are represented by XML elements. Listing 1-3 shows a quick example of a Java compilation.

Listing 1-3. *A Simple Ant Build File*

```
<project name="Example Application Build" default="default" basedir=".">

  <!-- Compile the stand-alone application -->
  <target name="default">
    <javac srcdir="./src" destdir="build"/>
    <echo message="Application compiled"/>
  </target>

</project>
```

The `<project>` element is the root element of every Ant build file and sets the default target for this build project. In this case, Ant executes the `default` target, which tells it to compile the code in the `src` directory and place it in the `build` directory. Once it has done this, it echoes a message to standard `out` to inform the user that everything went as planned.

Ant's tasks are split into three categories: core, optional, and custom. *Core* tasks are those tasks that the Ant development team supports and actively develops. The team has given a commitment to look after these tasks, improve them, and correct any bugs found by Ant users.

Optional tasks are bundled with Ant and depend on libraries that do not belong to the Ant project (core tasks have no such dependences), and they come bundled as part of the Ant distribution, as do the libraries, so you can still use them in your projects.

If the tasks that come bundled with Ant do not give you the options you want, you have two choices. First, you can use Ant to run a command-line tool if one exists that does what you want to do. Second, you can write your own task, which simply means you would write a Java class that implements the desired behavior. You can then use this *custom* task in future projects and distribute it.

Writing a custom task has the same advantages that Ant has over other build tools in that your new task can go wherever Ant can. If your project demanded a step that was possible only at the command line on Windows, then you could not build it on Unix unless you wrote a custom task. Java and Ant are portable; Windows tools aren't necessarily so.

Summary

This chapter provided a quick introduction to building software projects, automating the build process, using build tools, using `make`, and using Ant. It is simply a taster for the rest of the book, where you will see the practicalities of using Ant.

Build tools have helped many programmers over the years. Though they may not allow you to write your code any faster, they do take some of the pain out of turning that code into working software.

The next chapter describes how to obtain Ant and install it.

CHAPTER 2

Installing Ant

The previous chapter described what Ant is and the reasons for its development. Therefore, it is now time to install Ant. Ant is available in binary form as compiled Java classes that you download to your computer and store in your file system. This form of distribution provides you with the latest stable build of Ant, so you can be confident that it has been well tested and that any new features will be stable. You can also obtain the latest build of Ant as a binary distribution, which is available as a nightly build.

If, however, you want to build Ant from source, you can. You have two options if you want to install it from source: the latest stable build, which corresponds to the stable binary build, and a nightly build, which you can download or retrieve from a CVS repository.

The binary installation is straightforward, so I will cover that first. Then, I will explain how to install Ant from source. This is a useful exercise because it means you can have the latest version of Ant if you should so desire and because the Ant project's build file gives a good overview of the Ant project's build structure. Recall that one of the properties of a build file is that it describes the structure of a project's build process and as such is a useful aid for examining a project.

Installing a Binary Ant Distribution

Binary distributions of Ant come as archive files that you can extract to your file system. Ant is a top-level Apache project, so you can download the binary files from `ant.apache.org`.

Downloading a Binary Distribution

Once you are on the Ant home page (`ant.apache.org`), click the Binary Distributions link on the left side. Figure 2-1 shows the binary download page.

The download script will have selected an appropriate mirror for you to use, which, unless you have strong objections, should be fine.

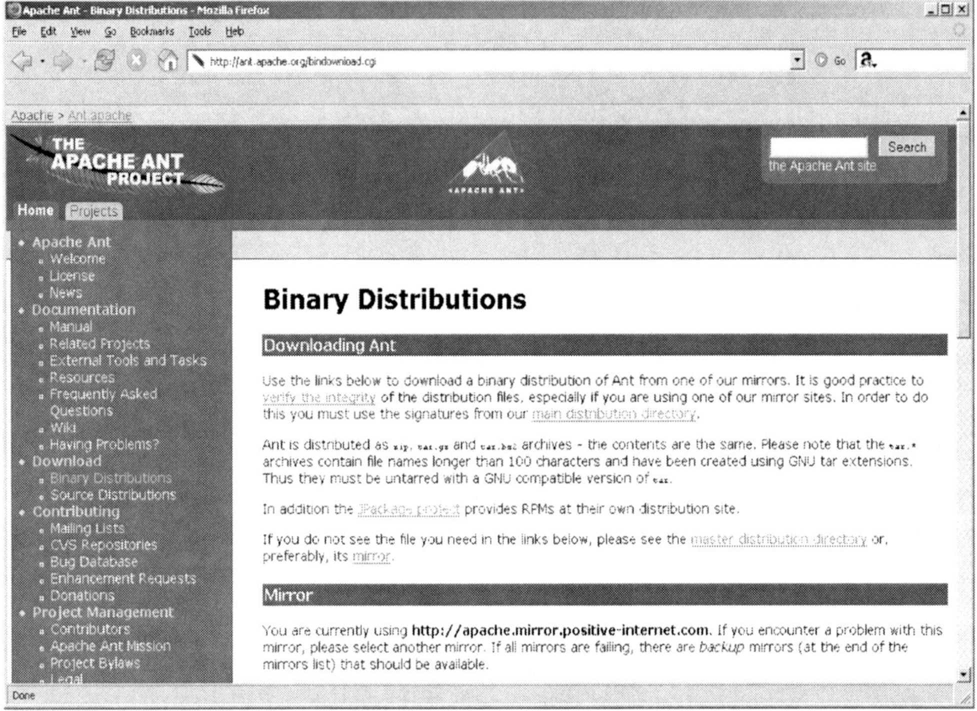

Figure 2-1. *The Ant binary download screen*

Downloading a Stable Build

As shown in Figure 2-2, the next section of the binary download page contains links to the latest stable version of Ant. This version has been tested and verified. Any new features are stable and will not exhibit unpredictable behavior, so you can be confident this version will work as expected.

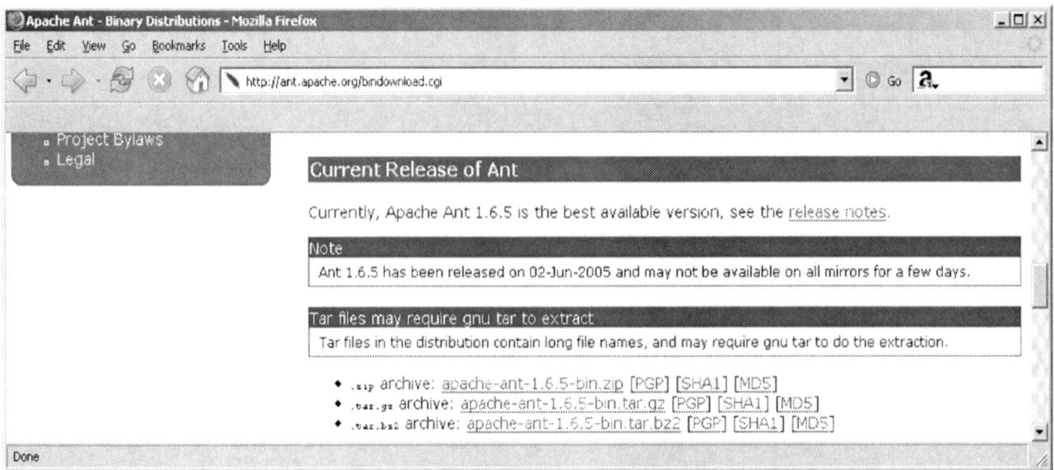

Figure 2-2. *The Current Release of Ant section of the binary download page*

Select the form of archive you want to download. In general, Windows users should download the *.zip archive, and Unix users should choose whichever of *.tar.gz or *.tar.bz2 they prefer. As the download page says, you should use a GNU-compatible version of tar to unpack the archive because some of the filenames are longer than 100 characters long.

Downloading a Nightly Build

If you want the latest features, some of which won't be available in the stable build, you may want to download a nightly build. Figure 2-3 shows the Nightly Builds section of the binary download page, along with a section that allows you to download older versions of Ant.

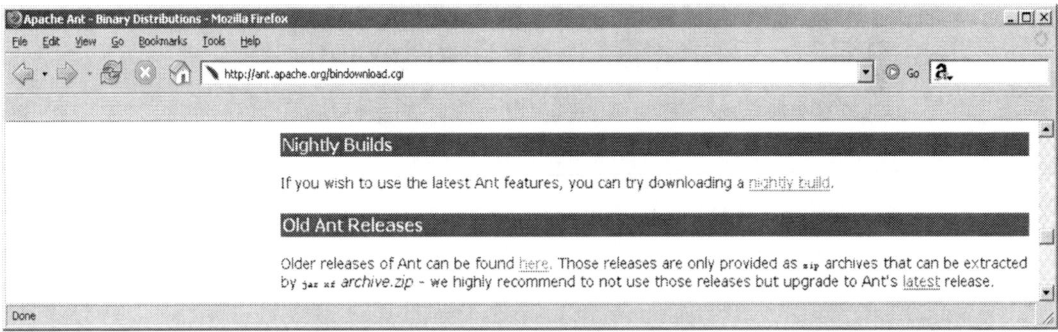

Figure 2-3. *The Nightly Builds section of the binary download page*

If you click the "nightly builds" link, this will take you to the nightly builds directory of the Apache server. To download the latest build, click the link that represents the newest version of Ant. Each link is in the form YYYYMMDD so that you can choose the appropriate directory to browse. Navigate to the bin directory, and choose which type of archive to download. In this case, the choice is between *.zip and *.tar.gz. Again, you should use a GNU-compatible version of tar to extract the *.tar.gz archive.

Verifying the Binary Distribution

Once you have downloaded the binary distribution, it is good practice to verify it has not been compromised. You can do this with the Pretty Good Privacy (PGP) application or the MD5 or SHA1 algorithms. This process is described in the "Using PGP to Verify the Binary Distribution" section.

Unpacking the Binary Distribution

Once you have the binary distribution, extract the archive to your file system. Windows users can use WinZip or similar to extract the *.zip file; Unix users should use a GNU-compatible tar with options appropriate to the compression format.

If you downloaded the *.tar.gz file, navigate to the directory where the archive is, and run the following:

```
> tar -xzf apache-ant-bin.tar.gz
```

This will extract the file to the current directory.

If you downloaded the `*.tar.bz2` file, navigate to the directory where the archive is, and run the following:

```
> tar -xjf apache-ant-bin.tar.bz2
```

This will extract the file to the current directory.

Verifying the Download

Once you have downloaded the file, it is good practice to verify that it has not been compromised. You can do this by using the PGP application or the MD5 or SHA1 algorithms.

Using PGP to Verify the Binary Distribution

PGP is a cryptographic suite written to ensure privacy over networks. It uses a public key encryption to ensure that only the intended recipient can read the messages you send. However, this is not how you will use it for verifying the download.

In this case, you will be using PGP as an authentication mechanism. Authentication allows you to compare information to see whether it is identical to the original information. The two main uses for authentication are checking passwords and verifying downloads. The principles are similar, though I will describe only download verification here.

When a file is ready for download, the file's owner can create a digital signature using PGP and their private key. In other words, PGP encrypts the file using the private key, and you can then decrypt it using the corresponding public key. However, this is not the whole story, because simply encrypting large zipped files would mean twice the amount of data to be downloaded and slow decrypting at the other end.

To solve this, PGP creates a message digest, otherwise known as a *hash*, from the file. This message digest is a fixed length of characters, no matter how large the file is, and the chances of a file having the same message digest as another are incredibly small. This character string varies in length depending on the algorithm used, but will be something like 160 characters long. PGP encrypts this message digest using the private key, which results in a small file.

When you download a file and ask PGP to verify it, PGP creates a digest of it and decrypts the original message digest. It then compares the two to verify that they are digests of the same file.

A successful verification means that the creator of the public key created the digest in the first place, because only this public key can decrypt the message digest as encrypted by the corresponding private key.

Figure 2-4 shows how PGP verifies a file once you have downloaded it.

The signature was created when the file was created and should be obtained from the source. This allows you to check that files hosted on a mirror have not been compromised. In the case of Ant, you should obtain the public key and signature files from the main Ant web site; the next sections explain the details of this.

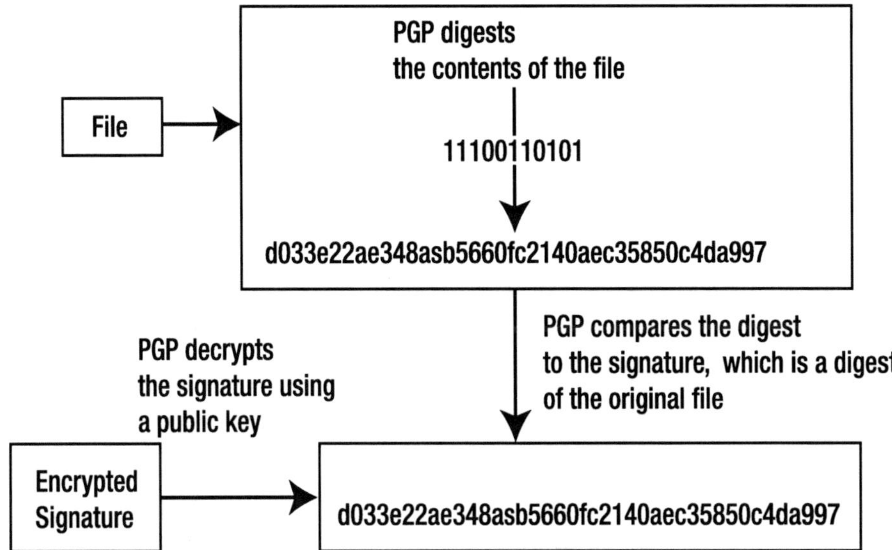

Figure 2-4. *Verifying a file has not been tampered with*

Obtaining PGP

The short history of PGP is fairly lively. As a result of governmental restrictions on cryptographic exports, the original PGP code was not available outside the United States. However, printed versions of the code were exported in books set in OCR font. As such, the code was obtained and compiled, becoming PGPi in the rest of the world.

Export restrictions have eased somewhat since the original release of PGP, and it is now much easier to obtain the code. Readers using Windows and Mac can obtain a GUI version of PGP from `www.pgp.com`. This site also has source downloads for all the major platforms, command-line tools included.

Readers in the United States or Canada can also visit the MIT site for PGP at `web.mit.edu/network/pgp.html` for binary and source distributions without the corporate razzle-dazzle.

Readers in parts more exotic can obtain PGPi from `www.pgpi.org`. This site contains many versions and options of PGP for many platforms. The main download index is at `www.pgpi.org/products/pgp/versions/freeware/`. Select your operating system and then the version you require.

As things stand, all readers should choose a version of PGP that runs on the command line. This makes it easy to automate verification, and you will also be able to follow along with the verification process used in this book.

Downloading the Keys and the Signature

Once you have installed PGP, download the Ant public key from `www.apache.org/dist/ant/KEYS` and the signature that corresponds to your Ant distribution. This will be an `*.asc` file. Figure 2-5 shows the file required for a Unix `*.tar.gz` binary distribution. The `KEYS` file will also be in your Ant distribution's base directory, though you should use the one from the Ant web site in preference to this one.

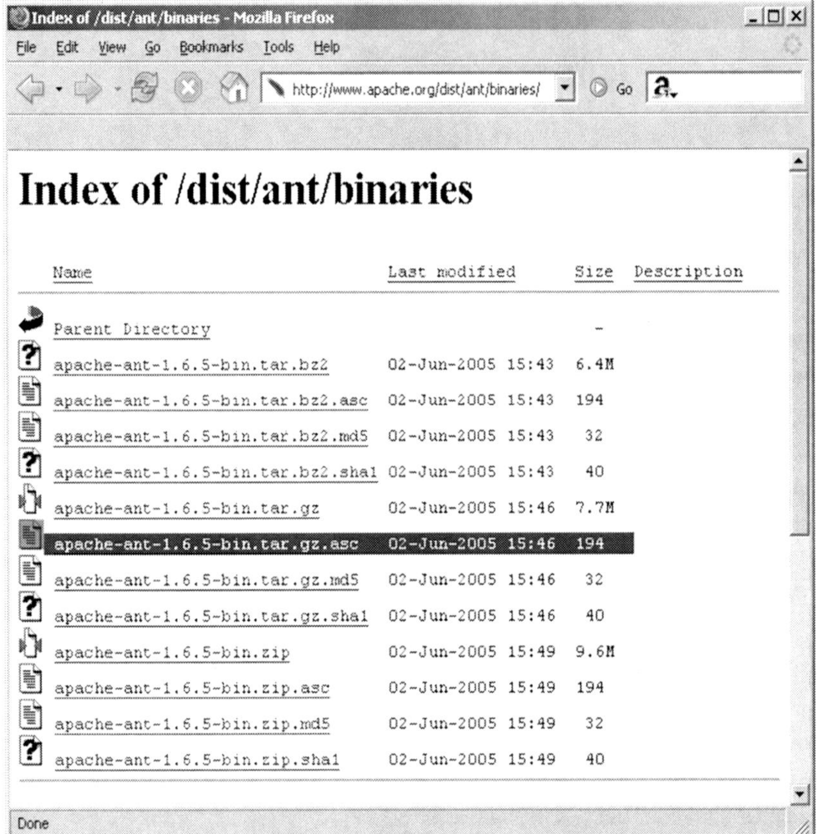

Figure 2-5. *A signature file for verifying a binary Ant distribution*

If you have downloaded a stable build, the PGP link next to the download link allows you to download the `*.asc` file appropriate to your distribution, as shown earlier in Figure 2-2. You can verify a nightly build using digests only (covered in the "Using MD5 and SHA1 to Verify the Download" section). However, nightly builds come directly from Apache, so you should put the same trust in Ant's nightly build downloads as you put in Ant's signatures.

■ **Caution** This form of verification is only as secure as the source of the keys and signature. The keys you download from the Apache web site will be not be trusted as far as PGP is concerned, because they will not come with trusted introductions. In other words, the keys and signature on the Ant web site are just as likely to be at risk as the file you are downloading from a mirror site. Bear this in mind during the following discussion.

Using PGP

The first step is to add the Ant public keys to your PGP key ring. (Excuse the casual use of new terms in this section, but if you'd like to know more about PGP, the manual is excellent and the web sites listed earlier can also help you.)

The following command adds the keys in the KEYS file to your PGP key ring:

```
> pgp -ka KEYS
```

To verify that the keys are on your key ring, run the following:

```
> pgp -kv
```

The Ant developers who have added public keys will be listed. Now that you have added the public keys, you can use them to verify the signature of the download. Run the following, where the *.asc file corresponds to the download:

```
> pgp apache-ant-bin.zip.asc
```

This will read the signature, find that the signature is not actually attached to a file, and then read in the file that corresponds to the signature file, minus the .asc section. The result of running the previous command is as follows:

```
Pretty Good Privacy(tm) Version 6.5.8
(c) 1999 Network Associates Inc.
Uses the RSAREF(tm) Toolkit, which is copyright RSA Data Security, Inc.
Export of this software may be restricted by the U.S. government.

File 'apache-ant-bin.zip.asc' has signature, but with no text.
Text is assumed to be in file 'apache-ant-bin.zip'.
Good signature from user "User Name <user@ant.com>".
Signature made 2004/07/16 08:00 GMT

WARNING: Because this public key is not certified with a trusted
signature, it is not known with high confidence that this public key
actually belongs to: "User Name <user@ant.com>".
```

Here you can see that PGP has assumed that the file the signature verifies is apache-ant-bin.zip. It verifies that the signature is correct and states when it was signed. You may be warned that the TZ environment variable is not set. This won't affect the verification process, but if this extra warning bothers you, add the TZ variable as specified in the PGP manual.

The most worrying thing about this output is that PGP does not trust this signature because the public key associated with it has not come from a trusted, signed source. If you will be working with Ant a lot, or if you just want to trust the Ant keys for completeness, you can sign the keys yourself. This will convince PGP that they are from a trusted source.

The first step is to create a private-public key of your own, if you do not already have one. Run the following, and fill in the details as appropriate:

```
> pgp -kg
```

You now have a private key that you can use to sign the keys and a public key you can give to others. To verify that you have added a key, run the key view command again:

```
> pgp -kv
```

Your new key will be shown in the list with the Ant keys and will be marked as the default key for signing, like so:

```
RSA 2048 OxF1964537 2005/03/28 *** DEFAULT SIGNING KEY ***
                               Matthew Moodie <matt@moodie.com>
```

To sign a key, run the following:

```
> pgp -ks
```

You will be asked for the ID of the user whose key you want to sign. You do not have to enter the whole name, because PGP will find the nearest ID to the string you enter and present you with the full version. You will be presented with the following warning to ensure that you know the provenance of the key you are about to sign:

```
READ CAREFULLY: Based on your own direct first-hand knowledge,
are you absolutely certain that you are prepared to solemnly certify
that the above public key actually belongs to the user specified
by the above user ID (y/N)? y
```

If you enter y, you will be prompted for the password you specified when you created your private key. Now that you have signed a key, PGP will allow you to use it to verify signatures. Run the verification command again.

```
> pgp apache-ant-bin.zip.asc
```

This time there will be no warning.

```
Pretty Good Privacy(tm) Version 6.5.8
(c) 1999 Network Associates Inc.
Uses the RSAREF(tm) Toolkit, which is copyright RSA Data Security, Inc.
Export of this software may be restricted by the U.S. government.

File 'apache-ant-bin.zip.asc' has signature, but with no text.
Text is assumed to be in file 'apache-ant-bin.zip'.
Good signature from user "User Name <user@ant.com>".
Signature made 2004/07/16 08:00 GMT
```

You can see who has signed the keys in your key ring with the following command:

```
> pgp -kc
```

The second part of this long output shows a list of keys, each of which starts with the key ID. Below each user ID is the ID of the signers of that key.

```
* 0xF1964537 ultimate  complete  Matthew Moodie <matt@moodie.com>
c            ultimate              Matthew Moodie <matt@moodie.com>
```

In this case, I am the only person who has signed my public key. The Ant keys will have a number of signers. However, PGP will not trust anyone except you as a key signer, which is another reason why PGP doesn't trust any of the keys on your key ring.

If you want a third party's key to sign other keys, you can change its trust level with the following command:

```
> pgp -ke <username>
```

You will be given another warning and asked what level of trust you would like to assign to this key.

```
Make a determination in your own mind whether this key actually
belongs to the person whom you think it belongs to, based on available
evidence. If you think it does, then based on your estimate of
that person's integrity and competence in key management, answer
the following question:

Would you trust "User Name <user@ant.com>"
to act as an introducer and certify other people's public keys to you?
(1=I don't know (default). 2=No. 3=Usually. 4=Yes, always.) ?
```

If you choose 4, this user can act as a signatory to other public keys, though you must have signed their key initially so that PGP trusts them in the first place. You can see how the layers of trust are built up and how important it is to trust the initial source of any key you receive.

Using MD5 and SHA1 to Verify the Download

MD5 and SHA1 are message digest algorithms that you can use to verify the integrity of a download. I covered message digests previously with reference to digital signatures, so I will go straight into the verification process.

The `md5/md5sum` and `sha1/sha1sum` tools are installed as standard on Unix; Windows users can obtain `md5` by following one of the links at the bottom of the Ant download page, as shown in Figure 2-6. One of the links is `www.fourmilab.ch/md5/`. The best way for Windows users to use SHA1 digests is to download `fsum` from `www.slavasoft.com/fsum/`.

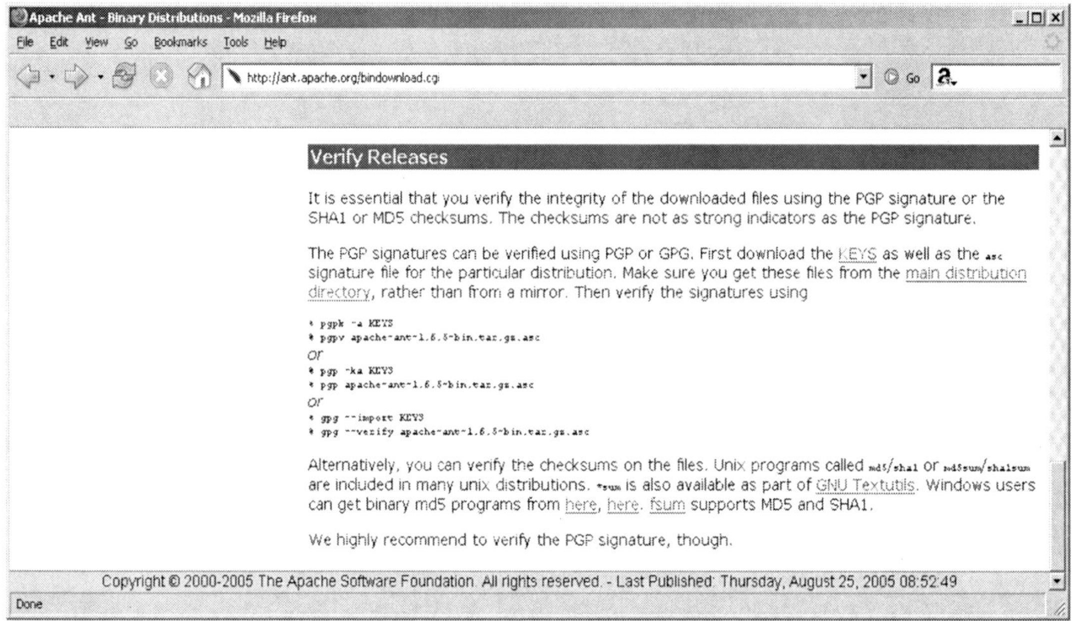

Figure 2-6. *You can obtain the* `md5` *tool from the links at the bottom of the page.*

You run the `md5` tool at the command line, and when you are verifying a download, you provide it with a 32-character MD5 hash.

If you have downloaded a stable build, the MD5 link next to the download link allows you to download the `*.md5` file appropriate to your distribution, as shown earlier in Figure 2-2. You can also verify a nightly build using MD5.

The `*.md5` file contains the message digest of the downloaded file, and you should provide this value to the `-c` option of `md5`, followed by the filename of the download.

```
> md5 -ce74b9bf7297b4d7883d84d88cf6601fc apache-ant-src.zip.md5
```

Unfortunately, this will not provide any output to the screen. If the test was successful, meaning the hash's value corresponded to the hash of the file, the return code is 0. If the test failed, the return code is 1.

To produce some human-readable output, you must write a script to verify the output of the test. Listing 2-1 shows a Windows batch file that tests the MD5 hash against the hash of the file.

Listing 2-1. `md5script.bat`*: Tests the Integrity of a Download*

```
@echo off

md5 -c%1 %2

IF NOT errorlevel 1 GOTO valid
echo Signature not valid.
GOTO end
```

```
:valid
echo Signature valid.

:end
```

To use this batch file, run the following command:

```
> md5script e74b9bf7297b4d7883d84d88cf6601fc apache-ant-src.zip
```

A successful test will result in the following:

```
Signature valid.
```

Listing 2-2 shows a Unix bash shell script that tests the MD5 hash against the hash of the file.

Listing 2-2. *md5script.sh: Tests the Integrity of a Download*

```
if md5 -c$1 $2
then
  echo Signature valid.
else
  echo Signature valid.
fi
```

To use this script, run the following command:

```
> md5script e74b9bf7297b4d7883d84d88cf6601fc apache-ant-src.zip
```

A successful test will result in the following:

```
Signature valid.
```

The procedure for sha1 is similar; just remember to use the sha1 utility on the *.sha1 file instead of md5 on the *.md5 file.

However, if you want to use fsum on Windows to check an SHA1 digest, the procedure is slightly more complicated. First, you have to edit the *.sha1 file as follows:

```
94ed9d65bc38246384af1078d546566fde050b2d ?SHA1*apache-ant-bin.zip
```

The change is to add ?SHA*filename after the SHA1 hash. This tells fsum which file was used to generate the hash. It will then calculate the hash of this file and compare it to the hash in the file. The relevant command is as follows:

```
> fsum -sha1 -c apache-ant-bin.zip.sha1
```

```
SlavaSoft Optimizing Checksum Utility - fsum 2.51
Implemented using SlavaSoft QuickHash Library <www.slavasoft.com>
Copyright (C) SlavaSoft Inc. 1999-2004. All rights reserved.

OK          SHA1        apache-ant-bin.zip
```

The test passed in this case. If the test failed, you wouldn't see any output after the fsum copyright lines.

Installing a Source Ant Distribution

You can install Ant from source in a number of ways, depending on your personal preference. If you want the latest milestone build, then you have to download it from the Ant web site (ant.apache.org). However, if you want to try the latest version of Ant, then you can download a nightly build from the web site or obtain it from the Ant CVS repository. This allows you to work with the latest features of Ant that might not be available in the stable release. Nightly builds also contain the latest bug fixes.

Note Installing Ant from source is just as easy on Windows as it is on Unix, mainly because of Java's cross-platform properties. The only nonstandard Windows tool described is cvs, though you can obtain it easily. You'll find the details in the following relevant section.

The next section will describe how you can use the Ant web site to obtain a source distribution, be it a stable build or a nightly build. After that, I will describe how to use CVS to obtain a nightly build.

Downloading a Source Distribution

Once you are on the Ant home page, click the Source Distributions link on the left side. Figure 2-7 shows the source download page.

The download script will have selected an appropriate mirror for you to use, which, unless you have strong objections, should be fine.

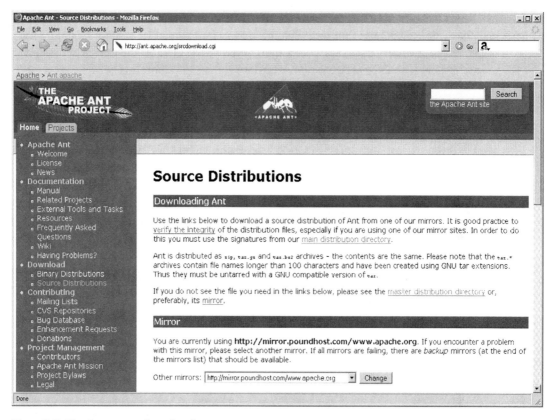

Figure 2-7. *The Ant source download screen*

Downloading a Stable Build

As shown in Figure 2-8, the next section of the source download page contains links to the latest stable version of Ant. This version has been tested and verified. Any new features are stable and will not exhibit unpredictable behavior, so you can be confident that this version will work as expected.

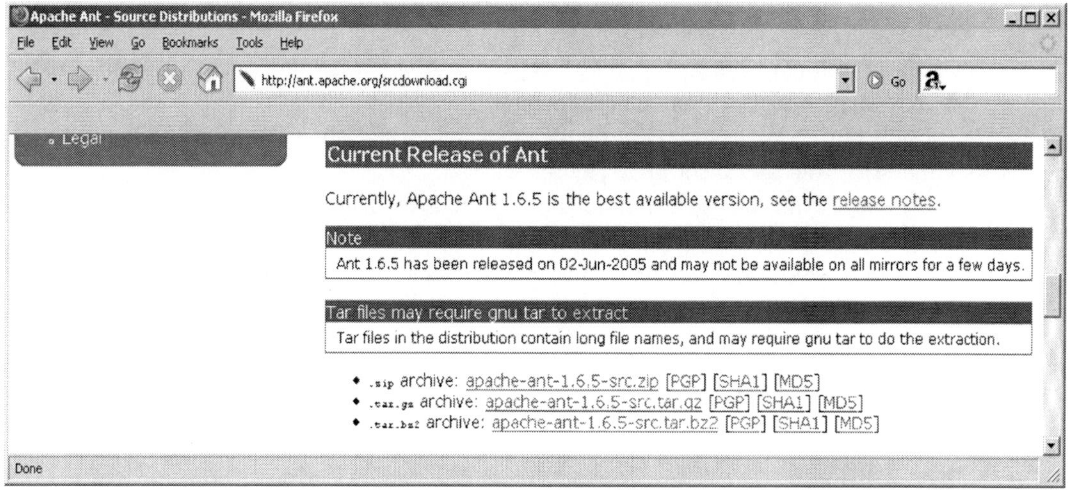

Figure 2-8. *The Current Release of Ant section of the source download page*

Select the form of archive you want to download. In general, Windows users should download the `*.zip` archive, and Unix users should choose whichever of `*.tar.gz` or `*.tar.bz2` they prefer. As the download page says, you should use a GNU-compatible version of `tar` to unpack the archive because some of the filenames are longer than 100 characters long.

Downloading a Nightly Build

If you want the latest features, some of which won't be available in the stable build, you may want to download a nightly build. Figure 2-9 shows the Nightly Builds section of the source download page, along with a section that allows you to download older versions of Ant.

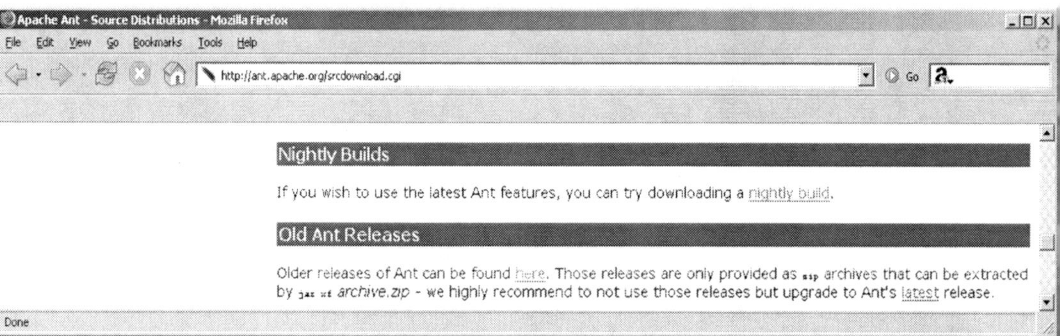

Figure 2-9. *The Nightly Builds section of the source download page*

If you click the link, this will take you to the nightly builds directory of the Apache server. To download the latest build, click the link that represents the newest version of Ant. Each link is in the form `YYYYMMDD` so that you can choose the appropriate directory to browse. Navigate to the `src` directory, and choose which type of archive to download. In this case, the choice is between `*.zip` and `*.tar.gz`. Again, you should use a GNU-compatible version of `tar` to extract the `*.tar.gz` archive.

Downloading a CVS Snapshot

If you do not have CVS installed on your system, you can still download nightly snapshots of the CVS repository via the Ant CVS repository web site. These distributions are likely to be more unstable than both nightly and milestone builds.

Click the CVS Repositories link on the Ant web site, and you will see the CVS Repositories section of the web site, as shown in Figure 2-10.

This page gives you instructions on how to obtain the latest source code using CVS, which you will see in the "Using CVS to Obtain a Source Distribution" section. For now, click the link to `cvs.apache.org/snapshots/ant/`. You should see a list of the latest snapshots of the CVS tree, as shown in Figure 2-11.

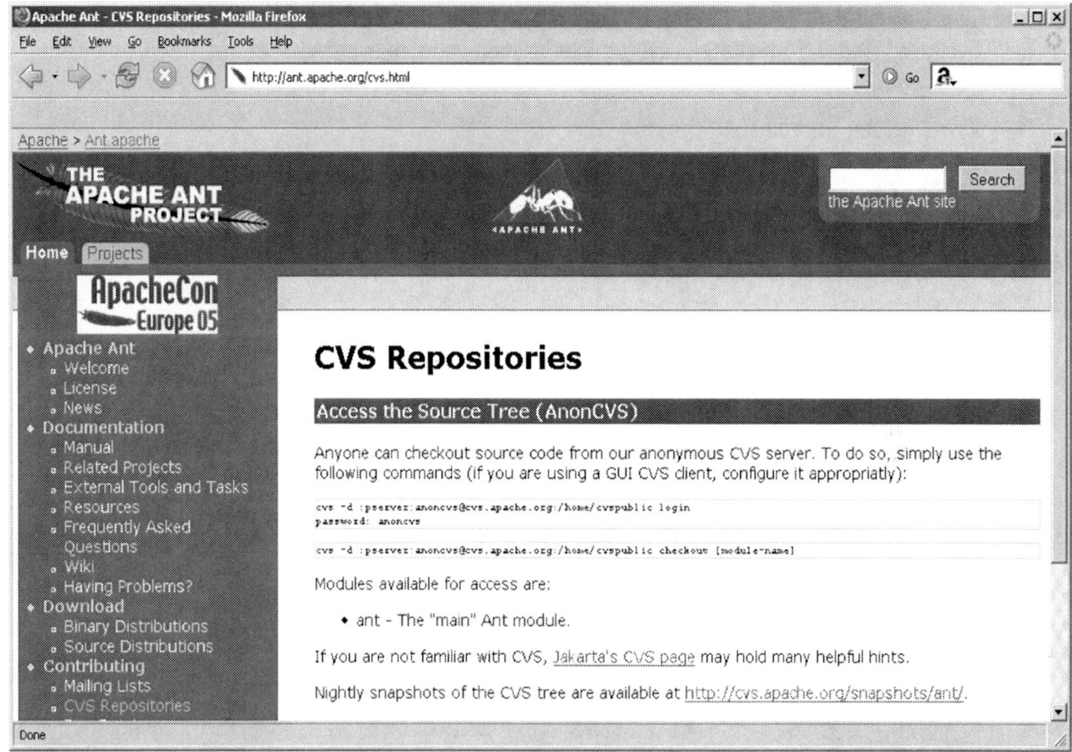

Figure 2-10. *The CVS Repositories section of the Ant web site*

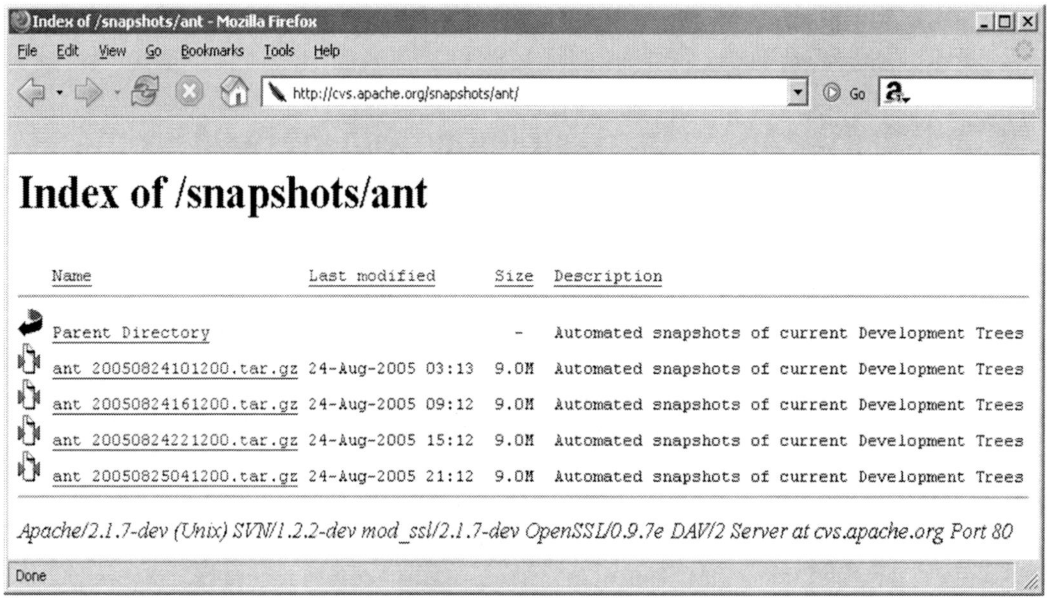

Figure 2-11. *CVS nightly snapshots on the Apache server*

These are all `*.tar.gz` files, though this shouldn't be a problem even for Windows users because WinZip, for example, can cope with these kind of archives without any problems.

Verifying the Source Distribution

It is good practice to verify the source bundle has not been interfered with once you have downloaded it. You can do this with the PGP application or the MD5 or SHA1 algorithms. This process is covered in the previous "Verifying the Download" section.

Using CVS to Obtain a Source Distribution

Using CVS to obtain a source distribution is painless. Most Unix systems have the `cvs` tool installed by default. Windows users can obtain it from `www.cvshome.org`.

The code obtained from the CVS repository is likely to be more unstable than a nightly build and certainly more unstable than a stable milestone build.

The following command logs you into the Apache CVS repository. When asked for the password, enter `anoncvs`.

```
> cvs -d :pserver:anoncvs@cvs.apache.org:/home/cvspublic login
password: anoncvs
```

If you log in successfully, you won't see a confirmation. Now that you have established a connection with the server, you can check out the Ant source code. Run the following to download the source to the current directory:

```
> cvs -d :pserver:anoncvs@cvs.apache.org:/home/cvspublic checkout ant
```

`cvs` will display its progress to the console, which allows you to see the various files and directories that are being downloaded.

Building the Ant Source Distribution with the Build Script

Now that you have the source distribution on your file system, you can build Ant. If you are installing Ant for the first time, you will have to use the build script (`build.bat` on Windows and `build.sh` on Unix). If you have a distribution of Ant already, then you can use the `build.xml` build file. The "Upgrading Ant" section covers the latter situation.

Installing Ant from source for the first time presents an interesting problem: if you don't have a build tool, how do you build Ant? To solve this problem, the Ant source distribution comes with a build script that compiles the source distribution.

Run the build script appropriate for your system as follows:

```
> build
```

This will first compile the core Ant classes from source, before using them to build the rest of the distribution. This happens in two stages. First, the `build` script calls the `bootstrap` script, which in turn compiles the bare minimum of Ant classes required and then calls `org.apache.tools.ant.Main` to build the core of the Ant distribution. Listing 2-3 shows the important part of `build.xml` that creates the bootstrap build.

Listing 2-3. *The bootstrap Target from build.xml*

```
<target name="bootstrap" description="--> creates a bootstrap build">
  <antcall inheritAll="false" target="dist-lite">
    <param name="dist.dir" value="${bootstrap.dir}"/>
  </antcall>
</target>
```

While this may not mean much just now, a quick discussion of this will show how the Ant build process first builds the minimum bootstrap distribution and then builds the main distribution. The `bootstrap` target uses the `<antcall>` element to call the `dist-lite` target, but it overrides the `dist.dir` property for the duration of the call. This ensures that the bootstrap build is placed in a scratch bootstrap area away from the main distribution. Listing 2-4 shows the relevant line from the Windows `bootstrap` script.

Listing 2-4. *The bootstrap Script Calls the Main Ant Class to Build the Bootstrap Build*

```
"%JAVA%" %ANT_OPTS% org.apache.tools.ant.Main ➥
-emacs %ANT_CMD_LINE_ARGS% bootstrap
```

The `bootstrap` argument at the end causes Ant to run the `bootstrap` target listed in Listing 2-4. The final bootstrap build is placed in the `bootstrap` directory. The JAR files required to build the main Ant distribution are placed in `bootstrap/lib`, and the scripts are placed in `bootstrap/bin`.

In the second stage, the `build` script calls the `bootstrap/bin/ant` script, which runs the default Ant task in `build.xml` using the line shown in Listing 2-5.

Listing 2-5. *bootstrap/bin/ant.bat Calls Ant's Default Target*

```
"%_JAVACMD%" %ANT_OPTS% -classpath "%ANT_HOME%\lib\ant-launcher.jar" ➥
"-Dant.home=%ANT_HOME%" org.apache.tools.ant.launch.Launcher ➥
%ANT_ARGS% %ANT_CMD_LINE_ARGS%
```

The default target for the Ant build is `main`, and this target simply calls the `dist-lite` target. However, this time the `dist.dir` property is set to the final distribution directory that will contain the Ant distribution. Listing 2-6 shows the relevant details.

Listing 2-6. *The Targets That Build the Main Ant Distribution*

```
<project name="apache-ant" default="main" basedir=".">

  <property name="dist.dir" value="dist"/>

  <target name="main"
          description="--> creates a minimum distribution in ./dist"
          depends="dist-lite"/>

</project>
```

In this case, the `dist-lite` target builds the main Ant distribution and places it in the `dist` directory, as specified by the `dist.dir` property. The `dist` directory contains the `bin` and `lib` subdirectories, which form the Ant distribution. The `dist` directory is your `ANT_HOME`, unless you copy the files to another location.

Taking Final Steps After Installation

The final step of installation is to set the `ANT_HOME` environment variable. This allows Ant to find the classes that it depends on, which means you can run it from anywhere on your file system.

Setting %ANT_HOME% on Windows

To set `%ANT_HOME%` on Windows, open Start ➤ Settings ➤ Control Panel ➤ System. Click the Advanced tab, and select Environment Variables. You will then see the Environment Variables dialog box, as shown in Figure 2-12.

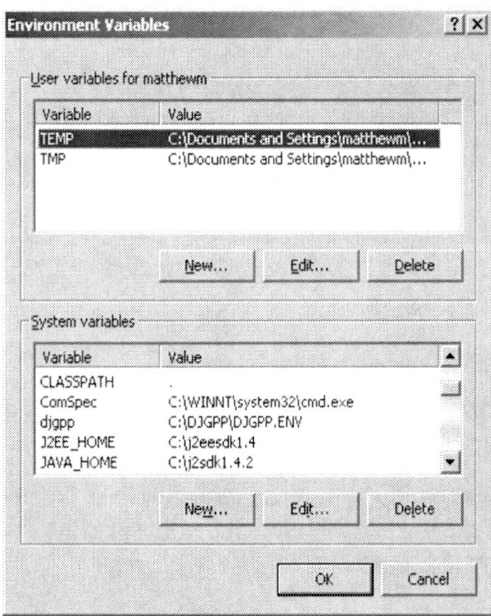

Figure 2-12. *The Windows Environment Variables dialog box*

If you want to add the environment variable just for you, click the New button under the User Variables for *User* section. Alternatively, if you want every user on your system to have access to it, click the New button under the System Variables section. Whichever you choose, enter the details of your Ant distribution, as shown in Figure 2-13.

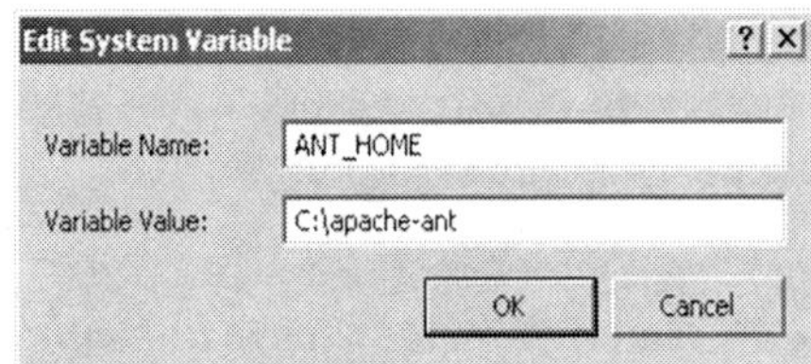

Figure 2-13. *Adding %ANT_HOME% as a system environment variable*

Click OK, and close down the system application. To test that you have successfully added the variable, run the following at the command line:

```
> echo %ANT_HOME%
```

This should display the name of the directory that you specified. To run Ant, you can use the %ANT_HOME% variable like so to test the installation:

```
> %ANT_HOME%\bin\ant -version
```

For more flexibility, you can add the Ant %ANT_HOME%\bin directory to your %PATH% environment variable using the system application, just as you added the %ANT_HOME% variable. This means you can call the ant command from any directory like so:

```
> ant -version
```

If these commands do not display the version number of Ant you installed, check the value of %ANT_HOME% and that the %ANT_HOME%\bin\ant file is accessible.

Setting $ANT_HOME on Unix

To add the $ANT_HOME environment variable, use the following command (in bash):

```
# ANT_HOME=/usr/java/apache-ant
# export ANT_HOME
```

You can also add these commands to ~/.bashrc or /etc/profile, or you can create a shell file, antEnv.sh, and place it in /etc/profile.d. The /etc/profile directory will run this file automatically at boot time to make the $ANT_HOME variable available to all users.

Examining the Ant Distribution

The Ant distribution is fairly simple and contains four directories: bin, docs, etc, and lib. The ANT_HOME directory also contains a number of files, most of which are licenses, though KEYS, README, welcome.html, and WHATSNEW are worth an explanation.

- KEYS: This file contains the public keys associated with the Ant project. See the "Verifying the Download" section for more details.
- README: This is a quick introduction to Ant with details of what it is and what it does.

- `welcome.html`: This is a fuller, more well-rounded version of `README`. It contains a fair bit of useful information, including what is new in this release of Ant. You should read this when you do a significant upgrade to see what new features are in the new version.
- `WHATSNEW`: This is a change log that describes the changes, new features, and bug fixes that have been made over a number of Ant versions, starting with the change from Ant 1.1 to Ant 1.2.

Looking at the bin Directory

The `bin` directory contains scripts for Unix and Windows that run Ant. The `ant.*` and `antRun.*` scripts have the same functions on both platforms, though the `*.cmd` scripts are slightly different.

Understanding the ant Scripts

The `ant.*` script runs the main Ant class and starts the build process. It takes a number of command-line parameters, all of which I will discuss in the next chapter. The `ant.cmd` script is a Windows NT script that calls the other `*.cmd` files to perform the same tasks as the other `ant.*` scripts.

Understanding the antRun Scripts

The `antRun.*` script runs an OS-specific command. The `<exec>` Ant task uses it to access system tools that may be required during a build. Its first argument is the directory from where the command should be run, and the other arguments are arguments to this command. For example:

```
> antRun . echo "Hello, world."
"Hello, world."
```

This runs the `echo` command from the current directory with the string `"Hello, world."` as the input to the command.

Understanding the runant Scripts

The `runant.*` scripts are Perl and Python scripts that run Ant, just as the `ant.*` scripts do. If you want, you could use them as CGI scripts; however, as the scripts point out, this would be somewhat daft.

Looking at the docs Directory

The `docs` directory contains an offline version of the Ant manual. The pages are mainly HTML, with the exception of a PDF task reference document.

Looking at the etc Directory

The `etc` directory contains a number of XSL transformation documents that some Ant tasks use to transform their results. For example, the JUnit test tasks are designed to test the results of the build process, and they use the XSL documents in this directory to form result documents.

Looking at the lib Directory

The `lib` directory contains the huge number of JAR files that Ant needs to do its work. Some of them are part of the Ant project itself, and others are from different Jakarta projects, such as Jakarta ORO and Jakarta Bean Scripting Framework, and from different Apache projects, such as the Apache Log4j logging framework and the Xerces XML processor.

The `lib` directory is in Ant's classpath, and you must copy any third-party or custom task JAR files into this directory for Ant to be able to use them.

Upgrading Ant

If the Ant developers release a new version of Ant, it is a fairly straightforward task to upgrade. The instructions in the installation sections apply to any new release. The most important task to remember is to reset the value of the `ANT_HOME` environment variable. Once you have installed a new version of Ant, you must point to the new location using this variable.

You should also remember to add the Ant directory to your path, should you want to run Ant from anywhere on your file system. If you do this, ensure that the old version of Ant is no longer in the path, because this may lead to unforeseen problems when you try to use the new version.

One final issue to consider is whether you have added any functionality beyond the core and optional tasks. For example, to hot-deploy web applications on a running Tomcat server, you must have the Tomcat deployment tasks in Ant's classpath. This means the `catalina-ant.jar` file must be in the `ANT_HOME/lib` directory. Therefore, you must ensure it is copied into your new version of Ant, along with any other custom JAR files you use.

Once you have successfully installed and tested the new version, you can delete the old distribution to avoid confusion in the future. Should you need to refer to an older version, Apache maintains an archive at `archive.apache.org/dist/ant/`. You can also get there via the Ant download page.

Summary

This chapter covered how to install Ant in a number of ways. You can install a stable version of Ant that comes as a package of compiled Java classes, or you can compile the classes yourself. Both techniques provide you with a robust release of Ant that has been through extensive tests, so you can be sure of its reliability.

If you want to work with new features and the latest version of Ant, you can obtain nightly builds or newly written CVS snapshots of the code. These allow you to test the features of Ant that have not made it into the stable releases.

You also looked at download verification and the issues surrounding it. You have two ways to verify an Ant download: PGP and MD5/SHA1. PGP is the more robust of the two, but requires a fair amount of effort to set up if you do not already have it on your system.

The next chapter gets into the details of build file syntax and how to run Ant from the command line.

CHAPTER 3

Using Ant

Now that you have installed Ant, you are ready to start using it. However, Ant is nothing without its build files. You must provide Ant with a description of the project before you can start to build the project. With this in mind, in this chapter you'll look at the syntax of build files, with a quick refresher on XML just in case.

You write Ant's build files in an XML dialect that is fairly simple, yet can't be captured in a DTD. As mentioned in a previous chapter, a Java class implements each XML element in Ant's build file, which means the attributes can change depending on the underlying Java class. The attributes of nested elements can also change depending on which element contains them.

This chapter will cover running Ant from the command line and the basics of build files. This discussion will include those XML elements in a build file that are not tasks and the `<property>` task, mainly because it is such an important task that it is integral to almost any build file.

Running Ant from the Command Line

The usual method of running Ant is to use the `ant` shell script supplied in `ANT_HOME/bin`. If you plan to use Ant a lot, it is a good idea to place this directory on your path or place a shortcut to the script in a directory that is on your path.

The `ant` script has a number of options at the command line. You can see what these are by running `ant -h`. The basic syntax is as follows:

```
ant [options] [target [target2 [target3] ...]]
```

The list of targets tells Ant which targets to execute in the build file. (I'll discuss targets in the "Examining the Target Element" section.) Table 3-1 describes the options.

Table 3-1. *Ant's Command-Line Options*

Option	Description
`-help`, `-h`	Displays the help message.
`-projecthelp`, `-p`	Prints help information that describes the targets in the project build file.
`-version`	Prints version information.

Table 3-1. *Ant's Command-Line Options (Continued)*

Option	Description
`-diagnostics`	Prints information that you can use to diagnose problems. This includes the JAR files and system properties that Ant is using.
`-quiet, -q`	Suppresses most visible output that Ant produces. This does not apply to print commands that are part of the build.
`-verbose, -v`	Prints all possible output that Ant produces.
`-debug, -d`	Prints debugging information. You can configure the `<echo>` task with levels of output to help with debugging.
`-emacs, -e`	Strips all unnecessary trimmings from visible output. For example, when a task executes, Ant usually displays the task type. If you set this option, Ant will not display this information.
`-lib <path>`	Specifies a path to search for JARs and classes, in addition to your classpath and Ant's two default directories (see the discussion after this table).
`-logfile <file>` `-l <file>`	Sets the log file for this build.
`-logger <classname>`	Sets the class that does the logging for this build. Chapter 11 covers logging.
`-listener <classname>`	Adds a project listener. Chapter 11 covers listeners.
`-noinput`	Disables interactive input. Chapter 6 covers this topic.

`-buildfile <file>`
`-file <file>`
`-f <file>`
	Specifies the build file to use for this build. The value of `<file>` can be an absolute path or a path relative to the current directory. The default is a file called `build.xml` in the current directory.

`-D<property>=<value>`	Sets the value of property `<property>` to `<value>`. I will discuss properties in the "Working with Properties" section.
`-keep-going, -k`	Forces Ant to execute every target that does not depend on a failed target. This ensures that at least part of the build was successful.
`-propertyfile <name>`	Loads all the properties from specified property file. (I will cover property files in the "Working with Properties" section.) `-Dproperties` take precedence if there is a clash.
`-inputhandler <class>`	Sets the class that will handle input requests. This is an implementation of the `org.apache.tools.ant.input.InputHandler` interface. Chapter 6 covers this topic.
`-find <file>` `-s <file>`	Tells Ant to search for the specified build file toward the root of the file system and use it. This allows you to run a build on a project from deep within its directory hierarchy.
`-nice number`	Sets a value for niceness for the main Ant thread: `1` (lowest) to `10` (highest). `5` is the default.
`-nouserlib`	Tells Ant to run without using JAR files from `${user.home}/.ant/lib` (see the paragraph that follows this table).
`-noclasspath`	Tells Ant to run without using your classpath.

By default, Ant's classpath is built from the system classpath, from the path set with `-lib`, from the `${user.home}/.ant/lib` directory, and from the `ANT_HOME/lib` directory. The system classpath, represented by the `CLASSPATH` environment variable, is passed to Ant as transparent input to `-lib`. Ant looks through these directories and loads any classes and JARs, which means you don't have to specify each JAR's name.

`${user.home}/.ant/lib` varies depending on your operating system. On Unix it maps to a user's "home" directory; on Windows it varies depending on version. Windows 2000, for example, uses `C:\Documents and Settings\username`.

You can run Ant without any of these options. In this case, it will look for a build file in the current directory and run the default target.

Ant has three environment variables that you can use to set its default behavior.

- `ANT_ARGS` is a list of the arguments described in Table 3-1. Set this variable to include those options you use frequently.
- `ANT_OPTS` is a list of arguments that you want to pass to the JVM that will run Ant.
- `JAVACMD` is the absolute path to the Java executable you want Ant to use.

Introducing Ant's Build File Syntax

The XML specification allows you to describe data in a structured form. As such, it is an extremely effective format for build files, which, as you are now aware, describe the structure of the project build process.

Examining the Project Element

Each XML document must be well formed, meaning it must have a root element that contains all other elements and each element must be closed by a closing element or must be a stand-alone, self-closing element. The root element of every Ant build file is the `<project>` element, so every Ant build file must contain the lines shown in Listing 3-1 at a bare minimum.

Listing 3-1. *The Minimum Requirements for a Build File*

```
<?xml version="1.0"?>

<project>

</project>
```

If you want to use a DTD, you can generate an incomplete DTD using the `<antstructure>` task, or you can find a working example at `www.sdv.fr/pages/casa/html/ant-dtd.en.html`. The incomplete DTD may be enough for some purposes, but if you want to use an IDE to edit build files and add appropriate elements in the appropriate place, you will need to use the more complete version.

■ **Note** The Eclipse IDE (`www.eclipse.org`) has a useful Ant build file editor.

Listing 3-2 shows a build file that creates the incomplete DTD.

Listing 3-2. *Generating an Incomplete DTD*

```
<?xml version="1.0"?>

<project>
  <antstructure output="./project.dtd"/>
</project>
```

To run Ant and create the DTD, execute the `ant` command at the command line, as follows:

```
> ant
```

Ant will process the build file and create the DTD. You can now add a reference to the DTD in your build file, as shown in Listing 3-3.

Listing 3-3. *A Build File with a DTD Declaration*

```
<?xml version="1.0"?>
<!DOCTYPE project PUBLIC "-//ANT//DTD project//EN" "project.dtd">

<project>

</project>
```

This is also how you add the complete DTD if you have downloaded it. If you eventually add new custom tasks or third-party tasks to your build files, you will have to extend this DTD. All in all, you may find it more straightforward to not work with DTDs, and you'll find that few source bundles come with DTD declarations. For example, the Ant distribution does not use a DTD.

Ant will always run any tasks that you set as child elements of `<project>`, which means every run of the project will include these tasks. If you want to control which tasks Ant runs, or you want to group related build steps (and you do), then you need to use targets, as defined by the `<target>` element. `<target>` elements are child elements of `<project>`, and you place tasks inside them so that you have more control over your builds. You can set a target as a default so that Ant will run it if you do not specify a target at the command line. To do so, use the `<project>` element's `default` attribute.

You set the base directory of the current build with the `<project>` element's `basedir` attribute. If you do not specify a default directory, the default is the parent directory of the `build.xml` file.

Lastly, you can give the project a name, which is useful as a description. Listing 3-4 shows all these attributes.

Listing 3-4. *Setting a Project Name, a Base Directory, and a Default Target*

```
<?xml version="1.0"?>
<project name="Apache Ant Book Project"
         basedir="."
         default="build-dtd">

  <target name="build-dtd">
    <antstructure output="./project.dtd"/>
  </target>

</project>
```

If you call `ant` with no arguments, it will run the `build-dtd` target and create the `project.dtd` file.

Examining the Target Element

A *target* is a collection of Ant tasks that you want to run as a unit. Each target should represent a discrete step of your build process and no more. It's possible that a target could be a small part of a large step, but you should make sure it is a discrete unit and it does not finish another task's business or leave unfinished business for another task. For example, an initialization target usually creates all the scratch directories for the build. You do not want to let the initialization target create some directories and then create some more common directories with the compilation target. Keeping a build file cohesive is important—for your sanity if nothing else.

The `<target>` element is the XML representation of a target in the build file. As already mentioned, it is a child element of `<project>`. It also can contain as many task elements as are required. When Ant calls a target, each of these tasks runs in turn until they all complete or one fails. You can chain targets together so that one target will not execute until another has completed all its tasks successfully. By setting these dependencies, you can start to build a description of the build process.

The `<target>` element's only mandatory attribute is `name`. The name allows you to call the target from the command line (see the "Running Ant from the Command Line" section) or from within the build file. You can accomplish the latter with the `<project>` element's `default` attribute or with certain tasks (more on this in Chapter 9).

You can provide the target with a description using the `description` attribute, and Ant uses this description when you call it with the `-projecthelp` option. In this case, Ant will display only the names and descriptions of targets that have descriptions. Ant is assuming that if it isn't important enough to have a description, it isn't important enough to be shown as a major target that you would want to run.

If none of the targets has a description, you will see something like this:

```
> ant -projecthelp
```

```
Buildfile: build.xml

Main targets:

Other targets:

 build-dtd
 build.path
 build.path.unix
 path.namespace
 properties.built-in
 properties.custom
 properties.environment
 properties.localfile
 properties.localfile.env
 properties.localfile.prefix
 properties.resourcefile
 properties.url
```

If you add a description, such as the one shown in Listing 3-5, then only that target will be displayed.

Listing 3-5. *Adding a Description to a Target*

```
<target name="build-dtd" description="Create an Ant DTD">
  <antstructure output="./project.dtd"/>
</target>
```

Now if you run the `-projecthelp` command again, Ant will display only this target:

```
> ant -projecthelp
```

```
Buildfile: build.xml

Main targets:

 build-dtd  Create an Ant DTD
```

To run this target, execute the following in the same directory as the build file:

```
> ant build-dtd
```

The <description> element adds a master description to a build file if you use it as a child element of <project>.

```
<description>
  Apache Ant book example project. The main targets are listed below.
</description>
```

You may use more than one <description> element if you want. Each one will print its message above the target descriptions. Here's the relevant ant command to display the descriptions you have added:

```
> ant -projecthelp
```

```
Buildfile: build.xml

  Apache Ant book example project. The main targets are listed below.

Main targets:

 build-dtd  Create an Ant DTD
```

If you want Ant to always run one target before running another one, such as an initialization target before a compilation target, then you need to specify the name of the first target you want to run in the second target's depends attribute, as shown in Listing 3-6.

Listing 3-6. *Setting a Dependency*

```
<?xml version="1.0"?>

<project name="Apache Ant Project" basedir="." default="build-dtd">

  <target name="pre-dtd">
    ...
  </target>

  <target name="build-dtd" depends="pre-dtd"
          description="Create an Ant DTD">
    <antstructure output="./project.dtd"/>
  </target>

</project>
```

In this example, the build-dtd target depends on the pre-dtd target. Once pre-dtd finishes successfully, build-dtd runs any tasks that it contains. Here's the result of running Ant with the default target:

```
Buildfile: build.xml

pre-dtd:

build-dtd:

BUILD SUCCESSFUL
Total time: 6 seconds
```

You can set as many target names in depends as you want by separating each name with a comma. Ant works through them one at a time until they all succeed or one fails.

The <target> element has more attributes, but these use properties, which I haven't covered yet. I'll do so now.

Working with Properties

While you write an Ant build file in XML, Ant has a few tricks up its sleeve to make the build file as flexible as possible. This is particularly important when working with platform-independent build files. Hard-coding directory paths and filenames is not a good idea in any area of programming, and you should attempt to avoid it in your source code. If this is the case, you don't want to undo all your careful work by hard-coding values into your build files.

Ant has a number of ways for you to make your build files portable and easily maintainable. The first three I will describe allow you to specify properties that can easily be changed from build to build, which allows you to configure the build for the local environment. The fourth technique allows you to incorporate certain conditions in your build files so that different results are obtained depending on the local environment.

■ **Note** The first three techniques are by far the most common, but you may find conditional processing useful. You should at this stage, however, form the opinion that you can treat Ant as a scripting tool. It does not do much more than simple conditions, such as `if...then` constructs, and does not handle errors. Of course, extensions to Ant have been written to overcome some of these perceived problems, and it is up to you whether you think you need them. I will provide pointers to extensions at the appropriate stages in this book.

Before learning about the techniques, you will look at the Ant concept of properties. Ant tasks use Ant properties to set attribute values at run time, which means the values of those attributes are not hard-coded.

Note The ${} notation used by Ant means "display the value of this property." Remember this when using some of the property-checking techniques described in this chapter. It is quite easy to forget that you want to specify the name of the property rather than its value.

You may want to set the base directory of the build at run time to allow for changes in directory structure. To do so, you have to place a property marker in the `basedir` attribute of the `<project>` element, as shown in Listing 3-7.

Listing 3-7. *A Property Marker in the `<project>` Element*

```
<?xml version="1.0"?>
<project basedir="${base.dir}">

</project>
```

The `${base.dir}` string inserts the value of the `base.dir` property at run time. If the `base.dir` property has not been set, Ant uses the literal string. This may or may not be a problem depending on the situation. For example, many build files use properties to set the locations of scratch and distribution directories. Before you run Ant, you are expected to set these properties in one of the ways described next. If you do not, you may end up with a directory structure like Figure 3-1.

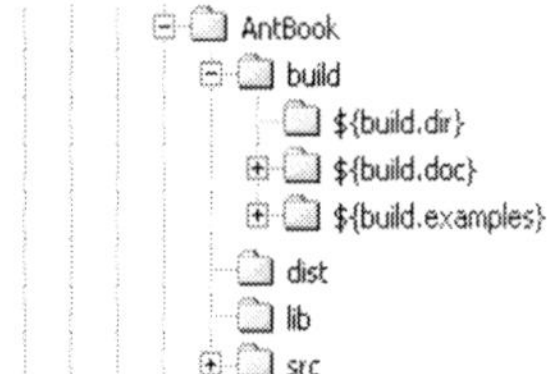

Figure 3-1. *Directory structure when properties are not set*

This is not a problem in the case of a build, because the directory names will remain constant throughout the build and you will be removing the scratch directory structure once you have finished the build anyway.

You may have a problem if the name of a JAR or WAR file must be set as a property or if you are referencing an existing directory in your build file. In the latter case, the build will fail if your source directory is called `src` and you are using a property called `src.dir`, because Ant will look for a directory called `${src.dir}` if the `src.dir` property is not set.

So, properties provide a standard build file that can be configured easily, removing the need for hard-coded strings. You should ensure that your properties are logically named so that other people can quickly and easily get an idea of how your project works when you are not there. You may even find that you benefit if you return to a project after a long break.

Naming properties as you would name Java packages is a good convention to use. For example, all properties that are associated with the initialization stage of the build could be prefixed `init.`, while those associated with the compilation stage could be prefixed `build.`. This separates them into discrete bundles and makes maintaining each build stage that much easier.

Using Built-in Properties

Ant provides you with certain built-in properties that you may find useful during your build process. They mainly provide information about the version of Ant and Java you are using and the current project, the latter of which you can use to set other paths in the project.

■ **Note** The built-in properties described in the following two sections have the common naming convention analogous to Java packages that I advocated previously. As such, you may want to avoid using the prefixes these properties use when naming your own properties.

Accessing Ant's Built-in Properties

Table 3-2 describes the five built-in Ant properties.

Table 3-2. *Ant's Built-in Properties*

Property	Description
`ant.file`	The absolute path to the current build file.
`ant.java.version`	The version of Java that Ant uses.
`ant.project.name`	The name of the project as set in the `<project>` element's `name` attribute. If you have not set this attribute, Ant will substitute the literal string `${ant.project.name}`.
`ant.version`	The version of this Ant installation. This is not just the version number and includes information such as the compilation date.
`basedir`	The base directory for this build, as defined in the `basedir` attribute of the `<project>` element. If you do not set this attribute, Ant uses the current directory.

These properties are unique to Ant and are shown in Listing 3-8. The `<echo>` task will display the specified message to standard out and is a good way to demonstrate the substitution that occurs when you use properties.

Listing 3-8. *Displaying Ant's Built-in Properties*

```
<?xml version="1.0"?>

<project name="Apache Ant Properties Project" basedir=".">

  <target name="properties.built-in">
    <echo message="The base directory: ${basedir}"/>
    <echo message="This file: ${ant.file}"/>
    <echo message="Ant version: ${ant.version}"/>
    <echo message="Project name: ${ant.project.name}"/>
    <echo message="Java version: ${ant.java.version}"/>
  </target>
</project>
```

Run the `properties.built-in` target, and you should see something like the following:

```
properties.built-in:
  [echo] The base directory: C:\AntBook
  [echo] This file: C:\AntBook\build.xml
  [echo] Ant version: Apache Ant version 1.6.3beta1 compiled on March 31 2005
  [echo] Project name: Apache Ant Properties Project
  [echo] Java version: 1.4
```

To see the substitution that Ant uses for the `ant.project.name` property, remove the `name` property from the `<project>` element. You will see something like the following when you run Ant:

```
[echo] Project name: ${ant.project.name}
```

Accessing System Properties

Ant also gives you access to the Java system properties as if you had called `java.lang.System.getProperties()`. This can, for example, allow you to build platform-specific paths and directory hierarchies. Listing 3-9 shows an example of this.

Listing 3-9. *Building a Platform-Specific Path*

```
  <target name="build.path">
    <echo message="File: ${basedir}${file.separator}build.xml"/>
    <echo message="Path: ${basedir}${file.separator}build.xml ➥
${path.separator}${basedir}${file.separator}build.properties"/>
  </target>
```

This is quite a handful, so it should be noted that you don't always have to work with platform-specific file and path separators. You may have to worry about separators if you build a path of any kind to pass to a command-line tool, because Ant treats the raw path you build as a string and does not do any substitutions.

On the other hand, when you build a path with any of Ant's tasks, Ant is quite happy to convert the separators into ones appropriate for the operating system on which it is running. Ant will also do the conversion if you pass the string that you have built to its tasks. Therefore, you could rewrite the previous listing, as shown in Listing 3-10, if you intend to use the path only with Ant tasks. The major problem with separators comes when you are using property files, which are covered in the "Setting Properties in Property Files" section.

Listing 3-10. *Building a Platform-Specific Path with Unix-Style File Separators*

```
<target name="build.path.unix">
  <echo message="File: ${basedir}/build.xml"/>
  <echo message="Path: ${basedir}/build.xml;➥
                      ${basedir}/build.properties"/>
</target>
```

Don't worry if the display shows a mixture of file separators. Ant is still treating these as strings. To see how Ant does the conversion, see the discussion of the `refid` attribute in the "Using a Reference" section.

■ **Note** The Ant manual comes with a complete list of system properties for your reference, along with a description of each. They may come up in later discussions in this book and will be explained at those times.

Setting Properties in the Build File

The first method of providing custom properties is with `<property>` elements in an Ant build file. Unlike the `<project>` and `<target>` elements, the `<property>` element is defined as a task. This means you can include `<property>` elements inside a target so that properties can be set conditionally, depending on certain conditions or depending on which target has been selected.

You can also set properties at the beginning of a build file so that they apply to the entire build. This means you can set important constant values in a central location so that they are easy to find and change, should the project change. You should remember that properties set inside a target override any properties set at the project level. Naming again comes into this, and you should consider whether your target-level properties should be identified as such by using a prefix to avoid confusion and possible namespace clashes.

■ **Note** Properties set in a target are available to targets that depend on it, as well as to targets that it calls (more on this in Chapter 9).

Using a Name-Value Pair

The simplest and most obvious use of the <property> task is to set a property using a name-value pair, as shown in Listing 3-11.

Listing 3-11. *Setting a Property with a Name-Value Pair*

```
<target name="properties.custom">
  <property name="build.no" value="1.1"/>
  <echo message="Build no. = ${build.no}"/>
</target>
```

You can set the value of a property to the value of another property. This can be useful if you will be referencing a verbose built-in property multiple times, much like Listing 3-9 did. This is as simple as placing a property marker in the value attribute of a <property> task, as shown in Listing 3-12.

Listing 3-12. *Setting a Property to the Value of Another Property*

```
<target name="properties.custom">
  <property name="fs" value="${file.separator}"/>
  <property name="ps" value="${path.separator}"/>

  <echo message="File: ${basedir}${fs}build.xml"/>
  <echo message="Path: ${basedir}${fs}build.xml${ps}➥
                 ${basedir}${fs}build.properties"/>
</target>
```

The fs and ps properties are set to the values of the file.separator and path.separator properties, respectively.

Using a File Location

The name property has two other potential partners you can use to set a property. The first is location, which you can use to set the value of a property to the location of a file. If you supply a relative path, Ant will expand the path to make it absolute and then store it as the value of the property. If you provide an absolute name, Ant will store it as is, though with the path separators adjusted for the platform as appropriate. Listing 3-13 shows how to set a property to a filename using a relative path.

Listing 3-13. *Setting a Property to a Filename Using a Relative Path*

```
<target name="properties.custom">
  <property name="project.dtd" location="project.dtd"/>
  <echo message="Location of project.dtd: ${project.dtd}"/>
</target>
```

This will display something like the following, showing that Ant has expanded the relative path to an absolute path:

```
[echo] Location of project.dtd: C:\AntBook\project.dtd
```

You can see how this is an important tool to have if your build file will be working with files on a number of operating systems, especially when building paths. If you want to ensure that the files you reference are indeed the files you think they are, you should use this technique. That way, different setups on different systems will not interfere with your build.

Using a Reference

The second partner to `name` is `refid`, which is a reference to an object defined elsewhere in the file. The reference allows you to reuse chunks of the build file (termed an *object* in this case) so that common classpaths and paths can be shared among targets. Many tasks have a `refid` attribute, and they all perform similar tasks. In the case of the `<property>` task, the `refid` attribute assigns the value of the referenced object to the property named with the `name` attribute. There is no point in assigning anything other than a pathlike structure in this case because you won't be able to use any other kind of reference once it has been stored in the property. The "Using Pathlike Structures" section covers pathlike structures.

Listing 3-14 shows that a path will be converted into the appropriate path for the current operating system. In this case, the path is a Unix-style path. If you are working on a Unix system, substitute the Windows path to see the example in action.

Listing 3-14. *Ant Converts a String into the Appropriate Path*

```
<target name="properties.custom">
  <!-- Windows users should leave this line uncommented -->
  <property name="build.path"
            value="${basedir}/build.xml:${basedir}/build.properties"/>

  <!-- Unix users should remove the above line
       and uncomment the below line -->
  <!--
  <property name="build.path"
            value="${basedir}\build.xml;${basedir}\build.properties"/>
  -->

  <path id="build.path.id">
    <pathelement path="${build.path}"/>
  </path>

  <property name="build.path.property" refid="build.path.id"/>

  <!-- The converted string that Ant uses as a path -->
  <echo message="Converted string: ${build.path.property}"/>

  <!-- The unconverted string, which Ant treats as a string -->
  <echo message="Path: ${build.path}"/>
</target>
```

The original build.path variable is a string property with Unix-style file and path separators (or Windows-style ones if you have changed the file on Unix). In this code, you create a path with a reference called build.path.id and pass the value of the build.path property into it. Ant converts this string to the local operating system format before storing it as a reference. Remember, this is not the same as a property, so you create a new property called build.path.property so that you can see the new, converted value of the path. In other words, the <echo> task does not support the refid property and so cannot display the contents of a reference, which in this case you want to do.

The result should be like this:

```
properties.custom:
  [echo] Converted string: C:\AntBook\build.xml;
                           C:\AntBook\1stApp\build.properties
  [echo] Path: C:\AntBook\1stApp/build.xml:
               C:\AntBook/build.properties
```

This is proof that Ant does the conversion: the unconverted path still contains the Unix-style path separator and has a mixture of file separators.

Accessing Environment Variables

The final technique available to you when setting properties in the build file is using the environment attribute of the <property> element. You should use this attribute by itself only and not in combination with any of the other techniques supplied. Ant won't let you use the environment attribute with any of the attributes described previously and doesn't guarantee results when used with any of the attributes described in the next section.

The environment attribute gives you access to the operating system's environment variables so that you can use them in your build process. For example, you may want to add a note about which architecture the build was carried out on or use the system classpath as the classpath when Ant compiles the Java classes.

The value you set in the environment attribute is the prefix you must use when referencing an environment variable in the build file. So, if you set the value of environment to env, you would reference the system classpath using ${env.CLASSPATH}. Ant is case-sensitive in this case, even if the host operating system is not.

Listing 3-15 shows how to access system environment variables.

Listing 3-15. *Gaining Access to the System's Environment Variables*

```
<target name="properties.environment">
  <property environment="env"/>
  <echo message="Built on: ${env.OS} ${env.PROCESSOR_ARCHITECTURE}"/>
  <echo message="ANT_HOME: ${env.ant_home}"/>
</target>
```

If you run this example, you will see something like the following, depending on your operating system:

```
properties.environment:
  [echo] Built on: Windows_NT x86
  [echo] ANT_HOME: ${env.ant_home}
```

Ant has not read the value of ANT_HOME because it is looking for an environment variable called ant_home.

The <property> task has other attributes, but you use them to load properties from a file rather than to set properties in the build file. The next section shows how to deal with these attributes.

Setting Properties in Property Files

Setting properties in the build file is a useful technique when you are working with common code repositories or servers. For example, if you have one CVS repository for all your code, you should set its value in the build file and discourage developers from changing it. In other words, setting properties in the build file is an excellent way of centralizing common, constant information and should be seen as such.

You can use properties for more than that, however. Not every piece of information in a build process is a constant value on every machine that the build file could possibly be run on. Users or developers may store third-party JAR files in different places to you and to other people who are likely to use the build file. Test servers may have different URLs depending on location because testing tends to occur on a local level, behind firewalls, and so on.

You will still have to use properties in situations like these, but you cannot specify these values in advance. The best way to work with localized information is to distribute a properties file with the names of the attributes and example values, which local users can change to suit their setup. Ant can then load these properties during the build. In addition to separating constants from local properties, properties files are easier to edit and more compact than their <property> task equivalents, as you will see next.

The most common technique is for developers and users to make a copy of the master properties file (build.properties.default), name it build.properties, and place it in the base directory. You must then make sure you import the build.properties file before the build.properties.default file. This means that local settings override the defaults (more on this in the "Examining Property Precedence" section). Another technique is to encourage developers and users to copy the build.properties file to their "home" directory and use the ${user.home} system property to reference its new location. This file then takes precedence over the default file.

You can of course set all your properties in a properties file if you want to enforce absolute centralization.

Note You'll look at the <property> attribute that imports the file after the discussion on property files. For now, assume that the properties are loaded in any examples.

Writing a Property File

Ant property files must conform to the same format as Java property files, as used by the `java.util.Properties` class. This means all characters must be in ISO 8859-1 format, and if they are not, you can use the `native2ascii` tool that comes with the Java distribution to convert the file.

Each property is represented by a name-value pair, separated with an equals sign, and comments are delimited with a hash character, as shown in Listing 3-16.

Listing 3-16. *The Basic Syntax of a Properties File*

```
# A comment is indicated by a hash mark
property.name=property.value
```

You can load a property file and, thus, the properties it contains in three ways: from a local file using a filename, from a URL, and from a file located on Ant's classpath.

One particularly nice feature of Ant property files is in-file property expansion. This feature means you can use properties set in a file to build the values of other properties set in that file. You can use this technique to your advantage in a number of situations, including building classpaths from third-party JARs and setting server names, both of which are shown in Listing 3-17.

Listing 3-17. *In-File Property Expansion in a Property File*

```
server.name=localhost
server.port=8080
server.scheme=http
server.manager.name=manager

server.url=${server.scheme}://${server.name}:${server.port}/➥
${server.manager.name}/

j2ee.jar=${env.J2EE_HOME}/lib/j2ee.jar
jsp.jar=${env.CATALINA_HOME}/common/lib/jsp-api.jar
servlet.jar=${env.CATALINA_HOME}/common/lib/servlet-api.jar
mysql.jar=${env.CATALINA_HOME}/common/lib/mysql.jar

build.classpath=${mysql.jar};${j2ee.jar};${jsp.jar};${servlet.jar}
```

The `server.url` and `build.classpath` properties are constructed from other properties in the properties file. Ant will import the properties and resolve them before running the build, so order is not important in the property file. However, order is important in the build file. When Ant imports the properties from the property file, it does so as part of the build sequence as set by you. Any properties you set *before* the import are available when the import occurs and so can be used to resolve property values. Any properties you set *after* the import are not available for resolving.

Caution Windows users cannot use back slashes in path names in property files, though back slashes are allowed in build files. This is consistent with ISO 8859-1, which uses back slashes as escape characters. If you use any back slashes, Ant will strip them out, leaving you with a horrible agglutinated mass. You have two options: you can use forward slashes as described or escape your back slashes with another back slash, like so: \\.

This process has implications for the property file shown in Listing 3-17. The four properties that hold the path to a JAR file depend on environment variables, and these are available only if you use the following before you import the property file:

```
<property environment="env"/>
```

Figure 3-2 shows the process. You can see how no environment variables are available in the process on the right, so the in-file expansion does not happen.

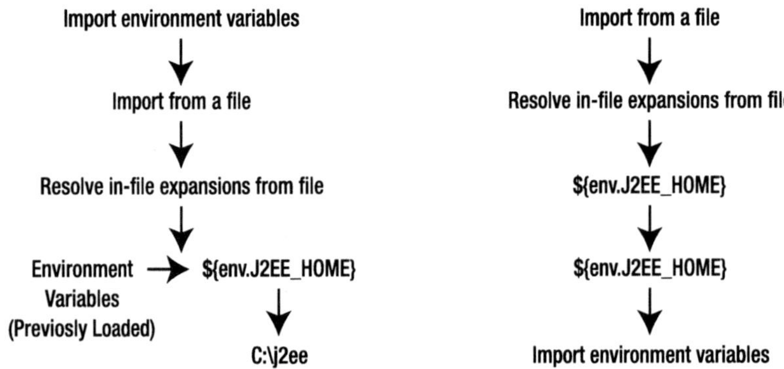

Figure 3-2. *In-file expansion and property loading order*

This is really just an extension of the behavior you saw when I discussed the `ant.project.name` property in the "Accessing Ant's Built-in Properties" section. If the property is not set, then Ant will treat the property marker as a string.

To ensure that you do not rely on outside properties, you can set all the required information in the property file, as shown in Listing 3-18.

Listing 3-18. *Removing the Need for Environment Variables*

```
j2ee.home=C:/j2ee
catalina.home=C:/jakarta-tomcat

j2ee.jar=${j2ee.home}/lib/j2ee.jar
jsp.jar=${catalina.home}/common/lib/jsp-api.jar
servlet.jar=${catalina.home}/common/lib/servlet-api.jar
mysql.jar=${catalina.home}/common/lib/mysql.jar

build.classpath=${mysql.jar};${j2ee.jar};${jsp.jar};${servlet.jar}
```

This keeps the property file internally consistent, which aids any maintenance you may undertake. However, this does not solve the problem if you still need to use environment variables, but want to ensure they are always loaded.

As mentioned, Windows users should be careful when specifying paths, such as in the value for `j2ee.home`. If you do not take this precaution, Ant will remove the back slash when you build a path. Here's what the path would look like after you have built it using in-file expansion:

```
[echo] Build classpath: C:j2ee/lib/j2ee.jar;
```

Notice the missing back slash. Now, if you feed this into a `<path>`, Ant will treat the colon as a Unix-style path separator followed by a back slash. It will then treat your path as two paths relative to the current `basedir` and expand them as follows, accounting for the local operating system:

```
[echo] Build classpath converted: C:\AntBook\ch03\C;
                                  C:\AntBook\ch03\j2ee\lib\j2ee.jar
```

One way to use environment variables and keep the property file internally consistent is to remove the "home" settings from the property file and use environment variable references in the build file. Listing 3-19 shows the new property file portion.

Listing 3-19. *Removing References to Application "Home" Directories*

```
# j2ee.home=C:/j2ee
# catalina.home=C:/jakarta-tomcat

j2ee.jar=lib/j2ee.jar
jsp.jar=common/lib/jsp-api.jar
servlet.jar=common/lib/servlet-api.jar
mysql.jar=common/lib/mysql.jar

# Remove the build.classpath property
# build.classpath=${mysql.jar};${j2ee.jar};${jsp.jar};${servlet.jar}
```

The consequences of this change are that you now can't build the classpath in the property file and must remember to append the environment variables in the build file. Listing 3-20 shows the new build file segment (assuming you have loaded the properties).

Listing 3-20. *Building the Classpath in the Build File with Environment Variables*

```
<property environment="env"/>
<path id="build.classpath.id">
  <pathelement path="${env.J2EE_HOME}/${j2ee.jar}"/>
  <pathelement path="${env.CATALINA_HOME}/${jsp.jar}"/>
  <pathelement path="${env.CATALINA_HOME}/${servlet.jar}"/>
  <pathelement path="${env.CATALINA_HOME}/${mysql.jar}"/>
</path>
```

Your choice of technique largely depends on whether you need environment variables. If you do, then you should really use the final technique described. If not, then filling in values, as shown in Listing 3-18, is the best option. Grouping "home" directories in one section of the property file adds to the centralization and maintainability of the file.

Loading Properties from a Local File

It is usual to provide a properties file with any source distribution, and most build projects will have a local properties file on the file system. If you are providing a local build file, you should provide a README or some other kind of information pointing to the settings in the properties file.

If you want to use a local property file, then you must specify its location with the file attribute of the <property> task. Listing 3-21 shows how to load the file from Listing 3-18 (the one that uses "home" directory properties).

Listing 3-21. *Loading a Local Property File*

```
<target name="properties.localfile">

  <property file="build.properties"/>

  <path id="build.classpath.id">
    <pathelement path="${build.classpath}"/>
  </path>

  <property name="build.classpath.property" refid="build.classpath.id"/>

  <echo message="Server URL: ${server.url}"/>
  <echo message="Build classpath: ${build.classpath}"/>
  <echo message="Build classpath converted: ${build.classpath.property}"/>
</target>
```

As mentioned previously, Ant properties are subject to namespace rules such as variables in programming, so there is a chance imported properties listed in a property file may conflict with properties that have already been set in the build file. To avoid this, you can append a prefix to the properties that you know come from the property file. To specify the prefix, add a prefix attribute in conjunction with the file attribute, as shown in Listing 3-22.

Listing 3-22. *Adding a Prefix to Imported Properties*

```
<target name="properties.localfile.prefix">

  <property file="build.properties" prefix="imported"/>

  <path id="build.classpath.id">
    <pathelement path="${imported.build.classpath}"/>
  </path>

  <property name="build.classpath.property" refid="build.classpath.id"/>
```

```
  <echo message="Server URL: ${imported.server.url}"/>
  <echo message="Build classpath: ${imported.build.classpath}"/>
  <echo message="Build classpath converted: ${build.classpath.property}"/>
</target>
```

Ant will add a period after the prefix without you having to specify that it should do so.

You can also load a property file that is located on your classpath (the one you used to run Ant). The `resource` attribute has the same function as the `file` attribute when you use it as you used the `file` attribute in the two previous examples, except that Ant searches your classpath for it and not Ant's base directory. Therefore, if you substitute the `resource` attribute for the `file` attribute and the current directory is in your classpath, you will not see any change in functionality. You can also use the `prefix` attribute with the `resource` attribute to manage property names.

`resource` also allows you to search a custom classpath to find a properties file using the `classpath` attribute or the `classpathref` attribute. `classpath` accepts a standard classpath and will convert the string into one that is appropriate for the local operating system. You can also specify a classpath with a nested `<classpath>` element, which performs the same operation as the `classpath` attribute. Listing 3-23 shows both of these techniques.

Listing 3-23. *Setting a Classpath Where a Properties File Is Located*

```
<target name="properties.resourcefile">

  <!--
  <property resource="build.res.properties" classpath="./lib"/>
  -->

  <property resource="build.res.properties">
    <classpath path="./lib"/>
  </property>

  <path id="build.classpath.id">
    <pathelement path="${build.classpath}"/>
  </path>

  <property name="build.classpath.property" refid="build.classpath.id"/>

  <echo message="Server URL: ${server.url}"/>
  <echo message="Build classpath: ${build.classpath}"/>
  <echo message="Build classpath converted: ${build.classpath.property}"/>
</target>
```

If you have a project classpath defined in an earlier `<path>` structure, then you can reference this by using the `classpathref` attribute instead of the `classpath` attribute.

```
<property resource="build.res.properties"
          classpathref="project.classpath"/>
```

Using a resource means that you can maintain some control over the property file if you want. For example, you could set it to read-only before placing it on the classpath. This ensures that Ant can use the properties it contains, but that users can't overwrite them.

■ **Note** If you load more than one property file, the order of loading determines which properties have precedence. If a property has already been loaded in a previous file, it is ignored if it is loaded in a subsequent file.

Loading Properties from a Remote File

If you like the sound of maintaining control over your property files or want to distribute them to various locations where the build will be taking place, then you can store them on a web server and get Ant to retrieve the properties from there. To retrieve properties from a remote file, set the value of the `url` property to the location of the property file. (This always requires a network connection.) You can also use the `prefix` attribute if you want. Listing 3-24 shows this technique.

Listing 3-24. *Retrieving Properties from a Remote File*

```
<target name="properties.url">

  <property url="http://localhost:8080/antBook/properties/build.properties"/>

  <path id="build.classpath.id">
    <pathelement path="${build.classpath}"/>
  </path>

  <property name="build.classpath.property" refid="build.classpath.id"/>

  <echo message="Server URL: ${server.url}"/>
  <echo message="Build classpath: ${build.classpath}"/>
  <echo message="Build classpath converted: ${build.classpath.property}"/>
</target>
```

Summarizing the Property Task

Table 3-3 summarizes the commands discussed previously and shows which ones are mutually exclusive. None of these attributes is required, though you must specify one of `environment`, `file`, `name`, `resource`, or `url`.

Table 3-3. *The <property> Task's Attributes*

Attribute	Description	Restrictions
classpath	Ant uses this classpath to search for the file named in resource. You can specify a classpath with a nested <classpath> element as well.	Valid only with the resource attribute. Only one of classpath and classpathref may be used.
classpathref	Ant uses this classpath to search for the file named in resource. It refers to a path set earlier in the file using a <path> element.	Valid only with the resource element. Only one of classpath and classpathref must be used.
environment	The prefix to use when referencing the operating system's environment variables.	Only one of environment, file, resource, or url may be used in a particular <property> task. May not be used if name is used.
file	A property file that contains the properties you want to load.	Only one of environment, file, resource, or url may be used in a particular <property> task. May not be used if name is used.
location	The value of the property is set to the absolute filename of this file. You can specify a relative filename, and Ant will expand it and store the value.	Used with name. Only one of location, value, or refid may be used with name. May not be used with any other attributes.
name	The name of the property to set.	May not be used with environment, file, resource, or url.
prefix	The prefix to add to imported properties. Ant adds a period after the prefix.	May be used only with file, resource, or url.
refid	A reference to an object defined earlier in the file.	Used with name. Only one of location, value, or refid may be used with name. May not be used with any other attributes.
resource	A file that Ant will look for on the current classpath. The classpath can be set with the classpath or classpathref attributes.	Only one of environment, file, resource, or url may be used in a particular <property> task. May not be used if name is used.
url	A URL where you have placed a property file that contains the properties you want to load.	Only one of environment, file, resource, or url may be used in a particular <property> task. May not be used if name is used.
value	The value you want to assign to the property.	Used with name. Only one of location, value, or refid may be used with name. May not be used with any other attributes.

Setting Properties at the Command Line

The final way to set properties is at the command line. You can specify individual properties using the `-Dproperty=value` syntax, or you can load the properties from a property file using the `-propertyfile` option. As noted at the beginning of the chapter, the `-Dproperty=value` syntax takes precedence. In fact, `-Dproperty=value` takes precedence over all property values in the build. For example, if you wanted to override the server name because the main development server is down, you can run the following:

```
> ant -Dserver.name=remotehost properties.localfile
```

```
[echo] Server URL: http://remotehost:8080/manager/
```

This has overridden the value imported from a property file that was loaded in the build file.

The property to supply at the command line does not have to be set in the build file. In some cases, you may want to specify a property's value at the command line only; the best example of this is when you want to supply a username and password for a server or a database. A build file is not a very secure location for sensitive information, such as passwords, because it is written in plain, human-readable text.

Being able to supply passwords at the command line significantly improves your security, though you should remember that the command may still reside in your shell's history for anyone to see. Physical access to your terminal should be just as important as electronic access.

Examining Property Precedence

As mentioned, properties set at the command line override any properties in the build file, including those imported from a properties file. I've also touched on how loading a property file overrides properties set in the build file and any properties that are loaded subsequently. The precedence picture is almost complete, though remember this general rule:

Properties that are defined first take precedence.

Therefore, those defined at the command line have the highest precedence because they are defined before the build file is read. After this, the order of `<property>` tags is important. The first `<property>` tag has precedence over the second, and so on. Here are the contents of the `build.properties` file:

```
property.example=Local File
property.file.example=build.properties
```

And here's the `build.properties.default` file:

```
property.example=Default File
property.file.example=build.properties.default
```

Listing 3-25 shows an example that demonstrates precedence.

Listing 3-25. *Targets That Demonstrate Property Precedence*

```
<?xml version="1.0"?>

<project name="Apache Ant Properties Project" basedir="." default="print-file">

  <property name="property.example" value="Global"/>
  <property file="build.properties"/>
  <property file="build.properties.local"/>

  <target name="print-global">
    <echo message="In print-global"/>
    <echo message="The value of property.example is: ${property.example}"/>
  </target>

  <target name="print-target" depends="print-global">
    <property name="property.example" value="Target"/>

    <echo message="In print-target"/>
    <echo message="The value of property.example is: ${property.example}"/>
  </target>

  <target name="print-file" depends="print-target">
    <property name="property.file.example" value="build.xml"/>

    <echo message="In print-file"/>
    <echo>
      The value of property.file.example is: ${property.file.example}
    </echo>
  </target>

</project>
```

If you run this example, here's what happens:

```
> ant
```

```
Buildfile: build.xml

print-global:
     [echo] In print-global
     [echo] The value of property.example is: Global

print-target:
     [echo] In print-target
     [echo] The value of property.example is: Global
```

```
print-file:
     [echo] In print-file
     [echo]
     [echo]        The value of property.file.example is: build.properties
     [echo]

BUILD SUCCESSFUL
Total time: 1 second
```

You can see how the property.example value that you set in the first <property> element overrides the values in the two property files and the value set in the print-target target. This is because you set it first. Also note how the value of property.file.example from build.properties overrides the other settings because you define it before any other instances of this property.

Now move the <property> elements around like this:

```
<property file="build.properties"/>
<property file="build.properties.default"/>
<property name="property.example" value="Global"/>
```

Here's the result of running the build again:

```
Buildfile: build.xml

print-global:
     [echo] In print-global
     [echo] The value of property.example is: Local File

print-target:
     [echo] In print-target
     [echo] The value of property.example is: Local File

print-file:
     [echo] In print-file
     [echo]
     [echo]        The value of property.file.example is: build.properties
     [echo]

BUILD SUCCESSFUL
Total time: 1 second
```

This time the value from the local properties file is used. Now, run the build with command-line properties like so:

```
> ant -Dproperty.file.example=command-line
```

```
Buildfile: build.xml

print-global:
     [echo] In print-global
     [echo] The value of property.example is: Local File

print-target:
     [echo] In print-target
     [echo] The value of property.example is: Local File

print-file:
     [echo] In print-file
     [echo]
     [echo]         The value of property.file.example is: command-line
     [echo]

BUILD SUCCESSFUL
Total time: 1 second
```

Now the command-line property has taken precedence.

Using Properties to Control a Build

Any builds can become complex to match a complex project. However, you might not always want to execute every part of a build, or you may want to execute only certain parts if a condition is true (or false for that matter). You can of course create a build sequence using target dependencies, which means you can chain targets together. Using this mechanism, you can even integrate conditions that cause the build process to fork and create a different distribution. For example, the sample application that appears later in the book has a stand-alone Java client and a web-based interface, though they share database connection code. The build process for these two sections of the application starts with the common code before splitting, depending on which one you are building.

Figure 3-3 shows this situation.

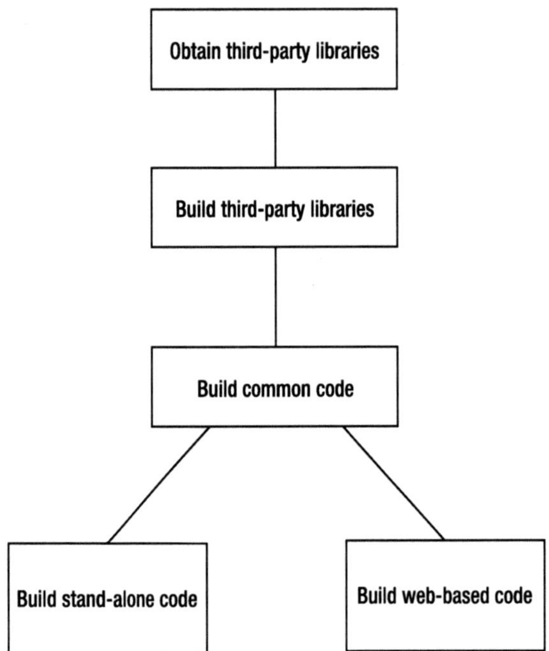

Figure 3-3. *A forking build process*

This build process is a simple enough one to model using dependences. In this case, you would simply set the depends attribute of the stand-alone target to the name of the target that builds the common code. The same is true of the web application target.

An alternative is to use the final two `<target>` element attributes: `if` and `unless`. These affect whether a target runs and depend on properties. Setting `if` to the name of a property means that *if* the property is set, then the target should run. Setting `unless` to the name of a property means that the target should run *unless* that property is set. It does not matter what value the property has, as long as it is set. `null` doesn't exist in Ant.

Note The value set in the `if` and `unless` attributes should be the name of a property, not the value a property contains. Do not use the `${}` notation unless you really mean to set the name of a property as the value of another property.

`if` overrides `unless` if they have the same property as a value, though you'll have absolutely no reason to want to do this. You should also be aware that these settings do not affect the running of any targets listed in the depends attribute, should it be specified. These are iterated over as normal, and it is only when they all succeed that Ant checks the `if` and `unless` attributes of this target.

Application builds are not always as simple as this, however. For example, you might want to obtain and build the third-party libraries only if you do not already have them. This means Ant will have to check whether a certain file exists in the build directory structure; if the file exists, Ant will skip the first two steps in Figure 3-3. This brings you to the first of the build control elements: `<available>`.

Using the Available Task

The `<available>` task sets the value of a property if a resource exists when you run the build process. This allows you to check for libraries and other files so that the build can proceed without any errors. It also means you can avoid unnecessary steps if the files you need are already available to Ant.

The default value of the property is `true`, which is enough for the purposes of the `if` and `unless` attributes, which check to see whether a property is set. In other words, they don't care what the value is. If, however, you want to set a different value, you can. For example, you may want to set the name of the resultant JAR file to a certain value depending on whether it contains newly built third-party libraries or whether it uses existing, older libraries. The value to append to the filename could be the value of the property set using the `<available>` task.

The available element has a number of attributes, each of which is described in Table 3-4.

Table 3-4. *The Attributes of the `<available>` Task*

Attribute	Description
`classname`	The Java class for which to look. You can set a classpath with the `classpath` or `classpathref` attribute. You must specify one and only one of the `classname`, the `file`, or the `resource` attribute.
`classpath`	The classpath that Ant will use when working with the `classname` or `resource` attribute. The default is the build's classpath. Any directories or JARs that you specify in this attribute are appended to the build classpath.
`classpathref`	The reference ID of a classpath that you have defined earlier in the build process.
`file`	The name of a file for which to look. You must specify one and only one of the `classname`, the `file`, or the `resource` attribute.
`filepath`	The path to use when looking for the file specified in the `file` attribute. The default is the base directory of the build.
`ignoresystemclasses`	If you set this to `true`, the search will ignore Ant's internal classes and will use the classpath specified only as part of this `<available>` element. The default is `false`.
`property`	The name of the property you want to set. This attribute is required.
`resource`	The name of a resource for which to look. This resource should be located within the JVM. You must specify one and only one of the `classname`, the `file`, or the `resource` attribute.
`type`	Set this attribute to `file` if you want Ant to search for a file. Set it to `dir` if you want Ant to search for a directory. If you do not set this attribute, Ant will search for both.
`value`	The value that this property will take if Ant finds the searched-for item. The default is `true`.

You can also specify the classpath and filepath elements as nested <classpath> and <filepath> elements, which means you can use reference IDs should you so want.

Listing 3-26 shows an example where Ant checks whether you already have a version of the JSTL. If you don't, Ant retrieves a copy of the source and builds it.

Listing 3-26. *Using the <available> Element to Check for the Existence of Third-Party Files*

```
<?xml version="1.0"?>

<project name="Apache Ant Available Project" basedir="."
         default="build-jstl">

  <property name="jstl.src" value="./src/jstl"/>
  <property name="jstl.jar" value="./lib/jstl.jar"/>

  <available property="jstl.src.exists" file="${jstl.src}"/>
  <available property="jstl.jar.exists" file="${jstl.jar}"/>

  <target name="checkout-jstl" unless="jstl.src.exists">
    <echo message="Checking out ${jstl.jar}"/>
    ...
  </target>

  <target name="build-jstl" depends="checkout-jstl" unless="jstl.jar.exists">
    <echo message="Building ${jstl.jar}"/>
    ...
  </target>

</project>
```

The build-jstl target depends on the checkout-jstl target, so the latter will execute first. This target will execute only if the <available> task has not found the source distribution of the JSTL. If it has, you have no need to download the source from the server. Even if an existing source distribution is found and Ant does not run the tasks contained in checkout-jstl, this counts as a successful target completion, so Ant tries to run build-jstl, safe in the knowledge that the source code is present.

Here Ant runs the build only if the JSTL binaries are not present, following a check by the second <available> task. If the binaries are not present, Ant uses the source code found or downloaded in the earlier step.

The following shows how to use the filepath attribute to replace the paths in the properties:

```
<property name="jstl.src" value="jstl"/>
<property name="jstl.jar" value="jstl.jar"/>

<available property="jstl.src.exists" file="${jstl.src}" filepath="./src"/>
<available property="jstl.jar.exists" file="${jstl.jar}" filepath="./lib"/>
```

This all assumes you want to download the source code of the JSTL in the first place. If you do not want to use the source code at any point, you won't have to get involved in this kind of checking and will just use the binary distribution.

Using the Uptodate Task

The `<uptodate>` task follows in the same vein as the `<available>` task in that it checks the status of files in the build and sets a property as appropriate. In this case, if a set of source files was modified after the set of files you are interested in working with, the `<uptodate>` element will set the property to `true`. You can then use the `if` and `unless` attributes of a target to control compilation and copying tasks, for example. As you can see, this task complements the `<available>` task well, which allows you to remove a certain amount of redundancy from your projects.

Ant does these kinds of checks as part of its task functionality. For example, when you are copying files, Ant will copy only those files that have changed. However, it still must spend time checking each file before deciding which files to copy. In large projects, this could take a long time. One way to cut down on this processing time is to use one sample file as the check for whether it is worth copying the whole project or just a section.

Table 3-5 shows the attributes of this task, though you may specify certain nested elements if you need to work with sets of files.

Table 3-5. *The Attributes of the `<uptodate>` Task*

Attribute	Description
`property`	The name of the property you want to set. This attribute is required.
`srcfile`	Ant will compare this file's timestamp with the timestamp of the file specified in the `targetfile` attribute. If this file's timestamp is earlier than the timestamp of the file named in `targetfile`, Ant will set the property. This attribute is required unless you specify a nested `<srcfiles>` element.
`targetfile`	If this file's timestamp is later than the timestamp of the file specified in `srcfile`, Ant will set the property. This attribute is required unless you specify a nested `<mapper>` element.
`value`	The value that this property will take if the timestamp of the file specified in `srcfile` is later than the timestamp of the file specified in `targetfile`. The default is `true`.

So, the `srcfile` attribute holds the original file, and you use the `<uptodate>` task to check whether the `targetfile` is more recent (that is, more up-to-date) than the source file. If it is more recent, the property is set.

The `<srcfiles>` nested elements are file sets and have the same attributes. Listing 3-27 shows how to set a file set and then use it later as part of an `<uptodate>` check.

Listing 3-27. *Using a File Set As Part of an <uptodate> Check*

```
<fileset dir="." id="uptodate.id">
  <include name="src/jstl/One.java"/>
</fileset>

<uptodate property="uptodate" targetfile="./One.java">
  <srcfiles refid="uptodate.id"/>
</uptodate>

<target name="compile" if="uptodate">
  <echo message="File changed: ${uptodate}"/>
</target>
```

The file that makes up the file set with the `uptodate.id` ID is the source file you want to check. If it has changed more recently than the file specified in the `targetfile` attribute of `<uptodate>`, then the property is not set and the `compile` target will not run. If the `targetfile` file is more recent than the source file, then the `compile` target will run.

Listing 3-28 shows this example using a nested `<mapper>` element.

Listing 3-28. *Using a File Set and Mapper As Part of an <uptodate> Check*

```
<fileset dir="." id="uptodate.id">
  <include name="src/jstl/One.java"/>
</fileset>

<uptodate property="uptodate">
  <srcfiles refid="uptodate.id"/>
  <mapper type="merge" to="./One.java"/>
</uptodate>

<target name="compile" if="uptodate">
  <echo message="File changed: ${uptodate}"/>
</target>
```

Here you've just transferred the value of the `targetfile` attribute to the `to` attribute of the mapper. This is actually what happens behind the scenes in Listing 3-27, because if you specify nested `<srcfiles>` elements and a `targetfile` attribute, Ant uses a merge mapper anyway.

Using the Condition Task

The `<condition>` task is like the `if` construct in programming and is described as a generalization of the two tasks described previously. This is true, and you can replicate the functionality of the `<available>` and `<uptodate>` tasks using the `<condition>` task if you want.

Table 3-6 describes the attributes of the `<condition>` task.

Table 3-6. *The Attributes of the* `<condition>` *Task*

Attribute	Description
`else`	If the nested condition is not matched, Ant will set the value of the property to this value. If you do not specify this attribute, then the property is not set.
`property`	The name of the property you want to set. This attribute is required.
`value`	The value that this property will take if the nested condition is matched. The default is `true`.

Using the Condition Task As an Available or Uptodate Task

The first example, shown in Listing 3-29, is a reworking of the `<available>` and `<uptodate>` examples from before, using the nested `<available>` and `<uptodate>` elements. These take the same attributes as before, except for `property` and `value`.

Listing 3-29. *Using the* `<condition>` *Task Instead of the* `<available>` *and* `<uptodate>` *Tasks*

```
<fileset dir="." id="uptodate.id">
  <include name="src/jstl/One.java"/>
</fileset>

<property name="jstl.src" value="jstl"/>
<property name="jstl.jar" value="jstl.jar"/>

<condition property="jstl.src.exists">
  <available file="${jstl.src}" filepath="./src"/>
</condition>

<condition property="jstl.jar.exists">
  <available file="${jstl.jar}" filepath="./lib"/>
</condition>

<condition property="uptodate">
  <uptodate>
    <srcfiles refid="uptodate.id"/>
    <mapper type="merge" to="./One.java"/>
  </uptodate>
</condition>

<target name="checkout-jstl" unless="jstl.src.exists">
  <echo message="Checking out ${jstl.jar}"/>
</target>
```

```
<target name="build-jstl" depends="checkout-jstl" unless="jstl.jar.exists">
  <echo message="Building ${jstl.jar}"/>
</target>

<target name="compile" if="uptodate">
  <echo message="File changed: ${uptodate}"/>
</target>
```

Using the <os> Test

If you are working with a project that needs to check the operating system on which it is built and carry out actions appropriately, then you can use the <os> nested element. Table 3-7 shows the attributes of the <os> element, which you can combine to create a specific test. As a result, none of these attributes is required.

Table 3-7. *The Attributes of the <os> Element*

Attribute	Description
arch	The architecture of the operating system for which you are testing.
family	The operating system's broad family. The possible values for this are listed after the table.
name	The name of the operating system for which you are testing.
version	The version of the operating system for which you are testing.

For arch, name, and version, Ant calls the appropriate line in the following and compares the value with that specified in the attribute:

```
System.getProperty("os.arch");
System.getProperty("os.name");
System.getProperty("os.version");
```

So, for the Windows 2000 machine that this book was written on, here are the appropriate values:

```
os.arch = x86
os.name = Windows 2000
os.version = 5.0
```

The family attribute allows you to be much broader in your scope and test against operating systems that are pretty similar to each other. You don't necessarily have to care which version of Windows or Unix is running and so don't need to research the exact values that the previous lines of code would return.

Table 3-8 lists the possible values for the `family` attribute.

Table 3-8. *Possible Values for the* `family` *Attribute of the* `<os>` *Nested Element*

Value	Description
`dos`	Matches all Microsoft DOS–based operating systems. This includes all versions of Windows and OS/2.
`mac`	Matches all Apple Macintosh operating systems.
`netware`	Matches Novell NetWare.
`openvms`	Matches OpenVMS.
`os/2`	Matches OS/2.
`os/400`	Matches OS/400.
`tandem`	Matches Hewlett-Packard's NonStop Kernel. This operating system used to be called Tandem.
`unix`	Matches all Unix-style operating systems. This includes Linux and the Mac Unix-style operating systems.
`win9x`	Matches Windows 95 and Windows 98.
`windows`	Matches all versions of Windows.
`z/os`	Matches z/OS and OS/390.

Listing 3-30 shows the `family` attribute in action.

Listing 3-30. *Using the* `<os>` *Element's* `family` *Attribute to Test the Operating System*

```
<condition property="is.windows">
  <os family="windows"/>
</condition>

<condition property="is.unix">
  <os family="unix"/>
</condition>

<target name="do-windows" if="is.windows">
  <echo message="This is Windows"/>
</target>

<target name="do-unix" if="is.unix">
  <echo message="This is Unix"/>
</target>
```

Using the <equals> Test

The <equals> nested element tests two strings to see if they are equal. This is a classic example of if functionality, and you can use it to check the values of properties or filenames. Table 3-9 shows the attributes of the <equals> element.

Table 3-9. *The Attributes of the <equals> Element*

Attribute	Description
arg1	The first string to test. This attribute is required.
arg2	The second string to test. This attribute is required.
casesensitive	Set this to true to make the test case-sensitive. The default is true.
trim	Set this to true to trim any whitespace from the strings. The default is false.

Using the <isset> Test

The <isset> element tests whether a property has been set in this project. You may find this test most useful when used in conjunction with other tests (you'll see how to do this in the "Using Logical Operators" section). For example, you may want to test to see whether a command-line property has been set and that a certain file exists and then run a target only if this is the case.

Table 3-10 shows the attribute of the <isset> element.

Table 3-10. *The Attribute of the <isset> Element*

Attribute	Description
property	The property to test. If it does not exist, the test fails. This attribute is required.

Using the <istrue> and <isfalse> Tests

The <istrue> and <isfalse> tests are related to and extend the <isset> test, but check that the value of the property is true or false, respectively. Ant also considers yes and on to equal true and considers no and off to equal false, so these values also satisfy these tests. <istrue> and <isfalse> share the attribute shown in Table 3-11, though they produce opposite effects.

Table 3-11. *The Common Attribute of the <istrue> and <isfalse> Elements*

Attribute	Description
value	The value to test. You can specify a property value using the usual ${} syntax or a constant to ensure the test always passes or fails, depending on your requirements.

Using the <isreference> Test

The `<isreference>` test checks whether the given ID is indeed a valid reference. You can also check whether this ID refers to a certain type of Ant structure.

Table 3-12 shows the attribute of the `<isreference>` element.

Table 3-12. *The Attributes of the <isreference> Element*

Attribute	Description
refid	The ID of the reference you want to test. This attribute is required.
type	The Ant type of the reference. If you do not specify this attribute, any type is considered.

The value of the type attribute should correspond to the name of the element that represents the Ant type. Listing 3-31 shows an example that tests for a file set.

Listing 3-31. *A File Set Reference Is Tested Using the <isreference> Test*

```
<condition property="is.fileset">
  <isreference refid="uptodate.id" type="fileset"/>
</condition>

<target name="fileset-prepare">
  <echo message="Value of is.fileset = ${is.fileset}"/>
</target>
```

The value of the `<isreference>` element's type attribute is set to `fileset`, which corresponds to the name of the element that represents a file set: `<fileset>`. So, the `is.fileset` property is set only if the `uptodate.id` reference ID refers to a file set. If you omit the `type` attribute, the property will be set if the `uptodate.id` reference ID is a valid ID. The type does not matter.

Using the <isfileselected> Test

The `<isfileselected>` test succeeds if a given file matches all the conditions specified as nested selectors (covered in Chapter 4). Use it as you would a file set. Table 3-13 shows the attributes of the `<isfileselected>` element.

Table 3-13. *The Attributes of the <isfileselected> Element*

Attribute	Description
basedir	The root of the directory structure to search. The default is the project's base directory.
file	The file you are checking. This attribute is required.

Using the <checksum> Test

This is identical to the `<checksum>` task described in Chapter 6, and I will cover the details then. You use this test to check that a file matches the checksum supplied as part of a download. You'll see this process when you examine the `<modified>` selector in Chapter 4.

Using the <http> Test

The `<http>` test checks that a web server provides a valid response and sets the property if this is the case. This allows you to check whether a server is listening to requests before you begin a download from it.

Table 3-14 shows the attributes of the `<http>` element.

Table 3-14. *The Attributes of the `<http>` Element*

Attribute	Description
`errorsBeginAt`	The lowest HTTP response code that indicates there was an error as far as this test is concerned. The default is `400`.
`url`	The URL of the server to query. This attribute is required.

Using the <socket> Test

The `<socket>` test checks that a process is listening at the specified server and port. Again, you can use this to check that you can run a target that requires this to be the case.

Table 3-15 shows the attributes of the `<socket>` element.

Table 3-15. *The Attributes of the `<socket>` Element*

Attribute	Description
`port`	The port to which you want to connect. This attribute is required.
`server`	The server to which you want to connect. This can be the hostname as defined under DNS, or it can be an IP address. This attribute is required.

Using the <filesmatch> Test

The `<filesmatch>` test checks whether two files are identical. The test follows three distinct steps, and as soon as a file fails one of these steps, the whole test fails. The steps are as follows:

1. Do both files exist? If one does not exist, the test fails.
2. Do both files have the same filename? If not, the test fails.
3. Are the files the same size? If not, the test fails.
4. Do both files have the same number of bytes in the same sequence? If not, the test fails.

As you can see, the first three steps are there to stop the test getting as far as a byte-for-byte check if at all possible, because that can become a costly operation for large files.

Table 3-16 shows the attributes of the <filesmatch> element.

Table 3-16. *The Attributes of the <filesmatch> Element*

Attribute	Description
file1	The first file in the test. This attribute is required.
file2	The second file in the test. This attribute is required.

Using the <contains> Test

The <contains> attribute represents another classic if function: checking whether a string contains another string. Table 3-17 shows the attributes of the <contains> element.

Table 3-17. *The Attributes of the <contains> Element*

Attribute	Description
casesensitive	Set this to true to ensure that this check is case-sensitive. The default is true.
string	The larger string in which you want to search. This attribute is required.
substring	The substring for which you want to search. This attribute is required.

Using the <length> Test

The <length> test checks the length of a string or a file. It is actually a task in its own right, but you can place it as a nested element of <condition> to use it as a test. This extends the functionality of the task in some ways, but reduces it in others. Table 3-18 shows the attributes of the <length> element.

Table 3-18. *The Attributes of the <length> Element*

Attribute	Description
file	The name of the file to test. You must specify one and only one of the following: a file attribute, a string attribute, or a nested file set.
length	The length you will be using as a comparison. This attribute is required.
string	The string to test. You must specify one and only one of the following: a file attribute, a string attribute, or a nested file set.
trim	Set this to true to remove whitespace from the string specified in string. This attribute is ignored if you specify a file attribute or a nested file set. The default is false.
when	The possible values are equal, greater, and less. The key to this attribute is to say, "Pass this test when the file/string is equal to/greater than/less than the length." The default is equal.

Using Logical Operators

As befits an implementation of the if programming construct, you can specify logical conditions that apply to all the previous tests. The three logical operators are <not>, <and>, and <or>.

The <not> element does not accept any attributes and takes exactly one child element, which may be any of the child elements of <condition>. That means this child element can contain other child elements should you want it to do so. For example, <not> can contain an <and> element that contains other conditions. The <not> element reverses the evaluation of the element it contains.

The <and> element does not accept any attributes and can take any number of child elements. These child elements can be any child element of <condition>, which of course means you can specify an <and> child element. The <and> element evaluates to true only if all its child elements evaluate to true, and it evaluates them in the order you specify them. Once a child element evaluates to false, the test ends, and the parent <and> element evaluates to false.

This has important ramifications if your <and> element contains resource-intensive checks, such as a byte-for-byte check using a <filesmatch> condition. You should always order your nested conditions starting with the least intensive checks to ensure that you do not waste processing time. It would be no fun to pass a byte-for-byte check and then fail an <isset> check. It's much better to do the checks the other way around.

The <or> element is even simpler than the <and> element. It does not accept any attributes and can take any number of child elements. Again, these child elements can be any valid child element of <condition>. In this case, the <or> element evaluates them in order and evaluates to true as soon as one of the child elements does. The subsequent child elements are not evaluated at all. Again, placing the least resource-intensive conditions first ensures that you do not perform an undue amount of processing when running a build.

Working with Property Sets

You can group properties for ease of use. You create a property set using a <propertyset> element and set its ID so you can use it later in your project. A property set acts upon the existing properties in a project and includes and excludes them depending on any patterns you set (patterns are covered in detail in Chapter 4).

The <propertyset> element has two attributes and one child element. Table 3-19 shows the attributes.

Table 3-19. *The Attributes of the <propertyset> Element*

Attribute	Description
dynamic	Tells Ant whether to recalculate the property set every time it is used. The default is true.
negate	Setting this attribute to true will reverse the selection of properties. In other words, only properties that don't match the nested criteria will be selected. The default is false.

You specify the selection criteria with nested <propertyref> elements (as well as nested <propertyset> elements). In this case, the containing <propertyset> element includes all those properties that match the values in the `<propertyref>` elements. The `<propertyref>` element has the attributes shown in Table 3-20, though you may specify only one of these at a time.

Table 3-20. *The Attributes of the `<propertyref>` Element*

Attribute	Description
`builtin`	Setting this to `all` will include all Ant's built-in properties. Setting it to `system` will include all the system properties. Setting it to `commandline` will include any properties that were supplied at the command line.
`name`	The property set will select this property only.
`prefix`	The property set will select properties that begin with this prefix.
`regex`	The property set will select properties that match this regular expression.

You can specify one mapper to change the property keys (see Chapter 11 for the details of mappers).

Using Pathlike Structures

Large projects usually have large numbers of files and directories; you will want to treat many of these as a group. For example, you may want to copy all the files with a certain extension into another directory, while ignoring all the other files.

You may also want to work with the same group of files or directories on more than one occasion during a build. For example, you may want to set a classpath for the project and use it in all your compilation tasks.

Ant deals with groups of files and directories using pathlike structures, many specialized forms of which are described in the next chapter. However, the two basic elements that use pathlike structures, `<path>` and `<classpath>`, are relevant to this chapter and are useful additions to the discussion.

Setting a Pathlike Structure

A *pathlike structure* is a reusable collection of files or directories that has a unique ID so that whenever you want to use it, you supply its reference ID. You can apply this to a number of situations; one example is as a constant value that you supply to compilation tasks. If you have a set location where you store all your libraries and classes, be they Java or C, then you store the value in a pathlike structure, which you then reference in the compilation steps of the build. In other words, the pathlike structure is acting as your classpath for the purpose of the compilation. You can use this technique to set search paths of all kinds; the "Setting Properties in Property Files" section provides some examples.

Another way you can use pathlike structures is when you want to perform multiple operations on the same group of files or directories. For example, you may want to confirm that a set of files exists before checking that the files are well-formed XML. Once you have done this, you may want to then transform this XML into HTML using an XSLT style sheet. By grouping these files as a pathlike structure, you can reference them using the unique ID, rather than using their filenames each time.

Both cases implement the spirit of reusability to lighten the maintenance load significantly. Centralizing groups of files and directories before carrying out operations with them or on them is extremely useful, which makes pathlike structures indispensable.

Just like any other reusable object, pathlike structures have scope. If you define a pathlike structure at the top level of your build file, that is, as a child element of <project>, then it is available to the whole build file. However, if you define it as a child element of a <target> element, it is available only in that target, in targets that depend on this target, and in any targets called by that target (see the <ant> and <antcall> tasks and Chapter 9).

Listing 3-32 shows a few examples of setting a pathlike structure. The <path> element can contain any number of <pathelement> and <path> child elements. You can use the id attribute of the <path> element to refer to the entire pathlike structure in subsequent pathlike structures or in tasks.

Listing 3-32. *Building Pathlike Structures*

```
<property environment="env"/>

<path id="build.path.id">
  <pathelement path="${env.ANT_HOME}/lib/ant.jar"/>
</path>

<!-- A short-form version of the above -->
<path id="build.path.id" path="${env.ANT_HOME}/lib/ant.jar"/>

<path id="build.path.complete">
  <path refid="build.path.id"/>
  <pathelement path="${env.ANT_HOME}/lib/mysql.jar"/>
</path>
```

The first two pathlike structures are the same, and you can refer to them using the build.path.id reference. Note the distinction with properties: you cannot obtain the value of a reference by wrapping it in ${} markers as you would for a property.

When you use a <path> element as a child of another path, it is usually to include a reference to an existing pathlike structure, as is the case in Listing 3-32. Here you use the refid attribute to substitute the value of the existing pathlike structure. Using the id attribute does not make sense here because the built path will be available under the ID of the parent <path> element. In the previous example, the second <path> element builds a new pathlike structure from the build.path.id pathlike structure and ANT_HOME/lib/mysql.jar. You can now refer to this pathlike structure by using build.path.complete.

Setting a Classpath Pathlike Structure

Certain tasks take a classpath as a <classpath> child element. The <classpath> element is analogous to the <path> element, except that it cannot appear as a child element of <project> or <target>, it cannot contain child <classpath> elements, and it cannot be given a reference ID.

The <classpath> element can contain a child <path> element, which you would use in the same way as the <path> child element in Listing 3-32. If you simply want to use an existing pathlike structure as a classpath pathlike structure, use the refid attribute. Listing 3-33 shows a number of classpath pathlike structures.

Listing 3-33. *Using an Existing Pathlike Structure As a Classpath*

```
<property environment="env"/>
<parenttask>
  <classpath>
    <pathelement path="${env.ANT_HOME}/lib/ant.jar"/>
  </classpath>
</parenttask>

<parenttask>
  <!-- A short-form version of the above -->
  <classpath path="${env.ANT_HOME}/lib/ant.jar"/>
</parenttask>

<parenttask>
  <classpath>
    <path refid="build.path.id"/>
    <pathelement path="${env.ANT_HOME}/lib/mysql.jar"/>
  </classpath>
<parenttask>

<parenttask>
  <classpath refid="build.path.id"/>
</parenttask>
```

All of these, bar the last example, are analogous to the <path> elements shown in the previous section. The major difference is that <classpath> elements must be the child elements of a containing task.

Summary

This chapter began with a look at Ant's command-line options. These allow you to customize and tweak Ant's functionality to a great extent. One of the most powerful options at the command line is the ability to specify property values and override the values of properties set within the file.

The rest of the chapter was dedicated to the basics of build files, which included the main nontask elements and property files. The main message to retain from this chapter is that you should endeavor to write the best build files you can. This means you will have to use many techniques borrowed from the world of coding. Ant allows you to reuse helpful pieces of the build file to cut down on redundancy and repetition and lets you import property values from a number of places. Both techniques lead to a loss of redundancy and an increase in centralization and maintainability. The more you group important configuration information in one place, the easier it is to maintain.

Ideally, you will get to a point where it is only the property file that changes when you send out the project, and not the build file.

CHAPTER 4

Examining Ant's Types

In the previous chapter, you saw how to run Ant and call targets within a build file. The build file is where you describe the structure of the project and how Ant should work with it, meaning it is the core of all your work with Ant. This chapter continues the examination of the build file, as does the next chapter, and explores the final set of nontask XML elements available to you.

Many Ant tasks require information of one kind or another. This information can be directory structures, filenames, property values, and much more. Providing this information is not what tasks are designed for; if nothing else, their name suggests action, movement, or activity, not passively sitting and holding information. They require information, and without it they cannot function. They are the verbs of the Ant universe.

Ant types are the placeholders for the information that Ant tasks require, and you specify them using nested XML elements. You can specify many of them as child elements of a number of Ant tasks, while others are quite specific in scope. Much of the information that Ant requires is directory and file structure, but you can also use Ant types to provide information on regular expressions and locations to redirect input.

As part of their role as information providers, Ant types are widely used as part of the pathlike structures you saw in the previous chapter. They extend the power and flexibility of pathlike structures, allowing you to work with a huge number of directory and file combinations. This aspect of Ant types is the main topic of this chapter, mainly because this is what you will be using Ant types for most of the time. With that in mind, let's look at these directory-based types.

Using Directory-Based Types

Ant works with the existing directory structure of your projects and performs operations on the files it contains. As I've mentioned on a number of occasions, the build file is a description of the project. Now that it is time to discuss Ant types, you will see how exactly to describe the project to Ant.

As is the case with many other aspects of Ant, the mechanism you use to work with files and directories is very flexible. For example, you can specify individual files, individual directories, groups of files, groups of directories, groups of files that exclude certain other files at run time, or any combination of these. If you want to work with a certain collection of files or directories, Ant will have the functionality to do it.

Using Pattern Sets

The base element that governs the use of many of the other directory-based types is the *pattern set*. A pattern set is a collection of patterns that Ant can use and reuse in tasks that perform operations on files. The fundamental concept in pattern sets, and most of the directory-based types described next, is the pattern.

Using Patterns

When working with files and directories, you will often find that you want to include only certain files or exclude others from the Ant task you are running. By specifying a pattern for each set of includes or excludes, you can cover the entire group rather than listing every single file. Patterns follow the common wildcard convention used for matching filenames that you will be familiar with, though Ant adds another useful feature to match multiple directories. Table 4-1 summarizes this simple convention.

Table 4-1. *Wildcard Characters Used in Ant Patterns*

Character	Description
?	Matches a single character and a single character only.
*	Matches zero or more characters.
**	Matches zero or more directories if used as a directory name in a pattern. Matches any file if used as a filename in a pattern.

These patterns are relative to the base directory of the task that contains the pattern. This can of course shift, depending on whether the task is using the project-level base directory or is using another base directory because of a child Ant type. You can also combine the two character patterns with other characters into one string. You cannot use the ** operator in the same pattern segment as the other characters because it expands the entire directory structure and is not a true pattern-matching operator. For example, `lib/?**` is not a valid pattern, but `lib/?/**` is. In the latter case, Ant splits the pattern into segments because of the file separator. The distinction between these operators will become clear as you work through some examples.

First, `?.jsp` matches `A.jsp`, `B.jsp`, and `C.jsp`, but not `.jsp` or `index.jsp`. The latter two filenames do not have a single character and a single character only before the `.jsp` extension, so the pattern does not match. The first three filenames do, so the pattern matches.

Second, the * wildcard will match with any combination, so `*.jsp` matches every one of the filenames used in the previous example. Each one of them has zero or more characters followed by `.jsp`. These operators will be fairly familiar and are widely used in a number of operating system tools, but it is the ** operator that makes Ant shine. One characteristic of the pattern-matching operators is that they match on a per-directory basis. This means that once Ant has matched a directory, it moves onto the next directory in the string. Consequently, an * at the end of a pattern will match only those files or directories that are in the final directory of the pattern. In other words, it does not move down through the directory structure matching everything.

Take the following directory structure as an example. The names in bold are files.

```
.
/lib
    /java
         One.java
         Two.java
    /native
           one.c
           two.c
```

The pattern `lib/*` will match the `java` and the `native` directories, but *not* the files they contain. Any operations using this pattern will affect the directories, which may lead to unexpected results if this is not what you intend. For example, if you attempt to copy `lib` using this pattern, you will copy the `lib` directory and the two subdirectories (and only those two subdirectories). You will end up with the `lib` directory and two empty subdirectories called `java` and `native` at their destination. This may be what you want, but then again it may not, so you must be careful when setting patterns like these.

Using the pattern-matching operators in combination is fairly simple. For example, emacs backup files have a tilde added to the end of their filename, which allows you to locate them and remove them from the file system when the time comes to clean up the file system or distribute your code. To match them and no other files, you could use `src/*.java?`, which would match all files with a `.java` extension in the `src` directory modified by emacs. However, any `.java~` files in subdirectories of `src` will not match this pattern.

Note The pattern-matching operators look only for files deeper in the directory structure than Ant's `basedir`. This means you cannot use the `..` directory name that represents the parent directory, because the parent directory is not scanned. If you include this directory name in your pattern, Ant will not match anything.

The ** operator is not a pattern-matching operator; rather, you use it to match paths and files in the file system. So, to give a basic example, ** will match everything from Ant's `basedir` upward, including all filenames. You can also specify this using a bit of Ant shorthand, like so: /. Any path ending in a \ or a / where a pattern is appropriate will be taken to mean ** or /**.

As an example, let's return to the directory structure. The ** operator can help you match all the files in subfolders of `lib` where the * operator could not. To match all subfolders and their contents, you would use `lib/**`. This pattern tells Ant to look in the `lib` folder and then move down the directory hierarchy until it reaches the end of every branch. Copying using this pattern will give you the directory hierarchy shown previously.

You can see from this example that the * operator, when used to match files and directories without modification, represents a single layer in the directory hierarchy at the point of reference, while the ** operator represents the entire directory hierarchy from the point of reference down.

You can of course limit the ** operator by adding file separators to the pattern, which will break the pattern into segments. Ant treats the ** operator in the same way as the pattern-matching operators in this respect, in that it completes every match for a pattern segment up to the file separator before trying to match the next pattern segment. For example, `src/**/java/*` will match paths such as `src/web/java/PhotoServlet.java`, `src/client/java/PhotoClient.java`, and `src/web/jsp/precompiled/java/Photo.jsp.class`. It will not match `src/web/jsp/precompiled/java/org/apache/jsp/Photo.jsp.class`. The section after the `java` directory in the latter case does not match the /* pattern segment.

Setting Patterns

Patterns are powerful things but are no use by themselves. They are simply pieces of information that you have to give to Ant to use, and in that respect, they are an integral part of the Ant types. You will find that every one of the types described in this chapter can use them.

As was noted earlier, the usual way to include a pattern in an Ant type is through a pattern set. This Ant type collects as many patterns as you want and uses them to specify which patterns you want to include in an operation and which ones you want to exclude from an operation.

To specify a pattern set, include a `<patternset>` element in your build file. You can set global pattern sets that many tasks and types in your project can reference, just as you could with paths (see Chapter 3). As you will see throughout the rest of the chapter, pathlike structures can use Ant types to build paths for use by tasks and as such use patterns and pattern sets extensively.

Using Includes and Excludes

The `<patternset>` element has four attributes, each of which you can use to manage the files and directories included in the task that uses the pattern. Table 4-2 shows these attributes. You can also use nested elements to specify these values (more on this later in this section).

Table 4-2. *Attributes of the `<patternset>` Element*

Attribute	Description
`excludes`	A list of patterns separated by commas or spaces. If a file matches any of these patterns, it is excluded from any task using this pattern. If you do not use this attribute, then no files are excluded. Note that Ant has a number of default exclude patterns, such as excluding CVS and Subversion repositories. These are described in the "Working with Default Excludes" section.
`excludesfile`	A file that specifies patterns to be used as for the `excludes` attribute. Each line in the file is a pattern. Only one file may be listed. If you want to use more than one file, insert `<excludesfile>` child elements.
`includes`	A list of patterns separated by commas or spaces. If a file matches any of these patterns, it is included in any task using this pattern. If you do not use this attribute, then all files are included.
`includesfile`	A file that specifies patterns to be used as for the `includes` attribute. Each line in the file is a pattern. Only one file may be listed. If you want to use more than one file, insert `<includesfile>` child elements.

Ant processes all the includes first and then applies the excludes to this list. Therefore, excludes always take precedence. One common error is to exclude everything and then include only the files you want by placing the include pattern after the exclude pattern like so:

```
<patternset excludes="**" includes="*.java"/>
```

Ordering the patterns in this way does not alter the way Ant processes them, and in this case you have excluded all the files in the project, regardless of what the includes attribute says. The includes mechanism implicitly excludes everything that does not match any of the includes patterns, so you have no need to specify any excludes, unless you want to modify the included set in a way that is not possible to do with the includes attribute (or the <include> element, as discussed in a moment).

The best way to approach it is to use the excludes mechanism as a refinement of your includes. As noted, this is how the mechanism works behind the scenes, so there's no point in trying to do anything else.

The nested elements have names that are analogous to those of the attributes listed in Table 4-2—that is, <exclude>, <excludesfile>, <include>, and <includesfile>—and share the attributes shown in Table 4-3. Note the singular versus plural distinction in the pattern attributes and elements. This is because the attributes can take a list of patterns, while the elements specify only one pattern.

You can use as many of these elements as you like in a <patternset> element. In the rest of the chapter, you will see that these child elements also appear as child elements of other Ant types.

Table 4-3. *The Common Attributes of <exclude>, <excludesfile>, <include>, and <includesfile>*

Attribute	Description
name	The pattern to use in the case of <exclude> and <include> or the name of the file to use in the case of <excludesfile> and <includesfile>. This attribute does not take a list of patterns, so Ant expects only a single pattern here.
if	Only use this pattern or read the file if this property is set.
unless	Only use this pattern or read the file if this property is not set.

These elements adhere to the same rules as noted for the attributes. You can build a set of includes and excludes with a combination of attributes and elements. For example, any patterns you specify in an includes attribute are added to the patterns used in a nested <include> element.

Here's an example of these nested elements:

```
<patternset id="src.files">
  <include name="${src}/**"/>
  <include name="build.*"/>
</patternset>
```

This pattern set includes all the files in the source tree and any file that matches the build.* pattern.

Working with Default Excludes

Ant will exclude a number of file and directory types by default. These include, for example, backup files or directories that make up a section of a CVS repository. It is assumed that you will not want to include them in any directory-based operation, because they are not functional files.

In other words, you do not want to compile them, copy them, or package them in a zip file. The downside is that you cannot delete them by default, though you can remove directories that contain them. You can, however, override this default behavior should you want to work with these default excludes. You can delete the directory patterns, such as **/CVS, by default.

The default exclude patterns are as follows:

```
**/*~
**/#*#
**/.#*
**/%*%
**/._*
**/CVS
**/CVS/**
**/.cvsignore
**/SCCS
**/SCCS/**
**/vssver.scc
**/.svn
**/.svn/**
**/.DS_Store
```

So, Ant will ignore files and directories that match these patterns, unless you are deleting a directory, in which case it will remove the directory and any files and subdirectories, regardless of whether they match any of these patterns.

The first example will be the one from the previous section where you wanted to copy the lib folder and its contents to a new location. Here's the directory structure again as a reminder:

```
.
 /lib
     /java
          One.java
          Two.java
     /native
            one.c
            two.c
```

Recall that the lib/* pattern copied the lib directory and the two subdirectories, but not the contents of the subdirectories. If you were to use the ** operator instead, meaning the pattern would be lib/**, Ant would recurse through the entire directory structure from the lib directory down, copying anything that it finds (minus any default excludes, of course).

Listing 4-1 shows the pattern sets for this example.

Listing 4-1. *Pattern Sets Demonstration, Contrasting the * and ** Patterns*

```
<patternset id="pattern.id.one.star">
  <include name="lib/*"/>
</patternset>

<patternset id="pattern.id.two.star">
  <include name="lib/**"/>
</patternset>
```

The resulting directory structures are therefore as follows:

```
.
 /onestar
        /lib
            /java
            /native

 /twostar
        /lib
        /java
             One.java
             Two.java
        /native
               one.c
               two.c
```

To use a pattern set, you must include it as a child element of one of the directory-based types, though, as you have seen, you can declare them at a project level and give them a reference ID. Some of these directory types are implicit pattern sets and so support the four child elements discussed previously (`<exclude>`, `<excludesfile>`, `<include>`, and `<includesfile>`) and the `<patternset>` element's attributes in addition to their own.

Working with Directory Sets

A *directory set* is a collection of directories on which you want to perform an Ant operation. It is important to note that not every Ant task that works with directories uses directory sets, so you may find it more convenient to use file sets instead (described in the next section), even for those tasks that support directory sets. If an Ant task has different behavior when using a directory set, the difference will be noted in the section where that task is described.

You specify a directory set with the `<dirset>` element, which either you can place as a child element of `<project>` and give an ID, or you can use as a child element of a task. Not all tasks that use directory sets can accept them as child elements and may accept only references to them. Table 4-4 describes those tasks that can use a directory set and how you specify one.

Table 4-4. *Ant Tasks That Can Use Directory Sets*

Task	Type	Description
apply	Core task	Applies a command to the directories in the directory set. You specify a <dirset> child element for this task (since Ant 1.6).
chmod	Core task	Modifies the permissions on the directories in the directory set. You specify a <dirset> child element for this task (since Ant 1.6).
javadoc	Core task	Creates Javadocs from the source files supplied. Directories supplied create package names in the Javadocs. You specify the directory set using the <packageset> child element. This element has a refid attribute that you can use to reference directory sets that you have previously defined.
pathconvert	Core task	Converts the path of the directory set into an OS-specific path. You must define a directory set elsewhere and use a reference to it with this task's refid attribute.
subant	Core task	Runs sub-builds. You specify a <dirset> child element for this task.
attrib	Optional task	Sets attributes for the directories in the directory set (the files contained within are not affected). This is a Windows-only task. You specify a <dirset> child element for this task.
chgrp	Optional task	Changes the group membership of the directories in the directory set (the files contained within are not affected). This is a Unix-only task. You specify a <dirset> child element for this task.
chown	Optional task	Changes the owner of the directories in the directory set (the files contained within are not affected). This is a Unix-only task. You specify a <dirset> child element for this task.

When you specify a <dirset> element, whether as a child element of <project> or as a child element of an appropriate task, it takes the <exclude>, <excludesfile>, <include>, and <includesfile> child elements and the excludes, excludesfile, includes, and includesfile attributes just as if it were a pattern set, in addition to those shown in Table 4-5.

Table 4-5. *The Attributes of the <dirset> Element*

Attribute	Description
casesensitive	Sets whether case is important in this directory set. To turn it on, use any of true, yes, or on; to turn it off, use any of false, no, or off. The default is true.
dir	The root directory of this directory set. This attribute is required.
followsymlinks	Sets whether Ant will include files linked symbolically. The default is true.

Listing 4-2 shows the same directory set twice, the first time using an explicit pattern set and the second time using an implicit pattern set. You can then refer to them by the ID specified by the id attribute.

Listing 4-2. *The Same Directory Set Using First an Explicit Pattern Set, Followed by an Implicit Pattern Set*

```
<dirset dir="." id="explicit">
  <patternset>
    <include name="lib/**"/>
  </patternset>
</dirset>
<dirset dir="." id="implicit">
  <include name="lib/**"/>
</dirset>
```

You can then reuse these directory sets in other directory sets within your build file, just as shown here:

```
<dirset refid="explicit"/>
<dirset refid="implicit"/>
```

Working with File Sets

File sets are much more general collections than directory sets, in that they group files and directories, while directory sets group only directories. They are also more flexible because they allow you to specify all sorts of additional conditions on the files to include and exclude from an operation.

You specify a file set using the <fileset> element, which either you can place as a child element of <project> and give an ID or you can use as a child element of a task.

When you specify a <fileset> element, whether as a child element of <project> or as a child element of an appropriate task, it takes the <exclude>, <excludesfile>, <include>, and <includesfile> child elements and the excludes, excludesfile, includes, and includesfile attributes just as if it were a pattern set, in addition to those shown in Table 4-6.

Table 4-6. *The Attributes of the <fileset> Element*

Attribute	Description
casesensitive	Sets whether case is important in this file set. To turn it on, use any of true, yes, or on; to turn it off, use any of false, no, or off. The default is true.
defaultexcludes	Sets whether this file set should use the default excludes (as described previously). Valid values are yes and no. The default is yes, meaning that Ant will use the default excludes.
dir	The root directory of this file set. You must specify one of dir or file.
file	A single file that will make up this file set. You must specify one of dir or file.
followsymlinks	Sets whether Ant will include files linked symbolically. The default is true.

Any patterns you use with a file set will apply the containing task to all the files and directories included and none of the ones excluded. Listing 4-3 shows how to create a file set that does not use the default excludes.

Listing 4-3. *A File Set That Turns Off the Default Excludes*

```
<fileset dir="." defaultexcludes="no">
  <include name="lib/java/*.java?"/>
</fileset>
```

This file set is also an implicit pattern set. As mentioned, a file set is a more general version of a directory set, and you can use one in all the tasks where you can use a directory set and many more besides. The other difference is their ability to contain selectors.

Using Selectors

Sometimes it is not enough to exclude or include files using criteria based on their names. For example, you may want Ant to move older versions of your project's distribution to an archive three months after their release before creating any more distributions. The best way to do this would be to select by date and not by version numbers or filenames, because that slows down the automation process.

Selectors are Ant's mechanism for selecting files and directories using criteria other than filenames. To specify a selector, you place it inside a selector container. The `<fileset>` element is a special selector container in that it can contain any number of other selector containers except another `<fileset>` element. It acts like an `<and>` selector container (covered in the next section), which means that all its child selectors must match for a file to be included. In other words, as soon as a file fails to match any of the nested selectors, Ant discounts it. This is an analogue to patterns, where a file must match all the include patterns to be included.

If you want to configure a projectwide selector for reuse, you can specify a `<selector>` element as a child element of `<project>`. This selector container can contain only one selector, which may be another container, and you must give it an ID so that you can reference it later in the project build. It also accepts `if` and `unless` attributes that work in the same way as with the include/exclude mechanism explained earlier in the chapter.

The `<selector>` tag is not restricted to being a child element of `<project>`, and you can use it within other selector containers to conditionally include files based on whether a property is set. The following builds a file set only if the `two.stars` property is set. (The `<filename>` element is explained next, but it includes the files specified by the pattern.)

```
<fileset dir=".">
  <selector if="two.stars">
    <filename name="lib/**"/>
  </selector>
</fileset>
```

Using the Contains Selector

The <contains> selector includes only those files that contain the text specified by the text attribute. Table 4-7 describes the attributes of this element.

Table 4-7. *The Attributes of the <contains> Element*

Attribute	Description
casesensitive	Sets whether case is important in this search. The default is true.
ignorewhitespace	Tells Ant whether to ignore whitespace in the searched-for string. The default is false.
text	The text for which to search. If a file contains this text, it is included. This attribute is required.

Here's an example that includes all the source files for a project, but only if they are covered by the Apache License:

```
<fileset id="javadoc" dir="${src}">
  <include name="shared/**"/>
  <include name="stand-alone/**"/>
  <include name="web/java/**"/>
  <contains text="Licensed under the Apache License"/>
</fileset>
```

Using the Date Selector

The <date> selector allows you to select files that were last modified during a specified time period. This time period can be a period before the specified date/time, a period after the specified date/time, or an exact match of the specified date/time. Table 4-8 describes the attributes of this element.

Table 4-8. *The Attributes of the <date> Element*

Attribute	Description
checkdirs	Sets whether Ant should check the date of modification on directories. The default is false.
datetime	The date/time that forms the upper or lower boundary of the selector. The default format is MM/DD/YYYY HH:MM {AM | PM}, though you can specify another pattern with the pattern attribute. You must specify only one of the datetime or millis attributes.
granularity	The margin of error to use when checking the modification time, measured in milliseconds. The default is 0 on non-DOS systems and 2000 on DOS systems.

Table 4-8. *The Attributes of the <date> Element (Continued)*

Attribute	Description
millis	The number of milliseconds since 1.1.1970 that forms the upper or lower boundary of the selector. You must specify only one of the datetime or millis attributes.
pattern	A date format compatible with the Java SimpleDate class to use with the datetime attribute. The default is MM/DD/YYYY HH:MM {AM | PM}.
when	Sets whether the time given in datetime or millis is the upper limit of the time period or the lower limit. If you want the time period to end with this date/time, set the value to before, meaning any file modified before this date/time is included. If you want the time period to start with this date/time, set the value to after, meaning any file modified after this date/time is included. If you want to include only files that were modified at this exact date/time, then set the value to equal, which is the default.

The following example includes all the HTML documentation of a project, but only if it is older than the date, which is specified in British format:

```
<fileset dir="${src.shared}/docs">
  <include name="*.html"/>
  <date datetime="01/02/2005" pattern="DD/MM/YYYY"/>
</fileset>
```

Using the Depend Selector

The <depend> selector selects files only if they have been modified after their namesakes in another location. This allows you to select only those files that have been updated in a new release of a project, for example.

You can nest mappers within this selector, though an identity mapper is used by default. (Chapter 11 covers mappers.) Table 4-9 shows the attributes of this selector.

Table 4-9. *The Attributes of the <depend> Element*

Attribute	Description
granularity	The margin of error to use when checking the modification time, measured in milliseconds. The default is 0 on non-DOS systems and 2000 on DOS systems.
targetdir	The base directory where Ant will begin its search for the older files. This attribute is required.

To use this selector, you specify a file set as normal and then use the targetdir attribute to tell Ant the location of the older distribution that it should compare with.

```
<fileset id="javadoc" dir="${src}">
  <exclude name="*/conf/**"/>
  <exclude name="*/docs/*"/>
  <include name="shared/**"/>
  <include name="stand-alone/**"/>
  <include name="web/java/**"/>
  <depend targetdir="${docs}/api"/>
</fileset>
```

Here you include a number of files from across a project, but only if they are newer than those in the `${docs}/api` directory.

Using the Depth Selector

The `<depth>` selector lets you choose files from a portion of the project's directory hierarchy, depending on the depth of nesting. Table 4-10 shows the attributes of this selector.

Table 4-10. *The Attributes of the `<depth>` Element*

Attribute	Description
`max`	The maximum number of directory levels that Ant will search. Files in deeper levels will not be included. The default is no limit.
`min`	The minimum number of directory levels that Ant will search. Files in higher levels will not be included. The default is no limit.

Here's an example that includes files only from the number of directories specified by the user at the command line:

```
<fileset dir="${docs.all.dir}">
  <patternset refid="docs.all"/>
  <depth max="${user.depth}"/>
</fileset>
```

Using the Different Selector

The `<different>` selector selects files only if they are different from their namesakes in another location. The criteria are as follows:

- If there is no file in the specified location, the file is different and is selected.
- If the files are different lengths, they are different.
- If you set the `ignoreFileTimes` attribute to `false`, then different timestamps will cause files to be different.
- If you set the `ignoreContents` attribute to `false`, Ant checks the files byte for byte.

Table 4-11 shows the attributes of this selector.

Table 4-11. *The Attributes of the `<different>` Element*

Attribute	Description
`granularity`	The margin of error to use when checking the modification time, measured in milliseconds. The default is `0` on non-DOS systems and `2000` on DOS systems.
`ignoreContents`	Tells Ant whether to carry out a byte-for-byte check. The default is `false`.
`ignoreFileTimes`	Tells Ant whether to check file timestamps. The default is `true`.
`targetdir`	The base directory where Ant will begin its search for the files to compare. This attribute is required.

The following uses all the documentation in a project, but only if it is different from the existing built Javadocs:

```
<fileset dir="${docs.all.dir}">
  <patternset refid="docs.all"/>
  <different targetdir="${docs}/api" ignoreFileTimes="false"/>
</fileset>
```

Using the Filename Selector

The `<filename>` selector is an include/exclude mechanism; however, unlike the `<include>` and `<exclude>` tags of pattern set fame, you can combine it with other selectors using selector containers. In other words, the `<filename>` selector selects files based on a pattern.

Table 4-12 shows the attributes of this selector.

Table 4-12. *The Attributes of the `<filename>` Element*

Attribute	Description
`casesensitive`	Sets whether case is important in this search. The default is `true`.
`name`	A pattern that Ant will use when searching for files. Any that match will be selected (or not, depending on the value of the `negate` attribute). This attribute is required.
`negate`	Reverses the selection decision if set to `true`. Therefore, if you set this to `true` and a file matches the pattern set in `name`, it is not selected. The default is `false`.

The following two file sets match the opposite files from each other:

```
<fileset dir="${build}/build-mysql-jdbc">
  <filename name="mysql-connector*/*.jar" negate="true"/>
</fileset>

<fileset dir="${build}/build-mysql-jdbc">
  <include name="mysql-connector*/*.jar"/>
</fileset>
```

Using the Present Selector

The <present> selector selects files that have a namesake (or not, depending on the setting) in a target directory, and for this reason it is case-sensitive. You can nest mappers within this selector, though an identity mapper is used by default. (Chapter 11 covers mappers.) Table 4-13 shows the attributes of this selector.

Table 4-13. *The Attributes of the <filename> Element*

Attribute	Description
present	Tells Ant whether to select a file if it has a namesake or whether to select a file if it doesn't have a namesake. Set this attribute to both to require that the file have a namesake or to srconly to require that it be a unique file. The default is srconly.
targetdir	The base directory where Ant will begin its search for the files to compare. This attribute is required.

The following uses all the documentation in a project, but only if corresponding built Javadocs aren't present in ${docs}/api:

```
<fileset dir="${docs.all.dir}">
  <patternset refid="docs.all"/>
  <present targetdir="${docs}/api" present="srconly"/>
</fileset>
```

Using the Containsregexp Selector

The <containsregexp> selector selects only those files that contain text matching a specified regular expression. It has only one attribute (see Table 4-14).

Table 4-14. *The Attribute of the <containsregexp> Element*

Attribute	Description
expression	The regular expression to be used as a test. This attribute is required.

Here's an example that includes all the source files for a project, but only if they are covered by the Apache License (though we are taking British spelling into account just in case):

```
<fileset id="javadoc" dir="${src}">
  <include name="shared/**"/>
  <include name="stand-alone/**"/>
  <include name="web/java/**"/>
  <containsregexp expression="Licensed under the Apache Licen[sc]e"/>
</fileset>
```

Using the Size Selector

The <size> selector places a limit on file size. Ant will not select any files that do not conform to this limit. Table 4-15 shows the attributes of this selector.

Table 4-15. *The Attributes of the <size> Element*

Attribute	Description
units	The units of the value attribute. k, M, and G represent multiples of 1,000; Ki, Mi, and Gi represent multiples of 1,024. The default is no units, which means the value attribute represents bytes.
value	The size of file that should be selected or not, depending on the value of the when attribute. If you do not set the units attribute, this value is in bytes. This attribute is required.
when	Sets whether the size is the upper limit or the lower limit. If you want to include files smaller than the size, set the value to less, meaning any file smaller than value is included. If you want to include files larger than the size, set the value to more, meaning any file larger than value is included. If you want to include only files with this exact size, then set the value to equal. The default is less.

Here you select only certain JAR files and only if they are smaller than 1 gigabyte:

```
<fileset dir="${httpunit.home}/jars">
  <include name="*.jar"/>
  <exclude name="junit.jar"/>
  <size value="1" units="Gi" when="less"/>
</fileset>
```

Using the Type Selector

The <type> selector allows you to select either files or directories, excluding the other type. You would usually use this in conjunction with another selector in a selector container, so I will cover it there. Table 4-16 shows the attribute of this selector.

Table 4-16. *The Attribute of the <type> Element*

Attribute	Description
type	This value can either be dir or be file. This attribute is required.

Using the Modified Selector

The <modified> selector is a much more complicated selector than the others already described, mainly because it gives you so many options and is so flexible. In essence, it uses a hash from a previous version, which it stores in a cache, and a hash of the current file to see if it has been altered.

As things stand, the cache is a simple property file that follows a key-value format.

```
file's absolute file name=hash
```

Here's an example cache file:

```
#Mon May 09 12:40:24 BST 2005
C\:\\AntBook\\ch04\\lib\\intext.txt=8653d5c7898950016e5d019df6815626
C\:\\AntBook\\ch04\\lib\\6.2.txt=777d45bbbcdf50d49c42c70ad7acf5fe
```

If a file was not in the cache, it passes the test, and the selector selects it and adds its hash to the cache for future use if you have specified that option in the selector.

The process that this selector uses to compare files is as follows:

- It obtains the absolute path for the current file.
- It obtains the cached digest from the cache, using the file's absolute path as the key (as shown previously).
- It obtains the digest of the current file using the configured algorithm.
- It compares the two digests with the configured comparator.
- It updates the cache if needed and if you requested as such.
- It selects the file if the comparison result indicates it has been modified.

The <modified> element takes the attributes shown in Table 4-17.

Table 4-17. *The Attributes of the <modified> Element*

Attribute	Description
algorithm	Sets the type of algorithm you want Ant to use when computing the digest. Setting this to hashvalue tells Ant to read the content of the file into a String and use String.hashValue() to compute a hash. This value is then stored. Setting this to digest tells Ant to use the java.security.MessageDigest to compute the value. You can set the specific message digest algorithm with a nested <param> element. The default is digest, which means Ant will create an MD5 hash if you don't use any <param> elements.
cache	Sets the type of cache to be used. Unless you have created a custom selector, the only option is a cache file as shown previously. The only valid value is propertyfile, which is the default. The location of the cache file is set with a nested <param> element. It is a file called cache.properties in the base directory of this build by default.
comparator	Sets the type of comparator. A value of equal is a straight object comparison, while a value of rule is a java.text.RuleBasedCollator comparison. The default is equal.

Table 4-17. *The Attributes of the <modified> Element (Continued)*

Attribute	Description
seldirs	Sets whether directories should be selected. The default is true.
update	Sets whether Ant updates the cache when values differ. The default is true.

You can specify each of these with a nested <param> element of the following form:

```
<param name="PARAM_NAME" value="VALUE"/>

<!-- An example -->
<param name="update" value="false"/>
```

In addition, you can change some other values with nested <param> elements. Table 4-18 shows the values for the <param> element's name attribute and what values the value attribute can take.

Table 4-18. *Using the <param> Element's name Attribute*

Value of the name Attribute	Possible Values for the value Attribute
algorithm.algorithm	MD5 or SHA. MD5 is the default.
algorithm.provider	The name of the provider. The default is null.
cache.cachefile	The name of the cache file. cache.properties in the base directory of this build is the default.

For example, if you want to use SHA and store the cache in a nondefault file, you could use the following:

```
<modified>
  <param name="cache.cachefile" value="custom.properties"/>
  <param name="algorithm.algorithm" value="SHA"/>
</modified>
```

Using Selector Containers

I have mentioned *selector containers* a few times, and now it's time to look at them. You will often find occasions where one selector is not enough and you want to select on a number of criteria, and this is where selector containers come in. They combine selectors and select only those files from the combination that meet their own criteria.

You have already seen the <selector> container, so let's move on to the others. Table 4-19 describes them and the attributes they can take.

Table 4-19. *Selector Containers*

Container	Attributes	Description
`<and>`		Any file that is selected matches every selector contained by the `<and>` element.
`<majority>`	`allowtie` (default `true`)	Any file that is selected matches the majority of the selectors contained by the `<majority>` element. The `allowtie` attribute resolves ties.
`<none>`		A file is selected only if it does not match any of the selectors contained by the `<none>` element.
`<not>`		This container can hold only one other selector and reverses the decision.
`<or>`		Any file that is selected matches one selector contained by the `<or>` element.

So, to return to the `<type>` selector, the following example includes only files in the `${src.web}/pages` directory that have been modified:

```
<fileset dir="${src.web}/pages">
  <and>
    <modified>
      <param name="cache.cachefile" value="custom.properties"/>
      <param name="algorithm.algorithm" value="SHA"/>
    </modified>
    <type type="file"/>
  </and>
</fileset>
```

Now this example will include all files that are covered by the Apache License or the GPL:

```
<fileset id="javadoc" dir="${src}">
  <include name="shared/**"/>
  <include name="stand-alone/**"/>
  <include name="web/java/**"/>
  <or>
    <containsregexp expression="Licensed under the Apache Licen[sc]e"/>
    <containsregexp expression="GNU GENERAL PUBLIC LICEN[SC]E"/>
  </or>
</fileset>
```

Of course, you may not want to include any open-source files at all.

```
  <fileset id="javadoc" dir="${src}">
  <include name="shared/**"/>
  <include name="stand-alone/**"/>
  <include name="web/java/**"/>
  <none>
    <containsregexp expression="Licensed under the Apache Licen[sc]e"/>
    <containsregexp expression="GNU GENERAL PUBLIC LICEN[SC]E"/>
  </none>
</fileset>
```

Implicit File Sets

Ant allows you to specify implicit file sets (much like implicit pattern sets). These are always directory-based tasks and will be noted in the appropriate section.

Working with Class File Sets

Class file sets are specialized file sets that add class files if they depend on a specified base class (the specified class is also included). You can then use this file set to create a zip or JAR file of classes for use later. With all related files collected together, you can be sure that the complete application is assembled and ready to go. It is usual to set an ID for a class file set and use it elsewhere in the build file.

To use class file sets, you have to have the Jakarta Byte Code Engineering Library (BCEL) classes, available from `jakarta.apache.org/bcel/`, in Ant's classpath. The easiest way to do this is to copy the `bcel.jar` file into the `ANT_HOME/lib` directory. You can of course also supply the path to this file using the `-lib` command-line option.

A class file set is represented by the `<classfileset>` element, which has one attribute in addition to the usual file set attributes, as shown in Table 4-20.

Table 4-20. *The Attribute of the `<classfileset>` Element*

Attribute	Description
`rootclass`	The name of the class that forms the base of this class file set. The default is `null`. This attribute is not required because you can specify a root class with nested elements (see the following discussion).

The nested elements of `<classfileset>` are `<root>` and `<rootfileset>`. The `<root>` element has a required attribute called `classname`, as shown in the next example:

```
<classfileset id="zip.classes.id" dir="${build.stand-alone}">
  <root classname="org.mwrm.client.Client"/>
</classfileset>
```

This snippet creates a class file set based on the `org.mwrm.client.Client` class. In other words, this file and only those files on which it depends will be part of this class file set.

The next example uses the <rootfileset> element, which is itself a file set of class files. The BCEL functionality will expect class files in this case and will exclude any nonclass files automatically, so ensure your patterns match class files.

```
<classfileset id="zip.classes.id" dir="${build.stand-alone}">
  <rootfileset dir="${build.stand-alone}"
               includes="org/mwrm/**/*.class"/>
</classfileset>
```

This example uses the entire project as the base for the class file set and includes all the class files and any other files on which they depend.

Working with File Lists

From the previous discussion, you can see that file sets are filters that exclude or include files according to a number of criteria. Those criteria are set in patterns or selectors, which can of course select individual files, though those files must exist. If you want to work with files that may or may not exist, then you need to use a *file list.*

File lists do not support pattern matching, so you must specify filenames. If you use a wildcard, you must use it literally. The <filelist> element takes the attributes shown in Table 4-21.

Table 4-21. *The Attributes of the <filelist> Element*

Attribute	Description
dir	The base directory. This attribute is required.
files	A comma- or whitespace-delimited list of files to include in this file list. This attribute is required unless you specify a nested <file> element.

You can nest a <file> element to specify a file. The following shows how you can use both approaches to include the same file:

```
<filelist dir="lib/java" files="One.java"/>

<filelist dir="lib/java">
  <file name="One.java"/>
</filelist>
```

Working with Zip File Sets

When you want to zip a collection of files using Ant, you can use a file set to build the collection. However, Ant also comes with *zip file sets,* which have extra functionality that adds more power and flexibility to the zip process. They are a special type of file set and take the same attributes as a file set, in addition to the attributes shown in Table 4-22.

You can use the <zipfileset> element as a child element of the four tasks that create archives (<zip>, <war>, <jar>, and <ear>).

Table 4-22. *The Attributes of the <zipfileset> Element*

Attribute	Description
dirmode	A three-digit octal string that specifies the user, group, and other modes for directories. This works only on Unix systems. The default is 755.
filemode	A three-digit octal string that specifies the user, group, and other modes for files. This works only on Unix systems. The default is 644.
fullpath	If this zip file set represents a single file, this attribute sets its location in the archive. This attribute and prefix are mutually exclusive.
prefix	If this zip file set represents a collection of files, the files are all prefixes with the value of this attribute. This attribute and fullpath are mutually exclusive.
src	A zip file whose contents will be extracted and added to this zip file set. This attribute and dir are mutually exclusive.

Summary

In this chapter, you looked at ways to pass information to Ant so that it can perform actions based on that information. Many of the build file elements described are information aggregators that group file and directory names according to patterns. In other words, they collect information on the files and directories you want to use. Once this information has been gathered, Ant passes it to the tasks so that they can carry out their functions.

You can select files in many ways; the first way you looked at was patterns. Ant uses the standard wildcard characters (* and ?) and introduces the ** operator that tells Ant to expand directory structures. These operators are powerful in combination and make working with files much easier.

Ant provides you with a set selectors that you can use to further refine your selection criteria. They allow you to select files and directories based on physical properties, such as size and date of modification, rather than just on name.

CHAPTER 5

Building a Project

The first four chapters in this book dealt with setting up and installing Ant, as well as the basic building blocks of a project's build file. Now it's time to work with an example project to demonstrate some of the major Ant tasks. The example application will also serve as a template for organizing other projects. This is of course only one way of doing it. As long as your projects are organized sensibly, you can carry out the same project build steps.

Many project teams split their projects into pieces that logically belong together. For example, an application may have a GUI as well as a web interface. In this case, the project team would place the core functionality that deals with the database into one section, and they would place GUI code and web interface code in two other, separate sections. This allows the separation of functionality and effort. In other words, everyone knows exactly where the boundaries are in the code and where the boundaries are in responsibility.

Ant is particularly useful in this regard because, as I've said before, it is designed to model the project structure. You can easily separate project sections in an Ant build file. This kind of organization makes your projects easier to manage, and you'll find that you can also conceptualize them better.

This chapter will deal with the initial stages of the project where you take the raw building blocks of an application and turn them into a packaged application for distribution or immediate use. You'll see how a project is organized along the lines of functionality, how Java code is compiled, and how other files are added to a distributable package.

Introducing the Example Application

The example application is a database-backed application that users can access with a command-line Java client or a JSP/servlet web application. This will allow you to work with the core database-access code and other common functionality while using two separate front-end interfaces. You could quite easily implement a GUI for this application as well. The application also includes documentation that you have to package with the appropriate distribution.

The application is simple, but it uses a wide range of features so you can get used to adding many kinds of components to a project. For example, it uses a stand-alone Java class with a `main()` method as the command-line client, JSP tag files, servlets, plain HTML, Java property files, and third-party open-source software. The main instructive point is the separation of functionality.

Introducing the Shared Code

The command-line client and the web interface share a few classes. One shared class contains the database-access code that connects to the database and pulls data from it. This class then passes the data to whichever client class instantiated it. By doing this, you centralize any SQL statements and database connection code so that all releases of the application behave in the same way. Figure 5-1 shows this simple abstraction.

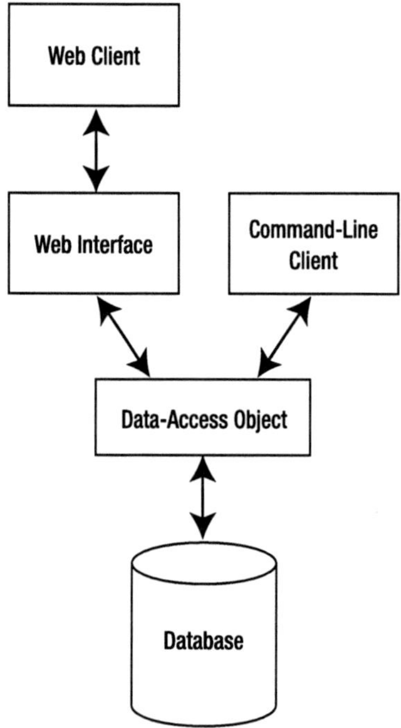

Figure 5-1. *Both interfaces use a common data-access object.*

You can see how the build process for both sides of the project will need to include the database layer shown here. In fact, Figure 5-1 describes the build process extremely well. The command-line client depends on the data-access code, so the target that builds the command-line client should depend on the target that builds the data-access object. The same goes for the web interface.

The two strands of the application also share a class that holds search choice constants. This means each client can offer the search options to users in an application-specific way, while using a common nomenclature underneath. For example, should a user want to order the results alphabetically, they would pass a command-line option to the command-line client, but would select a link or a drop-down box in the web interface. Once the application has divined which option the user has chosen, it sends the choice to the data-access layer, which also has access to the common choices. In other words, they all speak the same language. Figure 5-2 shows this new set of relationships.

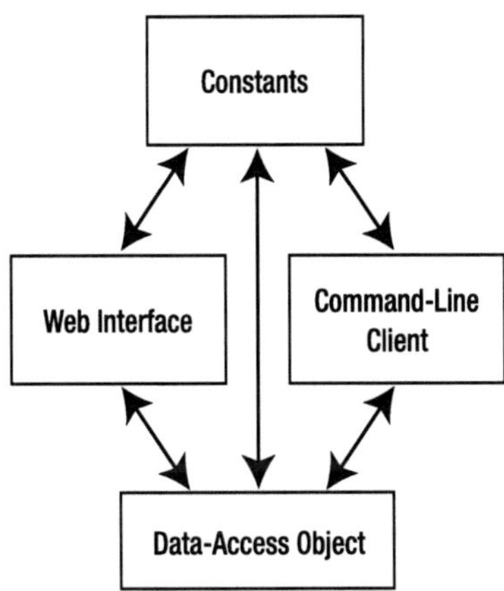

Figure 5-2. *Each component uses a set of constants to abstract the search choice.*

The final part of the shared code is a Java properties file that contains database connection information. The application uses JDBC to connect to the database, so providing the database driver and URL with a properties file is easy.

To start organizing the code, you need a src directory to store all your application's code. The first division you are going to use is, as you've just seen, shared code. Therefore, the shared child directory will contain the code that is common to all the incarnations of the application.

```
src/
    shared/
            conf/
                 database.properties
            java/
                 org/
                     mwrm/
                          shared Java classes
```

Introducing the Third-Party Libraries

The application uses third-party libraries from the Jakarta Project and MySQL. You can deal with third-party libraries in two ways: the first is to download a stable build manually and standardize the version across all those involved in a project. The second way of dealing with third-party libraries is to download the latest source files and compile them so that you have the latest, most up-to-date version of the software. This is an optional step, and you can easily factor it into the build process, as shown in Figure 5-3. I'll come back to this in the "Adding Third-Party Libraries to the Build" section.

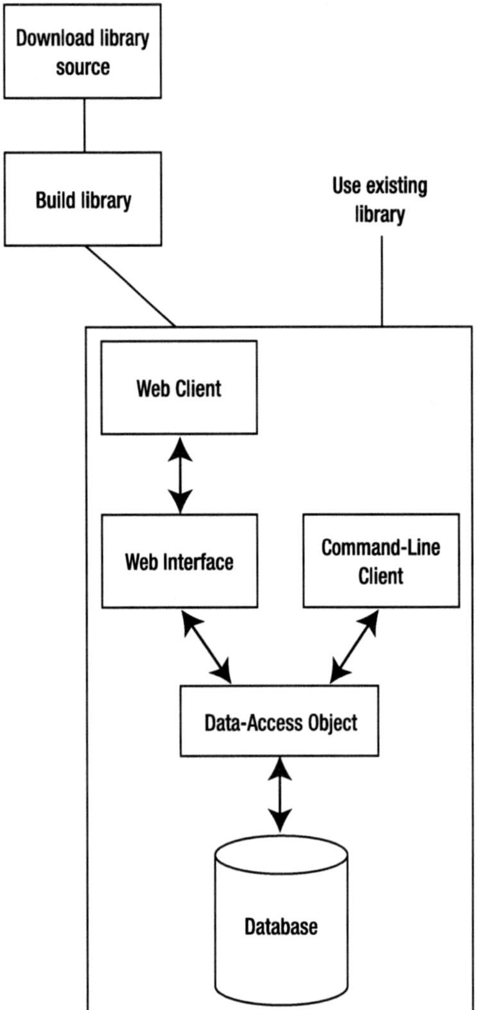

Figure 5-3. *Adding third-party libraries to a build*

Introducing the Stand-Alone Application

The stand-alone application is a command-line client that uses the data-access abstraction layer to connect to the database so that it can obtain data to display to the console. It takes a number of command-line options and displays the results according to the user's choice. It prints usage information if the user supplies invalid options.

To separate it from the shared code, place it in the following directory structure:

```
src/
    stand-alone/
                java/
                     org/
                         mwrm/
                              stand-alone client
```

Introducing the Web Application

The web application is the most complicated of the three divisions. It uses plain HTML, JSP pages, servlets, and tags to provide a rich web interface to the database. Each of these components will be in separate locations, and you'll bring them together when you build the web application.

Simple HTML, JSP pages, and tags guide the user through the application, though a servlet carries out the work of processing the data from the database and providing it for the JSP pages. Essentially, it performs similar work to the stand-alone client, meaning it takes the choice made by the user and obtains the relevant data from the database. Instead of displaying the data, however, the servlet places it in the session so that the rest of the web application has access to it.

Here's the structure of the web application project:

```
src/
    web/
        conf/
             web.xml
        images/
        java/
             org/
                 mwrm/
                      servlet classes
        pages/
              HTML pages
              JSP pages
        tags/
             tag files
```

Introducing the Final Directory Structure

Now that you've separated the three sections of code, the final directory structure looks as follows:

```
src/
    shared/
           conf/
                database.properties
           java/
                org/
                    mwrm/
                         shared Java classes
    stand-alone/
                java/
                     org/
                         mwrm/
                              stand-alone client
```

```
web/
    conf/
         web.xml
    images/
    java/
         org/
             mwrm/
                  servlet classes
    pages/
          HTML pages
          JSP pages
    tags/
         tag files
```

In addition to these directories, you'll need other directories at the same level as `src`. These will help you organize the project when you run the build.

- `build`: This is a scratch directory where you will assemble all the code before running the final packaging steps.
- `dist`: When you have built and packaged the application, you will place it in here prior to distribution or deployment.
- `lib`: You will place third-party libraries in this folder so you can include them in a distribution.

Compiling Java Applications with Ant

Ant provides you with the `<javac>` task so that you can compile Java source code into Java classes. However, before you look into that, you should be aware of a number of preliminary considerations, the first of which is setting up your working environment. This involves setting global properties in a properties file and creating scratch directories so that you have space to work without potentially disrupting the source code.

Setting Up a Working Environment

To begin, you need to create a `build.properties` file in the root directory of the build (that is, the one that contains the `src` directory). You will import the properties from here into the build to ease the maintenance burden of the project. You need to set the names of your top-level directories. Every path in the build file will build on these directories and are in turn properties. By making every path in the build file a property, you centralize the most important parts of the build into one location where you can look after them. If one section of the path changes, then you will have to change only one property in the properties file.

To compile the web portion of the application, you'll need to use the Servlet API and so should include a reference to it in the properties file. This JAR file is included with Tomcat, but if you are using another servlet container, you will have to change this value or download it from `www.ibiblio.org/maven/servletapi/jars/`. I'll cover downloading this as part of the build later in the "Compiling the Source" section.

Listing 5-1 shows what you have so far. Note how each subdirectory is built from another property and how the name of the JAR and WAR files is set here too.

Listing 5-1. *The Names of the Directories in `build.properties`*

```
# The source directory that contains the code
src=src

# Subdirectory properties
src.shared.root=${src}/shared
src.shared.java=${src.shared.root}/java
src.shared.docs=${src.shared.root}/docs
src.shared.conf=${src.shared.root}/conf

src.stand-alone.root=${src}/stand-alone
src.stand-alone.java=${src.stand-alone.root}/java
src.stand-alone.docs=${src.stand-alone.root}/docs

src.web.root=${src}/web
src.web.java=${src.web.root}/java
src.web.docs=${src.web.root}/docs
src.web.pages=${src.web.root}/pages
src.web.tags=${src.web.root}/tags
src.web.conf=${src.web.root}/conf

# The scratch directory
build=build

build.stand-alone.root=${build}/stand-alone

build.web.root=${build}/web
build.web.web-inf=${build.web.root}/WEB-INF
build.web.classes=${build.web.web-inf}/classes
build.web.tags=${build.web.web-inf}/tags
build.web.lib=${build.web.web-inf}/lib

# The final destination of our project files
dist=dist

# The location of third-party JAR files
lib=lib

# This name will be appended to the JAR and WAR files
appName=antBook
appName.jar=${dist}/${appName}.jar
appName.war=${dist}/${appName}.war
```

```
# The Tomcat home directory
catalina.home=C:\\jakarta-tomcat-5.5.9
servlet24.jar=${catalina.home}/common/lib/servlet-api.jar
# Use the following line if using Ant to download the JAR
#servlet24.jar=${lib}/servlet-api.jar
```

Now that you have the properties ready, you can include them in your project's `build.xml` file, as shown in Listing 5-2.

Listing 5-2. *Including the Properties in* `build.xml`

```
<?xml version="1.0"?>

<project name="Example Application Build" default="build-both" basedir=".">

  <property file="build.properties"/>
  </project>
```

This should be familiar to you from Chapter 3. Now it's time to actually use the properties.

Creating Directories

The `src` directory is the only top-level directory you can assume exists, because you want to leave open the option of downloading fresh JARs for the `lib` directory. The others are necessarily absent from the first build, so the upshot is you want to create `build`, `dist`, and `lib`.

Ant's directory-creation task is called `<mkdir>`; Table 5-1 lists its single attribute.

Table 5-1. *The* `<mkdir>` *Task's Attribute*

Attribute	Description
`dir`	The name of the directory to create, which is either relative to the base directory of this build or an absolute path. This attribute is required.

Listing 5-3 shows the `dir` target that will create the necessary directories.

Listing 5-3. *The* `<mkdir>` *Task Creates the Directory Structure*

```
<!-- Create the working directories -->
<target name="dir" description="Create the working directories">
  <echo message="Creating the working directories"/>
  <mkdir dir="${build.stand-alone.root}"/>
  <mkdir dir="${build.web.classes}"/>
  <mkdir dir="${dist}"/>
  <mkdir dir="${lib}"/>
</target>
```

The first <mkdir> task creates the build directory as well as the stand-alone directory it contains. The recursive nature of the <mkdir> task saves you a lot of effort and allows you to create large directory structures in only a few steps. The second <mkdir> task shows this in action as well.

Compiling the Source

Now that you have the directory structure in place, it's time to build the application. Ant's Java compilation task is <javac>, and it's as flexible as the javac command is at the command line. You'll keep the stand-alone application in its own target because it allows you to compile just the stand-alone application, should you want. This follows the project structure shown in Figures 5-1 and 5-2 and means you can include it in more than one project build path. For example, you may sometimes want to build it for testing, but not for distribution.

The <javac> task has the attributes shown in Table 5-2 (as well as the attributes of a file set, as detailed in Table 4-6 in Chapter 4), and many of them will be familiar from the command line. You can specify most of the attributes that take paths as nested elements as well.

Table 5-2. *The <mkdir> Task's Attribute*

Attribute	Description
bootclasspath	The boot classpath to use for this compilation. The default is the system boot classpath.
bootclasspathref	A reference ID to a path that you have defined elsewhere in the build file.
classpath	The classpath for this compilation. As with all Java applications, the classpath is an important issue to understand. More details follow this table. The default is the system classpath plus Ant's classpath (ANT_HOME/lib and the -lib command-line option).
classpathref	A reference ID to a path that you have defined elsewhere in the build file.
compiler	The compiler implementation to use. If you do not set this attribute, Ant will use the value of the build.compiler property, if set.
debug	Sets the javac -g flag and can be used in combination with debuglevel. This attribute makes sense only if your compiler supports debugging. The default is false, which sends -g:none to the compiler.
debuglevel	Sets the keywords to be appended to the -g command, if it is sent. If debug is set to false, this attribute is ignored. You specify either none or a comma-separated list of lines, vars, and source. The default is an empty string (that is, nothing is appended to the -g option).
depend	Tells the compiler to track dependencies, if it supports this feature. The default is false.
deprecation	Tells Ant whether to compile with deprecation information. The default is false.
destdir	The directory where you want Ant to place the compiled class files. The default is the same location as the source files, just as it is for javac at the command line.
encoding	The encoding of the source files. The default depends on your system.

Table 5-2. *The <mkdir> Task's Attribute (Continued)*

Attribute	Description
excludes	The excludes list for this compilation, where each entry is separated from the next one with a space or a comma. You may use wildcards. The default is to omit nothing except the default excludes.
excludesfile	The name of the file that contains the exclude patterns. The default is not to use a file.
executable	The full path to the javac executable should you set fork to true. The default is the executable of the JVM that is running Ant.
extdirs	A list of the directories that contain installed extensions. The default is the system extension setting.
failonerror	Tells Ant whether to carry on with the build if there was a compilation error. The default is true.
fork	Tells Ant to compile the classes with an external JDK compiler. The default is false.
includeAntRuntime	Tells Ant to add its runtime libraries to the classpath. The default is true.
includeJavaRuntime	Tells Ant to add the Java run-time libraries to the classpath. The default is false.
includes	The includes list for this compilation, where each entry is separated from the next one with a space or a comma. You may use wildcards. The default is *.java.
includesfile	The name of the file that contains the include patterns. The default is to not use a file.
listfiles	Tells Ant to list the files that it is compiling, rather than just the number of files. The default is false.
memoryInitialSize	The initial size for the external JVM should you set fork to true. Ignored if you do not.
memoryMaximumSize	The maximum amount of memory to be used by the external JVM should you set fork to true. Ignored if you do not.
nowarn	Tells Ant whether to send the -nowarn option to the compiler. The default is false.
optimize	Tells Ant whether to compile the source with optimization. The default is false.
source	The value of the -source command-line option. The default value depends on your own VM, and some will ignore it. You will know best as to what the value of this attribute should be.
sourcepath	The source path for this compilation. The default is the value of srcdir or any nested <src> elements.
sourcepathref	A reference ID to a path that you have defined elsewhere in the build file.
srcdir	The base directory of the Java source code. All paths used in the <javac> task are relative to this directory. This attribute is required.

Table 5-2. *The <mkdir> Task's Attribute (Continued)*

Attribute	Description
tempdir	The location of a temporary directory that Ant should use in the build. Ant uses it only if you set fork to true and the length of the command-line arguments exceeds 4 kilobytes.
target	The version of Java for which these files will be compiled. The default value depends on your own VM. You will know best as to what the value of this attribute should be. If you are using JVM 1.4 or greater, you should note that your classes won't work in a 1.1 JVM.
verbose	Tells the compiler to be more verbose. The default is false.

Whether you set these attributes depends on your project and how you would have compiled it at the command line. If you have certain compiler and JVM version concerns for your project and want to know more, the best place to look is the <javac> task's documentation.

If you are using JDK 1.3 or greater on Windows, unforked compilation will lock files in the classpath, so you can't move or delete them later in the build. If this is part of your build plan, set fork to true.

The <javac> task can also have the following child elements, some of which can replace their corresponding attributes:

<bootclasspath>
<classpath>
<exclude>
<extdirs>
<include>
<patternset>
<sourcepath>
<src>

<bootclasspath>, <classpath>, <extdirs>, <patternset>, <sourcepath>, and <src> are pathlike structures (see Chapter 4 for details on this type of structure) and can take references to other paths defined elsewhere in the build file.

Note The <javac> task uses the system classpath, Ant's own classpath (the contents of ANT_HOME/lib and the values supplied with the -lib command-line option), and any custom classpath you supply as an argument or nested element.

This is a good point to add the master build classpath that contains all the JAR files for compiling and running the application. Listing 5-4 shows the <path> element that sets the master classpath. You'll see the jsp20.jar property when you compile the JSTL source code.

Listing 5-4. *Building the Master Classpath with a <path> Element*

```
<!-- #################################### -->
<!-- The master build classpath           -->
<!-- #################################### -->

<path id="build.classpath">
  <pathelement location="${servlet24.jar}"/>
  <pathelement location="${jsp20.jar}"/>
  <pathelement location="${mysql.jar}"/>
  <pathelement path="${appName.jar}"/>
</path>
```

Listing 5-5 shows the <javac> task that you will use to compile the stand-alone application. Note how the shared code is compiled first.

Listing 5-5. *The <javac> Task Compiles the Stand-Alone Application*

```
<!-- ############################ -->
<!-- The stand-alone application -->
<!-- ############################ -->

<!-- Compile the stand-alone application -->
<target name="compile-stand-alone" depends="dir"
        description="Compile stand-alone application">
  <echo message="Compiling the stand-alone application"/>
  <javac srcdir="${src.shared.java}" destdir="${build.stand-alone.root}"/>
  <javac srcdir="${src.stand-alone.java}"
         destdir="${build.stand-alone.root}"/>
  </target>
```

The sample web application has a similar compilation, though it requires the servlet classes to be in the classpath. As such, Listing 5-6 shows the variants of <javac> that you can use to compile the web application.

Listing 5-6. *The <javac> Task Compiles the Web Application*

```
<!-- ############################ -->
<!-- The web application          -->
<!-- ############################ -->

<!-- Compile the web application -->
<target name="compile-web" depends="dir" description="Compile web application">
  <echo message="Compiling the web application"/>
  <javac destdir="${build.web.classes}">
    <src path="${src.shared.java}"/>
```

```
  </javac>
  <javac srcdir="${src.web.java}" destdir="${build.web.classes}">
    <classpath refid="build.classpath"/>
  </javac>
</target>
```

Recall that you built the servlet24.jar property from the catalina.home property in the property file because I assumed you have access to Tomcat. If you wanted to download the JAR file in the build, you could use the target in Listing 5-7 and add it to the depends attribute of the compile-web target. Remember to change the servlet24.jar property as well.

Listing 5-7. *Downloading the Servlet JAR File with the <get> Task*

```
<!-- ######################## -->
<!-- Download the servlet JAR -->
<!-- ######################## -->

<!-- Download the servlet JAR -->
<target name="download-servlet-jar" depends="dir"
        description="Download the servlet JAR">
  <echo message="Downloading the servlet JAR"/>

  <get src="http://www.ibiblio.org/maven/servletapi/jars/servletapi-2.4.jar"
       dest="${servlet24.jar}"
       verbose="true"/>
</target>
```

The <get> task is straightforward. The src attribute is the file you want to download, and the dest attribute is its name in your file system. These are the only two required attributes. The verbose attribute is set to false by default, though here you should see the details of the download for the sake of instruction. You can also take advantage of HTTP BASIC authentication with the username and password attributes, though you should set these only at the command line and not as properties or as hard-coded values in the file.

Now that you have compiled the code and placed the class files in the scratch directory, it's time to assemble the other parts of the project before you package them for distribution.

Adding Third-Party Libraries to the Build

If you are using third-party libraries in a build, you may want to build them at the same time as the main project, assuming the source code is available. However, building third-party libraries is not an important step when you are using a set, stable version of a third-party library to ensure standard behavior across a project team. You don't need to build the libraries from source during every run of the build, because you can set up a build path to do this, as the case may be.

Figure 5-4 shows a simple build path that allows you to choose between using the existing library in your base directory's lib directory and using a freshly downloaded source bundle.

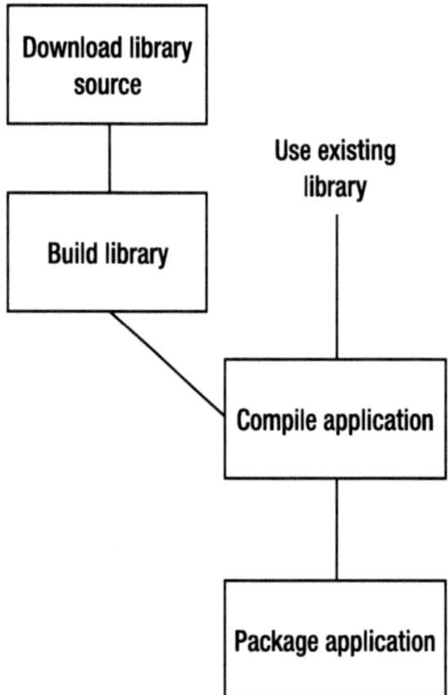

Figure 5-4. *Choosing between downloading source code and using preexisting binaries*

You can make this kind of choice in three ways: using properties, using the `<antcall>` task in a target, or using the `depends` attribute of `<target>`. This kind of choice is not unique to downloading third-party source code; you can apply it to many other situations. For example, you may want to exclude the documentation from some project builds, but not others.

The example project uses two third-party libraries: the MySQL JDBC connector and the JSTL tag library. You can obtain these easily as binary JAR files, but you can also get the latest CVS snapshot. The `<cvs>` task checks out source from a CVS repository and places it in your file system. Table 5-3 shows its attributes.

Table 5-3. *The `<cvs>` Task's Attributes*

Attribute	Description
`append`	Tells Ant whether it should append output messages to the file specified in `output` or `error`. The default is `false`.
`command`	The CVS command to execute, though you can add to this with, for example, the `package` attribute, as in Listing 5-9. The default is `checkout`.
`compression`	If you set this to `true`, it is equivalent to setting the `compressionlevel` to `3`. The default is `false`.
`compressionlevel`	Valid values are `1`–`9`. If you set it to anything else, it's equivalent to setting `compression` to `false`. Ignored if `compression` is set to `false`, and its default is `3` if `compression` is set to `true`.
`cvsRoot`	The root of the CVS repository you are querying. The default is `null`.
`cvsRsh`	The remote shell to use. The default is `null`.

Table 5-3. *The <cvs> Task's Attributes*

Attribute	Description
date	Tells Ant to check out the most recent files, as long as their modification times are not later than this date.
dest	The directory where you want to place the source code that is checked out of the repository. The default is your project's base directory.
error	The file where you want to direct error messages. The default is the Ant log (set at MSG_WARN).
failonerror	Tells Ant whether to carry on with the build if there was a CVS error. The default is false.
noexec	Tells Ant to make a report and not to change any files. The default is false.
output	The file where you want to direct output. The default is the Ant log (set at MSG_INFO).
package	The name of the package you want to check out of the CVS repository. The default is null.
passfile	The file where you have stored the CVS passwords, if any. The default is ~/.cvspass.
port	The port of the CVS server. The default is 2401.
quiet	Tells Ant to suppress information messages during the CVS process. The default is false.
reallyquiet	Tells Ant to not print any messages at all during the CVS process. The default is false.
tag	The tag of the package you want to check out of the CVS repository. The default is null.

All the following sections will require the property definitions in Listing 5-8.

Listing 5-8. *The CVS Homes of the Third-Party Libraries*

```
<!-- CVSROOT for the JSTL -->
<property name="cvsroot"
          value=":pserver:anoncvs@cvs.apache.org:/home/cvspublic" />

<!-- CVSROOT for the MySQL connector -->
<property name="mysql.cvsroot"
          value=":pserver:anonymous@cvs.sourceforge.net:/cvsroot/mmmysql" />
```

These are the login details for the CVS repositories of the third-party libraries. The actual targets for obtaining the source and compiling it won't change. Listing 5-9 shows the targets for obtaining the source code.

Listing 5-9. *The Targets for Obtaining the JSTL and the MySQL Connector Source*

```
<!-- Update or check out required sources from CVS for the JSTL -->
<target name="checkout-jstl" depends="dir"
        description="Update or check out required sources
                     from CVS for the JSTL">

  <echo message="Checking out the required JSTL sources from CVS"/>

  <cvs cvsroot="${cvsroot}" quiet="true"
       command="checkout -P ${jstl.build}"
       dest="${build}" compression="true" />

</target>
<!-- Update or check out required sources from CVS for the MySQL connector -->
<target name="checkout-mysql-connector" depends="dir"
        description="Update or check out required sources
        from CVS for the MySQL connector">

  <echo message="Checking out the required sources from CVS
               for the MySQL connector" />

  <cvs cvsroot="${mysql.cvsroot}" quiet="true"
       command="checkout" package="${mysql.build}"
       dest="${build}" compression="true" />

</target>
```

The task for the JSTL CVS contains the command `checkout -P ${jstl.build}`, and the MySQL CVS task builds the command using the `package` attribute.

You need to define some more properties in `build.properties`. The MySQL connector source comes with its own build file and uses a number of properties of its own. However, to finish the job you need three more, as shown in Listing 5-10. (You'll use `mysql.name` in the compilation process.) The JSTL build requires a few more properties, also shown in Listing 5-10. The JSP classes are taken from Tomcat, but if you have not installed Tomcat, you can get the JAR file from `www.ibiblio.org/maven/jspapi/jars/`.

Listing 5-10. *Properties for Obtaining and Building the Third-Party Libraries*

```
# Required for the JSTL build
jsp20.jar=${catalina.home}/common/lib/jsp-api.jar
# Use the following line if using Ant to download the JAR
#jsp20.jar=${lib}/jsp-api.jar
jstl.build=jakarta-taglibs/standard
library.src=src
examples.src=examples
doc.src=doc
build.library=${build}
```

```
# Required for the MySQL connector build
mysql.build=mm.mysql-2
mysql.name=mysql-connector
mysql.jar=${lib}/${mysql.name}-bin.jar
```

You can modify the download-servlet-jar target from Listing 5-7 to download the JSP JAR file if you want, as shown in Listing 5-11.

Listing 5-11. *Downloading the JSP JAR File with the <get> Task*

```
<!-- ######################## -->
<!-- Download the JSP JAR     -->
<!-- ######################## -->

<!-- Download the JSP JAR -->
<target name="download-jsp-jar" depends="dir"
        description="Download the JSP JAR">
  <echo message="Downloading the JSP JAR"/>

  <get src="http://www.ibiblio.org/maven/jspapi/jars/jsp-api-2.0.jar"
       dest="${jsp20.jar}"
       verbose="true"/>
</target>
```

You can now run these two targets and obtain the source code of the JSTL and the MySQL JDBC connector. Once you have the source, you can build them. Luckily, both are based on Java and come with their own Ant build files for seamless integration into your project.

To use another project's build file in your own project, you use the <ant> task. This task will run the default target of the target project, but it can also run a specific target if you want. In the case of this sample project, you want to pass all the properties to the new builds because you want to customize them to your own requirements. (The JSTL build also requires certain properties before it will build successfully.) You can disable property sharing like this if you are worried about naming clashes (by setting the inheritAll attribute to false). Naming clashes will occur because the properties from the calling project override those in the called project.

The <ant> task can have nested <property> elements, which Ant always passes to the called project, no matter what settings you have. These will override any properties in the called file just as if they were buildwide properties.

■ **Note** Properties passed to Ant at the command line are always passed to the called project. They will even overwrite the nested <property> elements.

Table 5-4 shows the attributes of the <ant> task.

Table 5-4. *The <ant> Task's Attributes*

Attribute	Description
antfile	The name of the build file to use, which is relative to the directory specified in the dir attribute. The default is build.xml.
dir	The base directory for the project you are calling. It should contain the file you specify in the antfile attribute. The default is the calling project's base directory.
inheritAll	Tells Ant whether to pass properties to the called project. The default is true.
inheritRefs	Tells Ant whether to pass references to the called project. The default is false.
output	The file where you want to direct output (set at MSG_INFO). The default is null.
target	The name of the target you want to call in the called project. The default is the called project's default target.

So, calling another project's build file is extremely easy. The hardest part of it is working out which properties you need to customize or supply for the called project to build. If you are calling one of your own projects, that shouldn't be a problem because they will mostly be in place to start. Third-party libraries require a bit more investigation (as shown by the properties the JSTL build requires, as listed in Table 5-4).

Listing 5-12 shows the two <ant> tasks that build the third-party libraries and the tasks that copy them to your lib directory. (I'll discuss the <copy> task in the "Assembling the Project" section.)

Listing 5-12. *The Targets for Building the JSTL and the MySQL Connector*

```
<!-- Build the JSTL from source -->
<target name="build-jstl" depends="checkout-jstl"
        description="Build the JSTL from source">
  <echo message="Building the JSTL from source"/>

  <ant antfile="build.xml" dir="${build}/${jstl.build}"/>

  <copy todir="${lib}">
    <fileset dir="${build}/${jstl.build}/${build}/lib">
      <include name="*.jar"/>
    </fileset>
  </copy>
</target>

<!-- Build the MySQL connector from source -->
<target name="build-mysql-connector" depends="checkout-mysql-connector"
        description="Build the MySQL connector from source">
  <echo message="Building the MySQL connector from source"/>
```

```
  <!-- The MySQL connector file needs this directory to exist -->
  <!-- Therefore we need to create it -->
  <mkdir dir="${build}/dist-mysql-jdbc"/>

  <ant antfile="build.xml" dir="${build}/${mysql.build}"/>

  <copy tofile="${mysql.jar}">
    <fileset dir="${build}/build-mysql-jdbc">
      <include name="mysql-connector*/*.jar"/>
    </fileset>
  </copy>
</target>
```

Both `<ant>` tasks call the appropriate `build.xml` file located in the directory you downloaded, as defined by the `jstl.build` and `mysql.build` properties. As noted, some research into the properties of the third-party libraries was required before you could run the build. Similar research was required before you could use the `<copy>` task to move the JAR files into the `lib` directory. As you can see, the location of the JARs is not common to both libraries, so you had to use different patterns to locate them.

The MySQL connector uses a version number in the names of its directories and JAR files, so you have to remove any dependencies on this naming convention. The wildcard characters are perfect for this. The JSTL isn't so complicated but has two binary JARs, both of which you must copy.

Using Properties to Decide

The `if` and `unless` attributes of `<target>` allow you to control whether a target will execute, depending on the presence or absence of a named property (see Chapter 3). Therefore, you can force Ant to skip steps in the build process by providing properties at the command line with the `-D` option. So, instead of the forked build path shown in Figure 5-3, you will have a linear build path that ignores some steps, depending on your choice of properties.

The `compile-stand-alone` target is the end of the stand-alone application's linear build path, so it must depend on the `build-mysql-connector` target, which in turn depends on the `checkout-mysql-connector` target. Therefore, you must change the `depends` attribute of `compile-stand-alone` as follows:

```
<target name="compile-stand-alone" depends="build-mysql-connector"
        description="Compile stand-alone application">
```

The same applies to the `compile-web` target, but it also needs the JSTL:

```
<target name="compile-web" depends="build-jstl, build-mysql-connector"
        description="Compile web application">
```

Now, when you run Ant on each of these targets, you will always run the download and build targets as well. To control this, you need to use properties at the command line. Listing 5-13 shows the `if` attributes of the targets that download and build the third-party libraries.

Listing 5-13. *The* `if` *Attribute Determines Whether a Target Runs*

```
<target name="checkout-jstl" depends="dir" if="jstl"
        description="Update or check out required sources
        from CVS for the JSTL">
</target>

<target name="build-jstl" depends="checkout-jstl" if="jstl"
        description="Build the JSTL from source">
</target>

<target name="checkout-mysql-connector" depends="dir" if="mysql"
        description="Update or check out required sources
        from CVS for the MySQL connector">
</target>

<target name="build-mysql-connector" depends="checkout-mysql-connector"
        if="mysql" description="Build the MySQL connector from source">
</target>
```

Now, if you set the `mysql` property at the command line, the MySQL-specific targets will run. The same goes for the `jstl` property.

```
> ant -Djstl=true -Dmysql=true compile-web
```

If you don't set them, Ant will not run the targets.

Using the <antcall> Task

The `<antcall>` task is similar to the `<ant>` task, except that it calls a target in the current project's build file. This is a useful technique when you have a forked build process. You cannot use `<antcall>` outside a target, though you won't have reason to do so. It has the attributes shown in Table 5-5.

Table 5-5. *The* `<antcall>` *Task's Attributes*

Attribute	Description
`inheritAll`	Tells Ant whether to pass properties to the called project. The default is `true`.
`inheritRefs`	Tells Ant whether to pass references to the called project. The default is `false`.
`target`	The name of the target you want Ant to run. This attribute is required.

To use `<antcall>` to control the build, place an `<antcall>` task for each target you want to call in a master target, as shown in Listing 5-14.

Listing 5-14. *Using `<antcall>` to Control a Project*

```
<target name="stand-alone-complete"
        description="Compile stand-alone application,
        using CVS version of the MySQL connector">
  <echo message="Compiling stand-alone application,
                 using CVS versions of the MySQL connector"/>
  <antcall target="build-mysql-connector"/>
  <antcall target="package-stand-alone"/>
</target>

<target name="web-complete"
        description="Compile web application,
                     using CVS versions of the MySQL connector and the JSTL">
  <echo message="Compiling web application,
                 using CVS versions of the MySQL connector and the JSTL"/>
  <antcall target="build-mysql-connector"/>
  <antcall target="build-jstl"/>
  <antcall target="package-web"/>
</target>
```

To build the third-party libraries as well as the application, you just need to run the following:

```
> ant stand-alone-complete
> ant web-complete
```

If you want to build just the application, run the following:

```
> ant package-stand-alone
> ant package-web
```

To increase the build functionality, you can add a master target that will run these commands for you if you want to build the stand-alone application at the same time as the web application. Listing 5-15 shows how to do this.

Listing 5-15. *Master Targets for Building Both Applications*

```
<!-- ######################################## -->
<!-- Targets that work with both applications -->
<!-- ######################################## -->

<target name="build-both"
        description="Compile both applications,
                     without CVS versions of the MySQL connector and the JSTL">
  <echo message="Compiling both applications,
                 without CVS versions of the MySQL connector and the JSTL"/>
  <antcall target="package-stand-alone"/>
  <antcall target="package-web"/>
</target>
```

```
<target name="build-all"
        description="Compile both applications,
                     using CVS versions of the MySQL connector and the JSTL">
  <echo message="Compiling both applications,
                using CVS versions of the MySQL connector and the JSTL"/>
  <antcall target="stand-alone-complete"/>
  <antcall target="web-complete"/>
</target>
```

You can quite easily extend this structure of <antcall> tasks to cover as many permutations as you like.

Using Dependencies

The third method for choosing which targets to run is the depends attribute of the <target> element. The principle behind this technique is similar to that of the <antcall> task. However, instead of grouping <antcall> elements, you specify target names in a master target's depends attribute.

In the example build file, this means you will replace every <antcall> with a setting in the target's depends attribute. Compare Listing 5-16 with Listings 5-14 and 5-15.

Listing 5-16. *Using the depends Attribute to Control a Build*

```
<target name="stand-alone-complete"
        depends="build-mysql-connector, package-stand-alone"
        description="Compile stand-alone application,
        using CVS version of the MySQL connector">
  <echo message="Compiling stand-alone application,
                using CVS versions of the MySQL connector"/>
</target>

<target name="web-complete"
        depends="build-mysql-connector, build-jstl, package-web"
        description="Compile web application,
                     using CVS versions of the MySQL connector and the JSTL">
  <echo message="Compiled web application,
                  using CVS versions of the MySQL connector and the JSTL"/>
</target>

<!-- ######################################## -->
<!-- Targets that work with both applications -->
<!-- ######################################## -->
```

```
<target name="build-both"
        depends="package-stand-alone, package-web"
        description="Compile both applications,
                     without CVS versions of the MySQL connector and the JSTL">
  <echo message="Compiled both applications,
                 without CVS versions of the MySQL connector and the JSTL"/>
</target>

<target name="build-all"
        depends="stand-alone-complete, web-complete"
        description="Compile both applications,
                     using CVS versions of the MySQL connector and the JSTL">
  <echo message="Compiled both applications,
                 using CVS versions of the MySQL connector and the JSTL"/>
</target>
```

So, when you run the build-all target, Ant calls stand-alone-complete, which calls build-mysql-connector, which calls checkout-mysql-connector, which calls dir. If the last three targets complete their tasks, stand-alone-complete calls package-stand-alone, which calls compile-stand-alone. The dir target has already completed successfully, so the compile-stand-alone target runs. If it and package-stand-alone complete successfully, half the targets in the build-all target's depends attribute have completed successfully. Ant then calls web-complete, and the process goes much like the one described for stand-alone-complete.

Choosing Which Technique to Use

The depends attribute is the usual method for controlling the flow of a project. Its advantages include performance, with dependencies being up to six times faster than <antcall> tasks. Another advantage of depends attributes is that they group all the dependencies in one place right at the top of a target in a location that is useful to a casual reader. If you use properties, it may not be clear that you are using them to control the whole build unless you document thoroughly. Even then, users may not even read the build file and will try to run the build without setting any properties.

You should use depends attributes as much as possible if your project is confined to a single build file. It is a more maintainable technique because of its centralized nature and unambiguous meaning. If your build is split between files (as described in Chapter 9), then you have no choice but to use <antcall> tasks, though you should still try to minimize them.

Assembling the Project

Many, many ways of assembling a project for distribution exist, and Ant covers each one. The first step is to collect every piece of the project. Once you have done that, you can then choose which method of packaging, if any, you are going to use. For example, you may have source distributions as tarballs or zip files, binary distributions as JAR files, and local test copies as unpackaged directories. Your source distributions may be released daily, while the binary distributions may go out only when there is a major revision, so you want to build this flexibility into your build process.

Manipulating File Location

Ant has the full range of directory- and file-manipulation tasks that you would expect of an operating system, so you can do anything in a build process that you can do at the command line. These tasks take full advantage of Ant's pattern-matching capabilities, as well as heavily used pathlike structures.

You have already seen the `<copy>` task when you used it to move the third-party libraries to your `lib` directory. Table 5-6 shows the attributes of this task. It can also take nested `<fileset>`, `<mapper>`, `<filterset>`, and `<filterchain>` elements.

Table 5-6. *The <copy> Task's Attributes*

Attribute	Description
`enablemultiplemappings`	If you have specified a `<mapper>` nested element, this attribute tells Ant to process all the possible mappings for the source path; otherwise it will process only the first file or directory. The default is `false`.
`encoding`	The encoding of the source files. The default is the JVM's default encoding.
`failonerror`	Tells Ant whether to carry on with the build if there was a copy error. The default is `true`.
`file`	The name of the file to copy. This attribute is required unless you nest `<fileset>` elements.
`filtering`	Tells Ant whether to use the project's global filters. It will always use nested `<filterset>` elements, regardless of its setting. The default is `false`.
`flatten`	Tells Ant whether to copy all the files into the directory specified by `todir`, ignoring the source directory hierarchy. The default is `false`.
`granularity`	The number of milliseconds that Ant should allow either way when it is deciding whether a file is out-of-date. The default is `2000` on DOS-based operating systems. It is `0` on all other systems.
`includeEmptyDirs`	Tells Ant whether to include empty directories in the copy. The default is `true`.
`outputencoding`	The encoding that Ant should use for the copied files. The default is the value of `encoding` if you have set it or the JVM's default if not.
`overwrite`	Tells Ant whether to overwrite existing files at the destination, even if they are newer than the files you are copying. The default is `false`.
`preservelastmodified`	Tells Ant to maintain the last modified time of the files you are copying. The default is `false`.
`todir`	The name of the directory to which you are copying. You must specify one of `todir` and `tofile`. I discuss the rules governing the two after this table.

Table 5-6. *The <copy> Task's Attributes*

Attribute	Description
tofile	The name of the file to which you are copying. You must specify one of todir and tofile. I discuss the rules governing the two after this table.
verbose	Tells Ant to list the files as it copies them. The default is false.

The general rule with the todir and tofile attributes is that if more than one file is to be copied, you must use the todir attribute. For example, more than one file will be copied if you use the file attribute and a <fileset> nested element or if a file set contains more than one file (if the file set contains a single file, you may use tofile). If only one file is to be copied, you can use whichever attribute you want. The tofile attribute will rename the file, while todir won't.

The stand-alone application is almost all in place by this point, but it still requires the Java properties file. Listing 5-17 shows the <copy> task that copies it into the working directory. There's more to this target, but that will wait until the "Creating JAR Files" section.

Listing 5-17. *Copying the Java Properties File Using the <copy> Task*

```
<!-- Package the stand-alone application -->
<target name="package-stand-alone" depends="compile-stand-alone"
        description="Package the stand-alone application">
  ...
  <copy file="${database.properties}" todir="${build.stand-alone.root}"/>
  ...
</target>
```

The web application has more files to work with, so a few more <copy> tasks exist, as shown in Listing 5-18.

Listing 5-18. *Copying the Web Application's Web Pages and Configuration Files*

```
<!-- Copy the web pages and configuration files -->
<target name="copy-web" depends="compile-web" description="Copy the web files">
  <echo message="Copying the web pages and configuration files"/>
  <copy todir="${build.web.root}">
    <fileset dir="${src.web.pages}"/>
  </copy>
  <!-- Copy the tags -->
  <copy todir="${build.web.tags}">
    <fileset dir="${src.web.tags}"/>
  </copy>
  <copy todir="${build.web.web-inf}">
    <fileset dir="${src.web.conf}">
      <include name="*.tld"/>
    </fileset>
  </copy>
```

```
  <!-- Copy the JAR files -->
  <copy todir="${build.web.lib}">
    <fileset dir="${lib}"/>
  </copy>
  <!-- Copy the properties file -->
  <copy file="${database.properties}" todir="${build.web.classes}"/>
  <!-- No need to copy web.xml, as the WAR task does this for us -->
</target>
```

These tasks are straightforward, though the final comment is worth discussing. When you create the WAR file of this web application in a moment, you will use the `<war>` task, which will pick up the `web.xml` file and place it in the WAR for you. If you wanted to use the expanded web application, then you would have to remember to copy the `web.xml` file into the expanded directory structure. It is also possible to assemble the entire WAR file in the `<war>` task, though you'll need zip file sets for this. You'll see zip file sets in the next chapter, so I'll defer this version of the `<war>` task until then.

One target that all Ant projects should have is a `clean` target. This will typically remove the working directories and remove any other unnecessary files. To do this, it will use the `<delete>` task, the attributes of which are shown in Table 5-7. (The deprecated attributes are not included, because they are replaced by nested file sets.) You can nest file sets in this task as well, and if you do, empty directories will be ignored by default (see the `includeemptydirs` attribute).

Table 5-7. *The `<delete>` Task's Attributes*

Attribute	Description
`deleteonexit`	Tells Ant to use the `File.deleteOnExit()` method to delete the file when the JVM terminates. The default is `false`.
`dir`	The name of the directory to delete. All its subdirectories are deleted as well. You must specify one of `dir` or `file` or supply a nested file set.
`failonerror`	Tells Ant whether to carry on with the build if there was an error. Is not used when `quiet` is set to `true`. The default is `true`.
`file`	The name of the file to delete. You must specify one of `dir` or `file` or supply a nested file set.
`includeemptydirs`	Tells Ant to delete empty directories if they match the pattern specified in a nested file set. The default is `false`.
`quiet`	This attribute is not quite the same as the `quiet` attribute of other tasks, and if set to `true`, it sets `failonerror` to `false`. If you set this to `true`, Ant does not display any error messages if a file or directory does not exist or can't be deleted, and the task continues processing. However, the `-verbose` and `-debug` command-line options override this attribute. The default is `false`.
`verbose`	Tells Ant to list the files as it deletes them. The default is `false`.

The example project uses a `clean` target, as shown in Listing 5-19.

Listing 5-19. *The clean Target Removes the Working Directories*

```
<target name="clean" description="Clean up the working directories">
  <echo message="Cleaning up"/>
  <delete dir="${build}"/>
</target>
```

Creating the JAR Files

Once you have assembled all the Java files you want to package into a JAR, you are ready to use the `<jar>` task. It has all the functionality of the `jar` command at the command line, so you will probably be familiar with what it does. Table 5-8 shows its attributes. You can use nested `<metainf>`, `<manifest>`, and `<indexjars>` elements.

Table 5-8. *The <jar> Task's Attributes*

Attribute	Description
`basedir`	The directory that will form the root of the resultant JAR file. The default is the base directory of the project.
`compress`	Tells Ant to compress the files as it adds them to the JAR file. If `keepcompression` is set to `true`, this applies to the entire archive, not just to the files you are adding. The default is `true`.
`defaultexcludes`	Tells Ant to use the default excludes (see Chapter 4). The default is `true`.
`destfile`	The name of the JAR file you want to create. This attribute is required.
`duplicate`	Tells Ant what to do if duplicate files are found. You can specify `add`, `preserve`, or `fail`. The default is `add`.
`encoding`	The encoding to use for filenames in the archive. The default is `UTF8`.
`excludes`	The excludes list for this task, where each entry is separated from the next one with a space or a comma. You may use wildcards. The default is to omit nothing except the default excludes.
`excludesfile`	The name of the file that contains the exclude patterns. The default is not to use a file.
`filesetmanifest`	Tells Ant how to react when it encounters a manifest file in a nested file set. `skip` ignores the file, `merge` tells Ant to merge the manifests, and `mergewithoutmain` merges the files without the main sections. The default is `skip`.
`filesonly`	Tells Ant to store only file entries. The default is `false`.
`includes`	The includes list for this task, where each entry is separated from the next one with a space or a comma. You may use wildcards. The default is all files.
`includesfile`	The name of the file that contains the include patterns. The default is not to use a file.
`index`	Tells Ant to create an index list to speed class loading (JDK 1.3 and greater). Only this JAR will be included in the list, unless you add nested `<indexjars>` elements. The default is `false`.

Table 5-8. *The <jar> Task's Attributes (Continued)*

Attribute	Description
keepcompression	Tells Ant to keep the original compression of the files you are adding. The default is false.
manifest	The name of the manifest file to use. It can be a manifest file in the file system or the name of a JAR file that contains the manifest you want to use. This JAR file must be specified in a nested file set and should contain a manifest at META-INF/MANIFEST.MF. The default is null.
manifestencoding	The encoding to use when reading the manifest. The default is the operating system's default.
roundup	Tells Ant to round up file modification times to the next even number of seconds. If you don't do this, the times will be rounded down in the JAR file. This means the JAR file will seem out-of-date when you run the target again. The default is true.
update	Tells Ant to overwrite files in the JAR file. The default is false.
whenempty	Tells Ant what to do if no files match. You can specify fail, create, or skip. The default is skip.

Listing 5-20 shows the full version of the package-stand-alone target.

Listing 5-20. *The package-stand-alone Target Creates the Stand-Alone Application's JAR File*

```
<!-- Package the stand-alone application -->
<target name="package-stand-alone" depends="compile-stand-alone"
        description="Package the stand-alone application">
  <echo message="Creating the stand-alone JAR file"/>
  <copy file="${database.properties}" todir="${build.stand-alone.root}"/>
  <jar destfile="${appName.jar}" basedir="${build.stand-alone.root}"/>
</target>
```

Creating WAR Files

Creating WAR files is usually the same as creating JAR files, because they share everything except the file extension. However, the <war> task has some unique attributes and nested elements. Table 5-9 shows the attributes.

Table 5-9. *The <war> Task's Attributes*

Attribute	Description
basedir	The directory that will form the root of the resultant WAR file. The default is the base directory of the project.
compress	Tells Ant to compress the files as it adds them to the WAR file. If keepcompression is set to true, this applies to the entire archive, not just to the files you are adding. The default is true.

Table 5-9. *The <war> Task's Attributes*

Attribute	Description
`defaultexcludes`	Tells Ant to use the default excludes (see Chapter 4). The default is `true`.
`destfile`	The name of the WAR file you want to create. This attribute is required.
`duplicate`	Tells Ant what to do if duplicate files are found. You can specify `add`, `preserve`, or `fail`. The default is `add`.
`encoding`	The encoding to use for filenames in the archive. The default is `UTF8`.
`excludes`	The excludes list for this task, where each entry is separated from the next one with a space or a comma. You may use wildcards. The default is to omit nothing except the default excludes.
`excludesfile`	The name of the file that contains the exclude patterns. The default is to not use a file.
`filesonly`	Tells Ant to store only file entries. The default is `false`.
`includes`	The includes list for this task, where each entry is separated from the next one with a space or a comma. You may use wildcards. The default is all files.
`includesfile`	The name of the file that contains the include patterns. The default is to not use a file.
`keepcompression`	Tells Ant to keep the original compression of the files you are adding. The default is `false`.
`manifest`	The name of the manifest file to use. The default is `null`.
`roundup`	Tells Ant to round up file modification times to the next even number of seconds. If you don't do this, the times will be rounded down in the WAR file. This means that the WAR file will seem out-of-date when you run the target again. If you do round up, you will have problems precompiling JSP pages, because they will always seem newer than the precompiled versions. The default is `true`.
`update`	Tells Ant to overwrite files in the WAR file. The default is `false`.
`webxml`	The location of the `web.xml` file for this web application. This attribute is required, unless you set `update` to `true`.

You can nest `<classes>`, `<lib>`, `<metainf>`, and `<webinf>` directories, which specify a file set that represents the files to be added to the `WEB-INF/classes`, `WEB-INF/lib`, `META-INF`, and `WEB-INF` directories, respectively. This means you can build the WAR file from disparate sources in the project's directory hierarchy, though the `<webinf>` element ignores any `web.xml` files contained in its file set. You'll see more of these nested elements in the next chapter once you have learned about zip file sets, which means you can build the WAR in one step without having to copy any files.

In the example application, however, most of the files already exist in the correct locations. Listing 5-21 shows how you build the WAR file for this application. Note the `webxml` attribute, which picks the `web.xml` file out and places it in the WAR.

Listing 5-21. *The <war> Task Assembles the Web Application's WAR File*

```
<!-- Build the WAR file -->
<target name="package-web" depends="copy-web" description="Build the WAR">
  <echo message="Building the WAR file"/>
  <war destfile="${appName.war}" basedir="${build.web.root}"
       webxml="${src.web.conf}/web.xml"/>
</target>
```

Building the Example Application

The final step in building both parts of the application is to link the packaging steps with depends attributes (or properties or <antcall> tasks, as per your preferences). The package-stand-alone and package-web targets don't download and build the third-party libraries, so you need to provide targets that do every step in the project build. Listing 5-22 shows the updated versions of stand-alone-complete and web-complete.

Listing 5-22. *The Updated Versions of stand-alone-complete and web-complete*

```
<target name="stand-alone-complete"
        depends="build-mysql-connector, package-stand-alone"
        description="Compile stand-alone application,
                     using CVS version of the MySQL connector">
  <echo message="Compiling stand-alone application,
                 using CVS versions of the MySQL connector"/>
</target>

<target name="web-complete"
        depends="build-mysql-connector, build-jstl, package-web"
        description="Compile web application,
                     using CVS versions of the MySQL connector and the JSTL">
  <echo message="Compiling web application,
                 using CVS versions of the MySQL connector and the JSTL"/>
</target>
```

Summary

In this chapter, you went through the processes that make up the main project build. You considered different techniques of structuring a build process and how to control which parts of the process run and which don't. This included using properties to selectively run targets, as well as the <antcall> task and the depends attribute of <target>, both of which are used in the same way.

You set up the example application's directory structure so that you could see these techniques on a project that has multiple applications within it. In this example, you have shared database-access code, a stand-alone application, and a web interface. These interfaces use third-party libraries for accessing the MySQL database and using the JSTL tag library. You saw how to check out the most recent version of these libraries from a CVS repository and the issues to watch for when working with third-party Ant builds.

This chapter did not include deploying or distributing the application, which I will cover in the next chapter, but did include creating JAR and WAR files of the binaries. You will also create packages of the source and include documentation in larger distributions in the next chapter.

CHAPTER 6

■ ■ ■

Deploying an Application

In the previous chapter, you examined how to build a project and place the binaries in JAR and WAR files. In this chapter, you will learn how to package an application in a distributable bundle, including the binaries, the documentation, and any appropriate licenses. (These may be included in a source JAR or WAR already, but you should include them just to ensure the entire bundle is covered.) Once you have a packaged distribution, you need to get it to your users. In the case of web applications, this may be as easy as hot deploying a WAR file to the web server, though other options include using FTP, using e-mail, and copying the distribution across a network.

Deployment choice of course depends on what kind of application it is and who the users are. Open-source projects are commonly placed in public places (CVS repositories, FTP servers, and web servers) for general download, while internal projects are placed in similar internal places or distributed directly to users. Source distributions are different again, in that internal projects may not even need a source distribution, though all distributions gain from including documentation.

In this chapter, you will create various distributions for your application that include zip and tar files for the documentation, source code, stand-alone application, web application, and entire binary distribution. Once you have these distributions, and you have digests for users to verify their integrity, you will distribute them via FTP and e-mail. You'll also see a few ways to deploy web applications.

Building Documentation Bundles

Adequate—or, even better, excellent—documentation is a must for any project, large or small, complicated or simple. This extends throughout the project, which means you should document your Ant setup as well as the rest of the project. Projects change hands, and just as undocumented code is an unfair legacy to pass on to the next maintainer/developer, undocumented build processes can impede progress on a project. Remember, the next maintainer/developer might be you in three months when you return to the project with hazy memories of code and build processes.

The documentation for Java projects, Ant build documentation aside, falls broadly into two categories: Javadocs and general documentation about the project. Javadocs should be part of your commenting regime in your source code, and you should keep them up to date as the code changes. The general documentation includes README files, licenses (if appropriate),

HTML manual pages, or Linux `man` entries. The HTML manual could be a copy of the web pages that provide download, build, and usage instructions, as well as links to the Javadocs.

■ **Note** The usual structure of documentation bundles is `<basedir>/docs/api`. This is the convention that this chapter will follow.

Creating Javadocs

The `javadoc` command-line tool is a useful method for building Java API documentation and is one with which you are no doubt familiar. It takes a huge number of options at the command line, and you will know best which ones apply to your Javadoc generation. Suffice it to say that Ant gives you options to replicate any functionality with its `<javadoc>` task, though, in this case, you won't see an entire table of its attributes. The table would be far too long and cumbersome for this discussion, so you should refer to `ant.apache.org/manual/CoreTasks/javadoc.html` for the entire list of attributes.

■ **Note** Sun has a tutorial on working with Javadocs at `java.sun.com/j2se/javadoc/`.

One great advantage of the `<javadoc>` task in Ant is that it makes combining packages from disparate locations easy. This is lucky because many projects have source files in different sections of the project. The example project is like this—it has a pool of shared code, as well as code for the web interface and the stand-alone client. Generating Javadocs that combine all these pieces of code is as simple as combining them in a single file set. The `<javadoc>` task then works on them all and creates a projectwide Javadoc bundle.

The example application has Javadoc comments throughout it. Listing 6-1 shows the properties used in the Javadoc build.

Listing 6-1. *Properties for the Javadoc Build*

```
# The directory where the docs will go
docs=${build}/docs

# Properties for customizing the Javadoc build
javadoc.doctitle=Welcome to the example application
javadoc.windowtitle=The example application
javadoc.j2se.version=1.5.0
javadoc.j2ee.version=1.4
```

Centralizing this kind of data means that your Javadocs will have a unified feel and that you can make changes easily and painlessly. You will place `javadoc.doctitle` and `javadoc.windowtitle` in the appropriate attributes and nested elements to customize the resultant HTML.

The Javadoc version information will help you link to Javadoc information outside the application so your users can quickly navigate to the information they require.

You may need to use the same file set for a number of Javadoc operations, so let's create a referenced file set to help with reusability. Listing 6-2 shows this file set.

Listing 6-2. *The Javadoc File Set*

```
<!-- ##################################### -->
<!-- Javadoc file sets                     -->
<!-- ##################################### -->

<fileset id="javadoc" dir="${src}">
  <exclude name="*/conf/**"/>
  <exclude name="*/docs/*"/>
  <include name="shared/**"/>
  <include name="stand-alone/**"/>
  <include name="web/java/**"/>
</fileset>
```

Listing 6-3 shows the `<javadoc>` task that builds the example application's Javadocs. You will do this only if your documentation is older than your source code. Unfortunately, the `<javadoc>` task does not check whether a file has changed since the last build, so you have to do it in this case. You'll use your documentation packages (covered in the "Creating Zip and Tar Files" section) as the reference point for the documentation. If your source code or handwritten documentation is newer than both packages, then you need new Javadocs. If it's not, then you can use the existing Javadocs. All the documentation targets will execute only if the `docs.notRequired` property is empty.

Listing 6-3. *Creating Javadocs for the Example Application*

```
<!-- ########################################## -->
<!-- Building the documentation bundle          -->
<!-- ########################################## -->

<!-- Checking that the documentation is up to date -->
<target name="check-docs"
        description="Check that the documentation is up to date">
  <echo message="Checking that the documentation is up to date"/>
  <condition property="docs.notRequired">
    <and>
      <uptodate targetfile="${dist}/${appName}-${package.docs}.zip">
        <srcfiles dir="${src}" includes="**"/>
      </uptodate>
      <uptodate targetfile="${dist}/${appName}-${package.docs}.tar.gz">
        <srcfiles dir="${src}" includes="**"/>
      </uptodate>
    </and>
  </condition>
</target>
```

```
<!-- Generate Javadocs for the application -->
<target name="javadocs" depends="dir,check-docs"
        description="Generate Javadocs for the application"
        unless="docs.notRequired">
  <echo message="Generating Javadocs for the application"/>
  <javadoc destdir="${docs}/api" windowtitle="${javadoc.windowtitle}">
    <fileset refid="javadoc"/>
    <doctitle>
      ${javadoc.doctitle}
    </doctitle>
    <classpath refid="build.classpath"/>
    <link href="http://java.sun.com/j2se/${javadoc.j2se.version}/docs/api"/>
    <link href="http://java.sun.com/j2ee/${javadoc.j2ee.version}/docs/api"/>
  </javadoc>
</target>
```

Here you create a file set including all the Java sources and excluding the configuration files in any `conf` directories and the documentation in the `docs` directory (which are part of the `javadoc` file set you defined in Listing 6-2). The `destdir` attribute is required, points to the directory that will contain the Javadocs, and corresponds to the `-d` command-line option. The `windowtitle` attribute corresponds to the `-windowtitle` command-line option, which sets the `<title>` tag in each HTML Javadocs page.

The `<doctitle>` nested element corresponds to the `-doctitle` command-line option, which sets the `<h1>` title of the Javadoc overview page. You can also specify this as a `doctitle` attribute.

The `<classpath>` nested element allows the Javadoc process to find classes outside the file set so that it can maintain object-oriented relationships. For example, servlets in the example application extend `javax.servlet.http.HttpServlet`, which should be represented in the Javadocs.

The final two nested elements are `<link>` elements that tell Ant to incorporate links to the Javadoc information on Sun's Java web site. This means readers of the documentation can click links to see details of those objects that are not part of the application. In this case, you have classes from the core Java distribution (J2SE) and the Servlet specification (part of J2EE). The only way to link to two sets of Javadocs in this way is to use the `<link>` nested element. If you had only one set of Javadocs to link to, you could use the `<javadoc>` task's `link` attribute instead.

If you aren't sure you have access to online documentation when building the Javadocs, then you have the option to use offline documentation instead. This scenario may occur if raw source code is given out to users, who will be required to build the entire distribution from scratch. You have two options here:

- Building the Javadocs with external links using offline `package-list` files to provide package structure
- Linking to offline documentation

The first method has the advantage that, should a user gain access to online documentation, their Javadocs will instantly be up to date. The disadvantage is that they will have links in their Javadocs to files they can't access. You should ensure that the local `package-list` files are up to date as well, because using old package definitions may lead to errors when connecting to the online version. Deprecated code documentation should be maintained, but you should not count on it being available forever.

The second method has the advantage that the user will instantly have access to descriptions of all the objects used in the project. The disadvantage is that these descriptions may not be as fresh as those in the online documentation.

All this is really a Javadoc discussion rather than an Ant discussion, but it is pertinent in the context of a build process. You can change your Javadoc target to work in both ways. Listing 6-4 shows the properties that you'll require for the following examples.

Listing 6-4. *Properties for Working with Offline Documentation*

```
javadoc.j2se.offline=C:/j2sdk1.5.0/docs/api
javadoc.j2ee.offline=C:/j2eesdk1.4/docs/apidocs
```

These two properties correspond to the root of the J2SE and J2EE Javadocs, respectively. Listing 6-5 shows how to implement the first method that you saw previously.

Listing 6-5. *Working with Offline* `package-list` *Files and Online Javadocs*

```
  <!-- Generate Javadocs for the application,
       using offline package-list files -->
  <target name="javadocs-offline" depends="dir,check-docs"
          description="Generate Javadocs for the application,
                       using offline package-list files"
          unless="docs.notRequired">
    <echo message="Generating Javadocs for the application,
                   using offline package-list files"/>
    <javadoc destdir="${docs}/api" windowtitle="${javadoc.windowtitle}">
      <fileset refid="javadoc"/>
      <doctitle>
        ${javadoc.doctitle}
      </doctitle>
      <classpath refid="build.classpath"/>
      <link href="http://java.sun.com/j2se/${javadoc.j2se.version}/docs/api"
            offline="true" packagelistLoc="${javadoc.j2se.offline}"/>
      <link href="http://java.sun.com/j2ee/${javadoc.j2ee.version}/docs/api"
            offline="true" packagelistLoc="${javadoc.j2ee.offline}"/>
    </javadoc>
  </target>
```

The bold lines introduce `<link>` elements that work with offline files. The `offline` attribute specifies whether offline files can be used if Ant cannot contact the resource in `href`. If you set `offline` to `true`, you can specify the location of the `package-list` files in the `packagelistLoc` attribute. The resulting `<a>` element's `href` attribute of the object or method is filled with the URL in the `<link>` element's `href` attribute, using the package structure found at `packagelistLoc`. This means Ant can create the entire Javadoc bundle without having to reference any online material.

To use only local files in the resulting `<a>` element's `href` attribute, you can use the two properties that represent the local files instead of the URL to the online documentation. This is the most pessimistic approach, where you say that the user of the Javadocs will never be able to read the online documentation. Listing 6-6 shows the relevant <link> elements.

Listing 6-6. *Working with Offline Documentation*

```
<!-- Generate Javadocs for the application,
      using offline package-list files -->
<target name="javadocs-offline" depends="dir,check-docs"
        description="Generate Javadocs for the application,
                     using offline package-list files"
        unless="docs.notRequired">
  <echo message="Generating Javadocs for the application,
                 using offline package-list files"/>
  <javadoc destdir="${docs}/api" windowtitle="${javadoc.windowtitle}">
    <fileset refid="javadoc"/>
    <doctitle>
      ${javadoc.doctitle}
    </doctitle>
    <classpath refid="build.classpath"/>
    <link href="${javadoc.j2se.offline}" resolveLink="true"/>
    <link href="${javadoc.j2ee.offline}" resolveLink="true"/>
  </javadoc>
</target>
```

You need to set the resolveLink attribute to true so that Ant does not treat the value of href as a relative path. You want it to realize that it is an absolute path and pass this to the javadoc command.

Finishing the Bundle

Once you have created the Javadocs for the distribution, you need to add your other documentation to it, if you have any. At the bare minimum, a project will at least have a README with installation and usage instructions. It may also have a license and HTML documentation that explains the project in more detail.

Adding the other documentation is a simple matter of copying the files from their location in the source tree into the working directory. This final directory should be the docs directory that contains the api directory. Listing 6-7 shows the <copy> tasks for this example's documentation.

Listing 6-7. *Assembling the Documentation*

```
<!-- Assemble the documentation -->
<target name="docs" depends="javadocs"
        description="Assemble the documentation" unless="docs.notRequired">
  <echo message="Assembling the documentation"/>
  <copy todir="${docs}">
    <fileset dir="${src.shared.docs}">
      <include name="*.html"/>
    </fileset>
```

```
    </copy>
    <copy todir="${docs}/stand-alone">
      <fileset dir="${src.stand-alone.docs}">
        <include name="*.html"/>
      </fileset>
    </copy>
    <copy todir="${docs}/web">
      <fileset dir="${src.web.docs}">
        <include name="*.html"/>
      </fileset>
    </copy>
  </target>
```

Now that you have all the documentation together, you can create distribution bundles. However, I'll finish the discussion of documentation by showing how to document the Ant build process for a project.

Writing Ant Documentation

As mentioned previously, documenting the build file and process is an invaluable part of the process. You can document the process in four ways:

- XML comments in the build file
- The `description` attribute of the `<target>` element
- The `<echo>` task
- A `README` or HTML description

The only time someone will see the XML comments in the build file is when they browse through the build file to make changes or examine the build process. If appropriate, you should make these comments fit this kind of audience. This may not always apply, but sometimes a person who is working with and changing a build file needs to know more than someone who just runs the build process. Thinking of XML comments as notes to your future self is a good way of looking at things. You can also use XML comments to divide the build file into logical segments, as you have done in the example application. Large, conspicuous XML comments delineate the shared code's targets from the stand-alone code's targets and also from the web code's targets.

Ant will show the message left in the `description` attribute of the `<target>` element when a user invokes the `-projecthelp` command-line option. Those targets with no description do not appear as a result of this command. You can use this to your advantage if there are targets within a build file that are part of a complex build path and should not be invoked on their own. Think of these targets in the same light as `private` methods in your class files, in that you have designed them so that only internal methods may call them. A user can of course open the build file to see all the targets inside, but complex build files don't lend themselves to casual browsing by curious users. Give out only the information that they require in the form of `description` attributes and `README` files.

The `<echo>` task is a great way of informing users (and yourself) of which step in the build process Ant has reached and what it is trying to achieve. Use this as a form of reassurance that things are going as planned. If you run many unsupervised builds, you may not need to bother with this or with the description method of documentation. As always, it comes down to your requirements.

Providing a verbose set of `README` files or HTML pages with instructions on the build (perhaps including the results of a `-projecthelp` run) will give everybody a head start when using the build file. This can be a detailed breakdown of all the targets and what is required to be in place before a user can run the build. This should include detailed descriptions of all the properties in any `*.properties` files that come with the build and any properties that can be supplied at the command line. (Usernames and passwords are particularly important in this regard.)

■ **Note** Chapter 10 includes a custom task that will display usage information for the current build and is designed so that it is the default target of a build. This means a user gets information on the build process by simply running `ant`, instead of potentially starting a lengthy build they may not want.

Creating Zip and Tar Files

Your choice of compressed file will largely depend on the target operating system. Windows users will prefer zip files, though most Windows systems can handle `tar.gz` files as well. If your preferred compression method is bzip2, you are certainly cutting down on the Windows users who will be able to open the file.

■ **Note** You can get bzip2 from `www.bzip.org/downloads.html`. It's available in source form or as binaries for some systems (Windows included). You won't need the binaries to use the Ant tasks, though you may need them to examine the results.

The example project will be available as `*.zip` files and `*.tar.gz` files, so you will have to keep things as centralized and uniform as possible. To that end, Listing 6-8 shows some properties for the properties file that you will use to name distribution bundles.

Listing 6-8. *Properties for Naming Distribution Bundles*

```
package.stand-alone=stand-alone
package.web=web
package.docs=docs
```

You will see more properties in Listing 6-9, but you'll set them in `build.xml` because they are not designed to be changed by the user, whereas you should expect that users may want to change filenames in the project.

One of the important things to consider when using zip files and tar files for the same things is that Ant's `<zip>` task can have nested `<fileset>` elements, but its `<tar>` task cannot and instead uses nested `<tarfileset>` elements. While these are extended file sets, they cannot take refid attributes to link them to predefined file sets. This means you cannot centralize lists of files as file sets and must use pattern sets instead. In turn, this means you have to centralize the dir attribute that the nested <fileset> and <tarfileset> elements will take.

Another difference between <zip> and <tar> is that <zip> takes nested <zipfileset> elements that are much more powerful and useful than <tarfileset> elements and allow you to do more when bundling the application. For example, <zipfileset> elements can incorporate the contents of existing zip files into the zip file that <zip> is building. This means you can reuse targets much as you do in other parts of the build process. In other words, you can build a zip file of the documentation in one target and then run that target every time you want to create that zip file, even if it is to add its contents to a larger zip file.

<tar>, on the other hand, cannot do this, so you must repeat lines and lines of <tar> tasks to replicate functionality that may already be present in another target. You'll see more of this as the example develops.

<zipfileset> elements do not suffer from the same weaknesses as <tarfileset> elements in that they can reference predefined <fileset> elements. Therefore, you can quickly and easily use any of the <zipfileset> element's functionality (described in a moment) to zip any set of files in the build process.

All this does not mean you cannot use the <tar> task, because it is useful in its place. If you are distributing to users with a Unix or Linux system, *.tar.gz files are the standard, and tar in combination with gzip creates smaller files than the zip algorithm.

Listing 6-9 shows the centralized properties and pattern sets for the parallel packaging processes. The presence of the <tar> task means you have to use pattern sets and properties.

Listing 6-9. *Centralized Properties and Pattern Sets for Bundling the Application*

```
<!-- ####################################################### -->
<!-- Properties and pattern sets for the packaging targets -->
<!-- ####################################################### -->

<!-- The value of each property in this section is the setting -->
<!-- for the 'dir' attribute of file sets and tar file sets -->

<!-- Property and pattern set for the documentation -->
<property name="docs.all.dir" value="${build}"/>
<!-- Tar file sets cannot use file sets, so we must use a pattern set -->
<patternset id="docs.all">
  <include name="docs/**"/>
</patternset>

<!-- Property and pattern set for the license and README -->
<property name="docs.misc.dir" value="${src}/shared/docs"/>
<!-- Tar file sets cannot use file sets, so we must use a pattern set -->
<patternset id="docs.misc">
  <include name="README"/>
  <include name="LICENSE"/>
</patternset>
```

```
<!-- Property and pattern set for the source, -->
<!-- build.xml, and build.properties -->
<property name="src.files.dir" value="."/>
<!-- Tar file sets cannot use file sets, so we must use a pattern set -->
<patternset id="src.files">
  <include name="${src}/**"/>
  <include name="build.*"/>
</patternset>

<!-- Pattern set for the binary JAR -->
<!-- Nothing else is needed because the directory that contains it -->
<!-- is already in the ${dist} property and it's used in a zip file set -->
<!-- as well as a tar file set -->
<patternset id="bin.jar">
  <include name="*.jar"/>
</patternset>

<!-- Pattern set for the binary WAR -->
<!-- Nothing else is needed because the directory that contains it -->
<!-- is already in the ${dist} property and it's used in a zip file set -->
<!-- as well as a tar file set -->
<patternset id="bin.war">
  <include name="*.war"/>
</patternset>
```

You'll use all these properties and pattern sets later, but it should be fairly clear what they do.

The `<zip>` and `<tar>` tasks are compression tasks at heart and so are fairly similar to the `<jar>` and `<war>` tasks you saw in Chapter 5. The main difference is the `<zipfileset>` and `<tarfileset>` nested elements, which add more functionality than simple compression.

You'll bundle the application using `<zip>` and `<tar>`, though when users extract the files contained within, they should see no difference in structure between the two. This means you have to have properties common to both stages of the build process (as discussed previously).

Zipping the Application

The `<zip>` task is the most powerful compression task in Ant's armory. Its main strength is its ability to include the contents of other zip files in the zip file it is currently building. As mentioned, you can then place modular sections of zip instructions in targets that you can execute at different stages of the build. In addition, you can add the whole range of file sets and pattern sets to a `<zip>` task, which means you have a flexible mechanism.

Table 6-1 shows the `<zip>` task's attributes. Deprecated attributes are not included.

Table 6-1. *The <zip> Task's Attributes*

Attribute	Description
`basedir`	The directory from which to zip the target files. The default is the base directory of the project.
`comment`	The comment to store as part of the zip file. The default is blank.
`compress`	Tells Ant to compress the files as it adds them to the zip file. If `keepcompression` is set to `true`, this applies to the entire archive, not just to the files you are adding. The default is `true`.
`defaultexcludes`	Tells Ant to use the default excludes (see Chapter 4). The default is `true`.
`destfile`	The name of the zip file you want to create. This attribute is required.
`duplicate`	Tells Ant what to do if duplicate files are found. You can specify `add`, `preserve`, or `fail`. The default is `add`.
`encoding`	The encoding to use for filenames in the archive. The default is the platform's default encoding.
`excludes`	The excludes list for this task, where each entry is separated from the next one with a space or a comma. You may use wildcards. The default is to omit nothing except the default excludes.
`excludesfile`	The name of the file that contains the exclude patterns. The default is to not use a file.
`filesonly`	Tells Ant to store only file entries. The default is `false`.
`includes`	The includes list for this task, where each entry is separated from the next one with a space or a comma. You may use wildcards. The default is all files.
`includesfile`	The name of the file that contains the include patterns. The default is to not use a file.
`keepcompression`	Tells Ant to keep the original compression of the files you are adding. The default is `false`.
`roundup`	Tells Ant to round up file modification times to the next even number of seconds. If you don't do this, the times will be rounded down in the zip file. This means the zip file will seem out of date when you run the target again. The default is `true`.
`update`	Tells Ant to overwrite files in the zip file. The default is `false`, which means Ant will add only newer files. If you have set `roundup` to `true` (the default), *newer* here means newer than two seconds.
`whenempty`	Tells Ant what to do if no files match. You can specify `fail`, `create`, or `skip`. The default is `skip`.

Most of this should be familiar from the JAR and WAR tasks. The difference comes when you add a `<zipfileset>` nested element. This useful nested element takes all the attributes of a file set, including a `refid` to another `<fileset>` or `<zipfileset>`. Table 6-2 shows its unique attributes.

Table 6-2. *The `<zipfileset>` Element's Attributes*

Attribute	Description
`dirmode`	A three-digit octal string that sets user, group, and other modes of the included directories once they are inside the archive. The default is 755. See `www.computerhope.com/unix/uchmod.htm` for information on numeric permissions.
`filemode`	A three-digit octal string that sets user, group, and other modes of the included files once they are inside the archive. The default is 644.
`fullpath`	The path and filename that the included file will have when Ant adds it to the archive. This is analogous to the `tofile` attribute of the `<copy>` task and can be used only if this zip file set contains a single file. The default is blank.
`prefix`	The prefix to add to all files in this zip file set when Ant adds them to the archive. For example, `prefix=lib` gives `antBook.jar` the path `lib/antBook.jar` when it is added to the archive. The default is blank.
`src`	The name of a zip file that contains files to include in the zip file being created. The contents of the file are included, not the file itself. To include the file, use the usual file set attributes. You can include and exclude patterns from the source archive with the usual file set attributes and nested elements. The default is blank.

You can also nest `<zipgroupfileset>` elements in the `<zip>` element. This allows you to include files from large numbers of zip files at once because this element represents a file set of zip files. This is in contrast to the `<zipfileset>` element, which can include the contents of a single zip file or a file set of uncompressed files. You will use a `<zipgroupfileset>` element as part of the following bundling process.

Here are the files you will create:

- `antBook-docs.zip`
- `antBook-docs.tar.gz`
- `antBook-src.zip`
- `antBook-src.tar.gz`
- `antBook-stand-alone-bin.zip`
- `antBook-stand-alone-bin.tar.gz`
- `antBook-web-bin.zip`
- `antBook-web-bin.tar.gz`

- antBook-bin.zip
- antBook-bin.tar.gz

Their names are pretty straightforward. The final two files contain the entire binary distribution.

Bundling the Source and Documentation

In this example, you will take advantage of the cumulative nature of the <zip> task by bundling each part of the application separately in different targets and including the contents of the resultant zip file as appropriate. For example, you will zip the documentation in one target and the source distribution in another, where you will combine the results of the first target into the final zip file. Listing 6-10 shows the two targets.

Listing 6-10. *Targets That Zip the Documentation and the Source Code*

```
<!-- ########################################## -->
<!-- Zip the distribution                       -->
<!-- ########################################## -->

<!-- Zip the documentation -->
<target name="zip-docs" depends="docs" description="Zip the documentation">
  <echo message="Zipping the documentation"/>
  <zip destfile="${dist}/${appName}-${package.docs}.zip">
    <!-- Include the documentation -->
    <fileset dir="${docs.all.dir}">
      <patternset refid="docs.all"/>
    </fileset>
    <!-- Include the license and the README -->
    <fileset dir="${docs.misc.dir}">
      <patternset refid="docs.misc"/>
    </fileset>
  </zip>
</target>

<!-- Zip the source and documentation together -->
<target name="zip-src" depends="zip-docs"
        description="Zip the source and documentation together">
  <echo message="Zipping the source and documentation together"/>
  <zip destfile="${dist}/${appName}-src.zip">
    <!-- Include the source code and the build files -->
    <zipfileset src="${dist}/${appName}-${package.docs}.zip"/>
    <fileset dir="${src.files.dir}">
      <patternset refid="src.files"/>
    </fileset>
  </zip>
</target>
```

The zip-docs target didn't have a call for <zipfileset> elements, so this code just used normal file sets. If you call zip-src, Ant will first run zip-docs, zip the documentation, and then place it in a zip file called dist/antBook-docs.zip. The tar example in the "Tarring the Application" section will also use the pattern sets in this target.

The <zipfileset> element in zip-src adds the files from dist/antBook-docs.zip to the <zip> task, and the file set adds the source code and build files. You now have two zip files in dist, which is a product of the cumulative approach you are taking. This is no bad thing, as projects often require documentation bundles.

Creating Digests for Distributions

When you downloaded and installed Ant in Chapter 2, you saw how to use message digests to confirm the integrity of a download. If you are offering your application for public consumption, or even to selected people, on a web site or FTP server, you might consider creating your own message digests to accompany your files.

Ant's <checksum> task allows you to create a message digest for your files using any algorithm your Java Cryptography Extension (JCE) provides. In fact, you can specify any JCE using the provider attribute. For the purposes of this chapter, you'll look only at the default JCE and the MD5 and SHA algorithms, mainly because that's how Ant's distributions are presented (I'll call SHA *SHA1* from now on for consistency with Ant's distributions.) Creating a PGP signature requires you to run the pgp executable, so I'll cover that in the next chapter when I discuss how to run native programs.

The <checksum> task has a number of complicated attributes, many of which are concerned with verifying data integrity. I won't cover these here; rather, you'll see examples of the attributes that produce digests. Listing 6-11 shows modified versions of the zip-docs and zip-src targets that create digests of the files.

Listing 6-11. *Creating Digests of the Zip Files*

```
<!-- Zip the documentation -->
<target name="zip-docs" depends="docs" description="Zip the documentation">
  <echo message="Zipping the documentation"/>
  <zip destfile="${dist}/${appName}-${package.docs}.zip">
    <!-- Include the documentation -->
    <fileset dir="${docs.all.dir}">
      <patternset refid="docs.all"/>
    </fileset>
    <!-- Include the license and the README -->
    <fileset dir="${docs.misc.dir}">
      <patternset refid="docs.misc"/>
    </fileset>
  </zip>
  <checksum file="${dist}/${appName}-${package.docs}.zip"
            forceOverwrite="true"/>
  <checksum file="${dist}/${appName}-${package.docs}.zip" forceOverwrite="true"
            algorithm="SHA1"/>
</target>
```

```
<!-- Zip the source and documentation together -->
<target name="zip-src" depends="zip-docs"
        description="Zip the source and documentation together">
  <echo message="Zipping the source and documentation together"/>
  <zip destfile="${dist}/${appName}-src.zip">
    <!-- Include the source code and the build files -->
    <zipfileset src="${dist}/${appName}-${package.docs}.zip"/>
    <fileset dir="${src.files.dir}">
      <patternset refid="src.files"/>
    </fileset>
  </zip>
  <checksum file="${dist}/${appName}-src.zip" forceOverwrite="true"/>
  <checksum file="${dist}/${appName}-src.zip" forceOverwrite="true"
          algorithm="SHA1"/>
</target>
```

The `file` attribute is the file you want to make a digest of, which will also provide the basis for the resulting digest file. The general rule is `filename.extension.algorithm`. This means the `antBook-docs.zip` file MD5 digest will be called `antBook-docs.zip.MD5`, and its SHA1 digest will be called `antBook-docs.zip.SHA1`. You can change the final extension from the algorithm name by setting the `fileext` attribute to something else. The `forceOverwrite` attribute makes sure the digest file is up to date.

The default algorithm is MD5, though you can set others with the `algorithm` attribute. In this code, you've set it to `SHA1` (a synonym for `SHA`, which you can also use). Now when you upload the zip files, you can include your digests along with them.

Bundling Binaries and Documentation

When you bundle binaries for distribution, you want them to include documentation. You can easily accomplish this, because the `zip-docs` target already creates a documentation bundle that you can include in a `<zip>` task. The first target shown in Listing 6-12 also includes the binary files that the `package-stand-alone` target creates, as well as the MySQL database connector. The second target includes the results of the `package-web` target, though you don't need to include JARs because they are inside the WAR file.

Listing 6-12. *Targets That Zip the Documentation and Binary Distributions*

```
<!-- Zip the binary stand-alone distribution with the documentation -->
<target name="zip-bin-stand-alone" depends="package-stand-alone,zip-docs"
        description="Zip the binary stand-alone distribution
                     with the documentation">
  <echo message="Zipping the binary stand-alone distribution
                 with the documentation"/>
  <zip destfile="${dist}/${appName}-${package.stand-alone}-bin.zip">
    <!-- Include the documentation -->
    <zipfileset src="${dist}/${appName}-${package.docs}.zip"/>
```

```
      <!-- Include the binary JAR files -->
      <zipfileset dir="${dist}" prefix="lib">
        <patternset refid="bin.jar"/>
      </zipfileset>
      <fileset dir=".">
        <include name="${mysql.jar}"/>
      </fileset>
    </zip>
    <checksum file="${dist}/${appName}-${package.stand-alone}-bin.zip"
              forceOverwrite="true"/>
    <checksum file="${dist}/${appName}-${package.stand-alone}-bin.zip"
              forceOverwrite="true" algorithm="SHA1"/>
  </target>

  <!-- Zip the binary web distribution with the documentation -->
  <target name="zip-bin-web" depends="package-web,zip-docs"
          description="Zip the binary web distribution with the documentation">
    <echo message="Zipping the binary web distribution with the documentation"/>
    <zip destfile="${dist}/${appName}-${package.web}-bin.zip">
      <!-- Include the documentation -->
      <zipfileset src="${dist}/${appName}-${package.docs}.zip"/>
      <!-- Include the binary WAR files -->
      <fileset dir="${dist}">
        <patternset refid="bin.war"/>
      </fileset>
    </zip>
    <checksum file="${dist}/${appName}-${package.web}-bin.zip"
              forceOverwrite="true"/>
    <checksum file="${dist}/${appName}-${package.web}-bin.zip"
              forceOverwrite="true" algorithm="SHA1"/>
  </target>
```

The zip-bin-web target doesn't hold anything new. However, the zip-bin-stand-alone target contains a <zipfileset> element that uses the prefix attribute. This allows you to place the stand-alone application's JAR file in the lib directory once a user decompresses the archive.

You can now build an entire binary distribution from the results of these two targets. They both produce zip files, which means you can use a <zipgroupfileset> element to merge their contents into one zip file. Listing 6-13 shows the relevant target.

Listing 6-13. *Bundling the Entire Binary Distribution*

```
  <!-- Zip the binary distribution with the documentation -->
  <target name="zip-bin" depends="zip-bin-stand-alone,zip-bin-web"
          description="Zip the binary distribution with the documentation">
    <echo message="Zipping the binary distribution with the documentation"/>
    <zip destfile="${dist}/${appName}-bin.zip"
         duplicate="preserve" update="true">
      <zipgroupfileset dir="${dist}" includes="*.zip"/>
```

```
  </zip>
  <checksum file="${dist}/${appName}-bin.zip" forceOverwrite="true"/>
  <checksum file="${dist}/${appName}-bin.zip" forceOverwrite="true"
            algorithm="SHA1"/>
</target>
```

So, here you include all the files contained in the zip files that the other targets created. To make sure the files exist, you set the depends attribute of the <target> element to run the previous targets. In this case you will have duplicates, but you can be fairly sure that the previous targets created the newest files possible, so you keep only one copy in the zip file by setting duplicate to preserve and setting update to true.

Bundling the Entire Distribution

The final step is to bundle the entire distribution. This is extremely easy because of the cumulative nature of the <zip> tasks you have used. Listing 6-14 shows how.

Listing 6-14. *Bundling the Entire Distribution*

```
<!-- Zip the binary and source distributions -->
<target name="zip-all" depends="zip-src,zip-bin"
        description="Zip the binary and source distributions">
  <echo message="Zipped the binary and source distributions"/>
</target>
```

Tarring the Application

Using the <tar> task is not quite as easy or efficient as using the <zip> task, but you will have to use it if you are distributing to Linux or Unix users. It has a lot of features that help you when you are building distributions for those platforms that do not apply to Windows distributions, and its compression algorithms are better than the <zip> task's. Table 6-3 shows its attributes.

Table 6-3. *The <tar> Task's Attributes*

Attribute	Description
basedir	The directory from which to tar the target files. The default is the base directory of the project.
compression	The method of compression to use, if any. This can be none, gzip, or bzip2. The default is none.
defaultexcludes	Tells Ant to use the default excludes (see Chapter 4). The default is true.
destfile	The name of the tar file you want to create. This attribute is required.
excludes	The excludes list for this task, where each entry is separated from the next one with a space or a comma. You may use wildcards. The default is to omit nothing except the default excludes.
excludesfile	The name of the file that contains the exclude patterns. The default is not to use a file.

Table 6-3. *The <tar> Task's Attributes (Continued)*

Attribute	Description
includes	The includes list for this task, where each entry is separated from the next one with a space or a comma. You may use wildcards. The default is all files.
includesfile	The name of the file that contains the include patterns. The default is not to use a file.
longfile	Tells Ant how to handle files that have names longer than 100 characters. You can use this to provide backward compatibility to early versions of tar. Options for backward compatibility are truncate, which cuts the filename down to 100 characters; fail, which stops the tar process if a filename is too long; and omit, which leaves out files that have long filenames. Setting any of these options means you will get predictable results when a user untars the archive. Other options are gnu, which makes a GNU tar-compatible tar file that may be untarred properly only by GNU tar, and warn, which does the same as gnu but warns you when it encounters a long filename. The default is warn.

It is the compression and longfile attributes that make this such a useful task for creating distributions that will go to Unix systems. Another nice feature from this point of view is the nested <tarfileset> element, though it does suffer from the drawbacks discussed previously. Table 6-4 shows its elements.

Table 6-4. *The <tarfileset> Nested Element's Attributes*

Attribute	Description
dirmode	A three-digit octal string that sets user, group, and other modes of the included directories once they are inside the archive. The default is 755.
fullpath	The path and filename that the included file will have when Ant adds it to the archive. This is analogous to the tofile attribute of the <copy> task and can be used only if this tar file set contains a single file. The default is blank.
gid	The GID for the tar entry. This is an integer. The default is null.
group	The group name for the tar entry. Note that this is not the same as the GID. The default is blank.
mode	A three-digit octal string that sets user, group, and other modes of the included files once they are inside the archive. The default is 644.
prefix	The prefix to add to all files in this tar file set when Ant adds them to the archive. For example, prefix=lib gives antBook.jar the path lib/antBook.jar when it is added to the archive. The default is blank.
preserveLeadingSlashes	Tells Ant to preserve leading slashes in filenames. The default is false.
uid	The UID for the tar entry. This is an integer. The default is null.
username	The username for the tar entry. Note that this is not the same as the UID. The default is blank.

This replicates a lot of the functionality of the <zipfileset> element but does not allow you to include files from other tar files. The compensation is the user and group functionality that you can implement.

Bundling the Source and Documentation

Without the cumulative nature of the <zip> task, you will build monolithic targets that create tar files from scratch every time and without any reusable targets. Listing 6-15 shows how the tar-src target builds an extra <tar> task onto the <tar> tasks in the tar-docs target. However, note how they use the same pattern sets and properties as the previous <zip> tasks.

Listing 6-15. *Targets That Tar the Documentation and the Source Code*

```
<!-- ######################################### -->
<!-- Tar and gz the distribution               -->
<!-- ######################################### -->

<!-- Tar the documentation -->
<target name="tar-docs" depends="docs" description="Tar the documentation">
  <echo message="Tarring the documentation"/>
  <tar destfile="${dist}/${appName}-${package.docs}.tar.gz" compression="gzip">
    <!-- Include the documentation -->
    <tarfileset dir="${docs.all.dir}">
      <patternset refid="docs.all"/>
    </tarfileset>
    <!-- Include the license and the README -->
    <tarfileset dir="${docs.misc.dir}">
      <patternset refid="docs.misc"/>
    </tarfileset>
  </tar>
  <checksum file="${dist}/${appName}-${package.docs}.tar.gz"
            forceOverwrite="true"/>
  <checksum file="${dist}/${appName}-${package.docs}.tar.gz"
            forceOverwrite="true" algorithm="SHA1"/>
</target>

<!-- Tar the source and documentation together -->
<target name="tar-src" depends="tar-docs"
        description="Tar the documentation">
  <echo message="Tarring the documentation"/>
  <tar destfile="${dist}/${appName}-src.tar.gz" compression="gzip">
    <!-- Include the documentation -->
    <tarfileset dir="${docs.all.dir}">
      <patternset refid="docs.all"/>
```

```
      </tarfileset>
      <!-- Include the license and the README -->
      <tarfileset dir="${docs.misc.dir}">
        <patternset refid="docs.misc"/>
      </tarfileset>
      <!-- Include the source code and the build files -->
      <tarfileset dir="${src.files.dir}">
        <patternset refid="src.files"/>
      </tarfileset>
    </tar>
    <checksum file="${dist}/${appName}-src.tar.gz" forceOverwrite="true"/>
    <checksum file="${dist}/${appName}-src.tar.gz" forceOverwrite="true"
              algorithm="SHA1"/>
  </target>
```

To replicate the cumulative nature of the zip process, in this code you set the depends attribute of tar-src to point to tar-docs. To combine the compression with the bundle, you set the compression attribute of the <tar> task to gzip.

Bundling Binaries and Documentation

To bundle the binaries with the documentation, you need to add more steps to the list of <tar> tasks from tar-docs. In addition, you need to run the tar-docs target to achieve the cumulative effect of a documentation distribution, as well as a binary distribution that contains documentation. Listing 6-16 shows the new targets. The highlighted lines are new and build on tar-docs.

Listing 6-16. *Targets That Tar the Documentation and Binary Distributions*

```
<!-- Tar the binary stand-alone distribution with the documentation -->
<target name="tar-bin-stand-alone" depends="package-stand-alone,tar-docs"
        description="Tar the binary stand-alone distribution
                     with the documentation">
  <echo message="Tarring the binary stand-alone distribution
                 with the documentation"/>
  <tar destfile="${dist}/${appName}-${package.stand-alone}-bin.tar.gz"
       compression="gzip">
    <!-- Include the documentation -->
    <tarfileset dir="${docs.all.dir}">
      <patternset refid="docs.all"/>
    </tarfileset>
    <!-- Include the license and the README -->
    <tarfileset dir="${docs.misc.dir}">
      <patternset refid="docs.misc"/>
```

```
    </tarfileset>
    <!-- Include the binary JAR files -->
    <tarfileset dir="${dist}" prefix="lib">
      <patternset refid="bin.jar"/>
    </tarfileset>
    <tarfileset dir=".">
      <include name="${mysql.jar}"/>
    </tarfileset>
  </tar>
  <checksum file="${dist}/${appName}-${package.stand-alone}-bin.tar.gz"
            forceOverwrite="true"/>
  <checksum file="${dist}/${appName}-${package.stand-alone}-bin.tar.gz"
            forceOverwrite="true" algorithm="SHA1"/>
</target>

<!-- Tar the binary web distribution with the documentation -->
<target name="tar-bin-web" depends="package-web,tar-docs"
        description="Tar the binary web distribution with the documentation">
  <echo message="Tarring the binary web distribution
                 with the documentation"/>
  <tar destfile="${dist}/${appName}-${package.web}-bin.tar.gz"
       compression="gzip">
    <!-- Include the documentation -->
    <tarfileset dir="${docs.all.dir}">
      <patternset refid="docs.all"/>
    </tarfileset>
    <!-- Include the license and the README -->
    <tarfileset dir="${docs.misc.dir}">
      <patternset refid="docs.misc"/>
    </tarfileset>
    <!-- Include the binary WAR files -->
    <tarfileset dir="${dist}">
      <patternset refid="bin.war"/>
    </tarfileset>
  </tar>
  <checksum file="${dist}/${appName}-${package.web}-bin.tar.gz"
            forceOverwrite="true"/>
  <checksum file="${dist}/${appName}-${package.web}-bin.tar.gz"
            forceOverwrite="true" algorithm="SHA1"/>
</target>
```

You have replicated the prefix trick from the `<zip>` task example here by setting the `prefix` attribute of the first `<tarfileset>` element in `tar-bin-stand-alone` to `lib`. You now have to package the entire binary distribution, as shown in Listing 6-17. This target is a combination of almost all the `<tarfileset>` elements you have written so far, which is a good illustration of the weakness of the `<tar>` task.

Listing 6-17. *Bundling the Entire Binary Distribution*

```
<!-- Tar the binary distribution with the documentation -->
<target name="tar-bin" depends="tar-bin-stand-alone,tar-bin-web"
        description="Tar the binary distribution with the documentation">
  <echo message="Tarring the binary distribution with the documentation"/>
  <tar destfile="${dist}/${appName}-bin.tar.gz" compression="gzip">
    <!-- Include the documentation -->
    <tarfileset dir="${docs.all.dir}">
      <patternset refid="docs.all"/>
    </tarfileset>
    <!-- Include the license and the README -->
    <tarfileset dir="${docs.misc.dir}">
      <patternset refid="docs.misc"/>
    </tarfileset>
    <!-- Include the source code and the build files -->
    <tarfileset dir="${src.files.dir}">
      <patternset refid="src.files"/>
    </tarfileset>
    <!-- Include the binary JAR files -->
    <tarfileset dir="${dist}" prefix="lib">
      <patternset refid="bin.jar"/>
    </tarfileset>
    <tarfileset dir=".">
      <include name="${mysql.jar}"/>
    </tarfileset>
    <!-- Include the binary WAR files -->
    <tarfileset dir="${dist}">
      <patternset refid="bin.war"/>
    </tarfileset>
  </tar>
  <checksum file="${dist}/${appName}-bin.tar.gz" forceOverwrite="true"/>
  <checksum file="${dist}/${appName}-bin.tar.gz" forceOverwrite="true"
            algorithm="SHA1"/>
</target>
```

An alternative solution to this problem takes advantage of the fact that each tar file is a repackaged version of the corresponding zip file. In this case, you will expand the zip file to a temporary location, such as /tmp, and then tar the expanded version. This is analogous to the way <zipfileset> elements allow you to add the contents of zip files to other zip files.

First, you need to specify the temporary directory as a property in the property file, like so:

```
tmp=C:/TEMP/antBook
#tmp=/tmp/antBook
```

Then you need to use the <unzip> task to extract the data from the zip files. Table 6-5 shows its attributes. This is a special task in that you can use it as <unjar>, <untar>, and <unwar> as well, with the attributes as described in the table.

Table 6-5. *The <unjar>, <untar>, <unwar>, and <unzip> Tasks' Attributes*

Attribute	Description
compression	The compression method that was used on the archive you are unpacking. The possible values are none, gzip, and bzip2. The default is none. This attribute is applicable only to the <untar> incarnation of this task.
dest	The destination directory for the files you are extracting. The attribute is required.
encoding	The encoding to use for filenames in the archive. You can specify native-encoding to use the platform's default encoding. The default is UTF8. This attribute is not applicable to the <untar> incarnation of this task.
overwrite	Tells Ant whether to overwrite files in the destination directory, even if they are newer than the archive's. The default is true.
src	The archive you want to expand. This attribute is required unless you nest some file sets.

Listing 6-18 shows the <unzip> task in action on the binary distribution of the web application. It unzips the binary zip file (created by zip-bin-web via the depends attribute) into a directory under ${tmp}. You should be careful to specify separate directories for each unzip target to ensure distributions aren't mixed up.

Listing 6-18. *Using the <unzip> Task to Help Create Tar Files*

```
<!-- ################################################### -->
<!-- Tasks that use the zip files to construct tar files -->
<!-- ################################################### -->

<!-- Tar the binary web distribution with the documentation -->
<target name="tar-bin-web-new" depends="package-web,tar-docs,zip-bin-web"
        description="Tar the binary web distribution with the documentation">
  <echo message="Tarring the binary web distribution with the documentation"/>
  <unzip src="${dist}/${appName}-${package.web}-bin.zip" dest="${tmp}/web"/>
  <tar destfile="${dist}/${appName}-${package.web}-bin.tar.gz"
       compression="gzip">
    <tarfileset dir="${tmp}/web"/>
  </tar>
  <checksum file="${dist}/${appName}-${package.web}-bin.tar.gz"
            forceOverwrite="true"/>
  <checksum file="${dist}/${appName}-${package.web}-bin.tar.gz"
            forceOverwrite="true" algorithm="SHA1"/>
</target>
```

You could of course remove everything from the ${tmp} directory prior to running the <unzip> task to ensure separation. Listing 6-19 shows the new target that will package the entire binary distribution, with a <delete> task added as contrast to Listing 6-18.

Listing 6-19. *Using the* `<unzip>` *Task to Help Create an Entire Binary Distribution*

```
<!-- Tar the binary distribution with the documentation -->
<target name="tar-bin-new"
        depends="zip-bin,tar-bin-stand-alone,tar-bin-web-new"
        description="Tar the binary distribution with the documentation">
  <echo message="Tarring the binary distribution with the documentation"/>
  <delete failonerror="false" includeemptydirs="true">
    <fileset dir="${tmp}" includes="**"/>
  </delete>
  <unzip src="${dist}/${appName}-bin.zip" dest="${tmp}"/>
  <tar destfile="${dist}/${appName}-bin.tar.gz" compression="gzip">
    <tarfileset dir="${tmp}"/>
  </tar>
  <checksum file="${dist}/${appName}-bin.tar.gz" forceOverwrite="true"/>
  <checksum file="${dist}/${appName}-bin.tar.gz" forceOverwrite="true"
            algorithm="SHA1"/>
</target>
```

As you can see, this is a lot more efficient and succinct than the previous version. The `<delete>` task needs to deal with a situation where the `${tmp}` directory does not exist (`failonerror` is set to `false`) and needs to remove empty directories along with the files they used to contain (`includeemptydirs` set to `true`).

The one slight disadvantage of this approach is that the tar targets always run the zip targets and increase the I/O operations on the file system. However, the zip targets are good at evaluating whether they should do a full zip, so this shouldn't be too much of a problem.

Bundling the Entire Distribution

The final target creates all the tar bundles from earlier in the chapter. This is a straight rewrite of the zip version, as shown in Listing 6-20.

Listing 6-20. *Bundling the Entire Distribution*

```
<!-- Tar the binary and source distributions -->
<target name="tar-all" depends="tar-src,tar-bin"
        description="Tar the binary and source distributions">
  <echo message="Tarred the binary and source distributions"/>
</target>
```

USING THE <WAR> TASK WITH ZIP FILE SETS

Now that you have seen zip file sets, you can rewrite the WAR target from the previous chapter. The `<war>` task's `<lib>` and `<classes>` child elements are file sets and do a lot of the work by filling the WAR file's `WEB-INF/lib` and `WEB-INF/classes` directories, respectively. The drawback of these nested elements is that you can use them only once, so you must collect all your files into a structure that can be represented sensibly by a file set if you want to use the files in these nested elements.

Remember, a file set will add the path to the file relative to its dir attribute, which can cause problems if files are in different locations. For example, take the following:

```
<classes dir=".">
  <include name="${build.web.root}/**"/>
  <include name="${database.properties}"/>
</classes>
```

You've had to use the project's base directory as the basis for this file set because this is the parent directory of the two includes. However, this causes problems in the WAR, which will have the following structure:

```
WEB-INF/classes/build/web/org/mwrm/Constants.class
WEB-INF/classes/build/web/org/mwrm/PropertiesLoader.class
...
WEB-INF/classes/src/shared/conf/database.properties
```

The paths to these files have been included, relative to the base directory of the file set. The solution is to choose the set of files that contains the greatest number of files and use that as the basis for the <classes> file set, which in this case is the set of class files, and then add the other files, such as database.properties, another way. The best way to add other files is to use <zipfileset> elements and set the prefix attribute to the path within the web application's structure that you require. You can extend this technique to other files in the web application.

In the following complete example, you add the database.properties file with a <zipfileset> element. As noted, if you were to include it as part of the <classes> element, Ant would add it as WEB-INF/classes/src/web/conf/database.properties, which is not what you want.

```
<!-- Build the WAR file in one step -->
<target name="package-web-test" depends="compile-web"
        description="Build the WAR file in one step">
  <echo message="Building the WAR file in one step"/>
  <war destfile="${appName.war}" basedir="${src.web.pages}"
       webxml="${src.web.conf}/web.xml">
    <lib dir="${lib}"/>
    <classes dir="${build.web.root}"/>
    <zipfileset dir="${src.web.tags}" prefix="WEB-INF/tags"/>
    <zipfileset file="${database.properties}" prefix="WEB-INF/classes"/>
    <zipfileset dir="${src.web.conf}" prefix="WEB-INF">
      <include name="*.tld"/>
    </zipfileset>
  </war>
</target>
```

The <zipfileset> elements here replicate the functionality of the <copy> tasks from the previous incarnation of this target, without having to do any copying.

Using the Zip and Tar Build Paths

Now you have two build paths that both create compressed bundles of files that you can distribute. You can run the entire build for both paths as follows:

```
> ant zip-all
> ant tar-all
```

Each command will create five files in the dist directory, making ten in all, named like so:

- antBook-docs.*
- antBook-src.*
- antBook-bin.*
- antBook-stand-alone-bin.*
- antBook-web-bin.*

Once you are happy with the outcome of the bundling process, it is time to get the distributions out to users and fellow developers.

Distributing the Application

As with most of the topics in this chapter, how you distribute your applications depends on a number of factors. These include whether it is a source distribution, documentation only, a command-line client, or a web application. The nature of the application also comes into play. In other words, you can usually place freely distributable open-source projects and freeware on a public FTP or HTTP server so that anyone can download them, while you can place in-house projects on a private FTP or HTTP server, copy them to a convenient location on an internal network, or mail them to those who have a stake in the project.

Placing the Application on an FTP Server

You can place a file on an FTP server in two ways: copy it to the relevant directory if the server is on your network or upload it to a remote server. I won't cover the copying option here because it is so straightforward, so let's look at using Ant's <ftp> task.

The <ftp> task is an optional task because it relies on code from the Jakarta Commons Net project and code from the Jakarta ORO project. If you want to use the <ftp> task, obtain the relevant JAR files from the distributions at jakarta.apache.org/site/downloads/downloads_commons.html and jakarta.apache.org/site/downloads/. Once you have them, place them in ANT_HOME/lib.

■ Note If you don't have a handy FTP server to use, the Apache Software Foundation has a Java implementation at incubator.apache.org/projects/ftpserver/. It of course comes with an Ant build file to create the binary files. The popular FileZilla project also offers a Windows FTP server at sourceforge.net/projects/filezilla/. Linux/Unix users have ftpd at their disposal.

The <ftp> task has a lot of attributes, but I'll concentrate on the most common and useful ones here. For full details, see the Ant manual. Listing 6-21 shows the properties in build.properties that you will need for this section.

Listing 6-21. *FTP Server Settings*

```
# FTP settings
ftp.server=localhost
ftp.src.dir=src
ftp.bin.dir=bin
```

Listing 6-22 shows the target to upload your application's documentation bundles to an FTP server.

Listing 6-22. *Sending the Documentation to a Remote FTP Server*

```
  <!-- #################### -->
  <!-- Distribution targets -->
  <!-- #################### -->

  <!-- ################### -->
  <!-- FTP targets         -->
  <!-- ################### -->

  <!-- Place the documentation on FTP -->
  <target name="ftp-docs" depends="zip-docs,tar-docs"
          description="Place the documentation on FTP">
    <echo message="Placing the documentation on FTP"/>
    <ftp server="${ftp.server}"
         userid="${ftp.user}"
         password="${ftp.password}"
         remotedir="${ftp.src.dir}"
         action="send">
      <fileset dir="${dist}">
        <include name="${appName}-${package.docs}.*"/>
      </fileset>
    </ftp>
  </target>
```

Here you set the server name to localhost with the server attribute, which is required. You'll provide the username and password at the command line for security like so:

```
> ant -Dftp.user=antBook -Dftp.password=antBOOk ftp-docs
```

The remotedir attribute specifies which directory on the FTP server you want to use, which is relative to the user's "home" directory on the FTP server. This approach does have its limitations. For example, every time you run this target, Ant will upload all the files to the FTP server. A better way to do this would be to upload only those files that have changed since the last upload. However, the files on FTP will have a timestamp relative to the FTP server's local time and so may appear to be much newer or much older than they really are, depending on where your machine is located.

Ant can overcome this problem with the help of two of the `<ftp>` task's attributes called `newer` and `timediffauto`. This is one reason you do not want to generate the Javadocs during every build. If you did, the Javadoc generation would change files that otherwise would be unchanged, and so Ant would upload them onto the FTP site.

Listing 6-23 shows them in action, along with the target to send the source bundles.

Listing 6-23. *Sending the Documentation and Source to a Remote FTP Server Only If They Are Newer Files*

```
<!-- Place the documentation on FTP -->
<target name="ftp-docs" depends="zip-docs,tar-docs"
        description="Place the documentation on FTP">
  <echo message="Placing the documentation on FTP"/>
  <ftp server="${ftp.server}"
       userid="${ftp.user}"
       password="${ftp.password}"
       remotedir="${ftp.src.dir}"
       action="send"
       newer="true"
       timediffauto="true">
    <fileset dir="${dist}">
      <include name="${appName}-${package.docs}.*"/>
    </fileset>
  </ftp>
</target>

<!-- Place the source code on FTP -->
<target name="ftp-src" depends="zip-src,tar-src"
        description="Place the source code on FTP">
  <echo message="Placing the source code on FTP"/>
  <ftp server="${ftp.server}"
       userid="${ftp.user}"
       password="${ftp.password}"
       remotedir="${ftp.src.dir}"
       action="send"
       newer="true"
       timediffauto="true">
    <fileset dir="${dist}">
      <include name="${appName}-src.*"/>
    </fileset>
  </ftp>
</target>
```

Setting `newer` to `true` tells Ant to overwrite files on the server only if the local files are newer. You use this in conjunction with the `timediffauto` attribute, which calculates the difference in time between the FTP server and the local machine for the purpose of determining which file is newer.

Placing the binaries on the FTP server is just as easy, as shown in Listing 6-24.

Listing 6-24. *Sending the Binaries to a Remote FTP Server*

```
<!-- Place the binaries on FTP -->
<target name="ftp-bin" depends="zip-bin,tar-bin"
        description="Place the binaries on FTP">
  <echo message="Placing the binaries on FTP"/>
  <ftp server="${ftp.server}"
       userid="${ftp.user}"
       password="${ftp.password}"
       remotedir="${ftp.bin.dir}"
       action="send"
       newer="true"
       timediffauto="true">
    <fileset dir="${dist}">
      <include name="${appName}*bin*"/>
    </fileset>
  </ftp>
</target>
```

This time you use the bin directory on the FTP server and a slightly different wildcard expression to catch all the binary bundles.

Finally, you want the end of the build path to be a target that builds everything and then uploads it all to the FTP server, as shown in Listing 6-25.

Listing 6-25. *The FTP Target Builds the Entire Application and Loads It onto the FTP Server*

```
<!-- Place everything on FTP -->
<target name="ftp" description="Place everything on FTP">
  <echo message="Placing everything on FTP"/>
  <antcall target="ftp-docs"/>
  <antcall target="ftp-src"/>
  <antcall target="ftp-bin"/>
</target>
```

Adding a Status Bar to the Build

One final touch for the FTP target is to add a splash screen with the <splash> task while the upload proceeds to give the user some stimulation. This will add processing and time to the build but is an interesting effect that you may want to use for your personal builds. The default is to show the splash screen for five seconds before the build begins, so you'll change that by setting the showduration attribute to 0 milliseconds, as shown in Listing 6-26.

Listing 6-26. *Adding a Splash Screen to the FTP Target*

```
<!-- Place everything on FTP -->
<target name="ftp" description="Place everything on FTP">
  <echo message="Placing everything on FTP"/>
  <splash showduration="0"/>
  <antcall target="ftp-docs"/>
  <antcall target="ftp-src"/>
  <antcall target="ftp-bin"/>
</target>
```

The status bar will progress for each target in the build. You can specify your own image using the imageurl attribute.

Adding Interactive Input to the Build

So far you have provided the username and password at the command line, but you can also prompt the user to enter their details as needed in the build. This is slightly more secure than providing them at the command line because they won't remain in your shell's history as do your command-line values (though of course this depends on your shell and security settings). However, they do still appear on the screen for passersby to read.

To work with interactive input, you use the <input> task. It takes four attributes, as described in Table 6-6.

Table 6-6. *The <input> Task's Attributes*

Attribute	Description
addproperty	The name of the property whose value will contain the information typed by the user. This allows you to capture user input. The default is to not set a property.
defaultvalue	The default value of the property named in addproperty. The default is blank.
message	The message that prompts the user for input. You can also specify this message in the body of the <input> element. The default is an empty message.
validargs	A comma-separated string that represents valid arguments for this prompt. You can use this to enforce certain usage. For example, y,Y,n,N limits the response to one of these four letters. Note that this task is case-sensitive. The default is an empty list, meaning any input is allowed.

The interesting thing about the addproperty attribute is that Ant ignores it if you specify the property some other way. Therefore, if you provide the property at the command line, Ant will not prompt you for it later in the build; it will use the command-line version automatically. Let's extend the ftp target as shown in Listing 6-27.

Listing 6-27. *Adding User Input to the* `ftp` *Target*

```
<!-- Place everything on FTP -->
<target name="ftp" description="Place everything on FTP">
  <echo message="Placing everything on FTP"/>
  <input message="Please enter your username." addproperty="ftp.user"/>
  <input message="Please enter your password." addproperty="ftp.password"/>
  <splash showduration="0"/>
  <antcall target="ftp-docs"/>
  <antcall target="ftp-src"/>
  <antcall target="ftp-bin"/>
</target>
```

By placing the prompt for input here, you can set the username and password for all the FTP operations in the other FTP-related targets called by `ftp`. Here are the edited highlights of an example run:

```
> ant ftp
```

```
Buildfile: build.xml

ftp:
     [echo] Placing everything on FTP
    [input] Please enter your username.
antBook
    [input] Please enter your password.
antB00k
```

The build should then continue, and Ant will add the files to the FTP server. If you supplied the username and password at the command line, you'd see how Ant ignores the `<input>` task because you have set the `addproperty` attribute.

```
> ant -Dftp.user=antBook -Dftp.password=antB00k ftp
```

```
Buildfile: build.xml

ftp:
     [echo] Placing everything on FTP
    [input] skipping input as property ftp.user has already been set.
    [input] skipping input as property ftp.password has already been set.
```

Distributing the Application via E-mail

If an FTP server is not appropriate for distribution, you may want to use the e-mail option. The `<mail>` task is a core task, meaning it has no external dependencies, but if you want to use MIME format or secure communications, you need the following:

- mail.jar from java.sun.com/products/javamail/
- JDK 1.4 or greater or jsse.jar from java.sun.com/products/jsse/
- activation.jar from java.sun.com/products/javabeans/glasgow/jaf.html

In this example, you will send attachments with the e-mail, so you will need to place these JAR files in ANT_HOME/lib. The <mail> task has a lot of attributes, but you need to set a lot of them, so you'll look at them in an example (see Listing 6-28).

Listing 6-28. *E-mail Properties*

```
mail.from=antBuild@example.com
mail.tolist=antUser01@example.com,antUser02@example.com
mail.message.docs=Here's the docs distribution
mail.mailhost=smtp.mail.example.com
mail.subject=Ant build
```

As before, you will provide the username and password at the command line. Listing 6-29 shows how to e-mail the documentation to the list of people in the mail.tolist property.

Listing 6-29. *E-mailing the Documentation*

```
<!-- #################### -->
<!-- Email targets        -->
<!-- #################### -->

<!-- E-mail the documentation -->
<target name="email-docs" depends="zip-docs,tar-docs"
        description="E-mailing the documentation">
  <echo message="E-mailing the documentation"/>
  <mail from="${mail.from}"
        tolist="${mail.tolist}"
        message="${mail.message.docs}"
        mailhost="${mail.mailhost}"
        user="${mail.user}"
        password="${mail.password}"
        subject="${mail.subject}">
    <fileset dir="${dist}">
      <include name="${appName}-${package.docs}.*"/>
    </fileset>
  </mail>
</target>
```

The nested file list will be included as an attachment, which is possible only if you are using MIME formats. The attributes of <mail> are straightforward, though if you need to use SSL encryption, you can set the ssl attribute to true. Note that you can also specify cclist and bcclist attributes, as well as a replyto attribute.

If you do not want to specify a message body as a property, maybe because it is a large body of text, you can place it in a file and refer to it with the `messagefile` attribute. Another alternative is to use a nested `<message>` element, as shown in Listing 6-30.

Listing 6-30. *Nesting a <message> Element*

```
<!-- E-mail the documentation -->
<target name="email-docs" depends="zip-docs,tar-docs"
        description="E-mail the documentation">
  <echo message="E-mailing the documentation"/>
  <mail from="${mail.from}"
        tolist="${mail.tolist}"
        mailhost="${mail.mailhost}"
        user="${mail.user}"
        password="${mail.password}"
        subject="${mail.subject}">
    <message>
      ${mail.message.docs}
    </message>
    <fileset dir="${dist}">
      <include name="${appName}-${package.docs}.*"/>
    </fileset>
  </mail>
</target>
```

The `<message>` nested element can also include a file if you specify one in its `src` attribute. You can also nest the `<to>`, `<cc>`, `<bcc>`, `<from>`, and `<replyto>` elements, each of which has a required `address` element and an optional `name` element.

E-mail addresses can be in any of the following formats:

- `address@xyz.com`
- `name <address@xyz.com>`
- `<address@xyz.com> name`
- `(name) address@xyz.com`
- `address@xyz.com (name)`

E-mailing the other parts of the distribution is similar to the process shown in Listings 6-23 and 6-24. Therefore, I won't cover these minor changes that amount to a change of e-mail body and change of nested file sets. Instead, let's move on to deploying the web application.

Deploying a Web Application

Web servers that run web applications usually have some method of hot deploying a web application on a running web application, and you will exploit in this ability in this section. The server in this example is Tomcat, available from `jakarta.apache.org/tomcat/`. You will employ three techniques for deploying on Tomcat, one of which will undoubtedly work on the server of your choice.

The important detail in this process is the location of the hot-deploy directory. In Tomcat's case, it is CATALINA_HOME/webapps, where CATALINA_HOME is Tomcat's installation directory. You will have to set this variable to run Tomcat, so you will take advantage of its presence in the build.

Copying the Expanded Web Application

If you are using the default Tomcat setup, you can copy the web application's files into the Tomcat webapps directory, and Tomcat will deploy it. If you want to check that you can hot-deploy in this way, open the CATALINA_HOME/conf/server.xml file. Find the <Host> element of your server, and check that the autoDeploy attribute is set to true. Here's the default setup:

```
<Host name="localhost" appBase="webapps"
      unpackWARs="true" autoDeploy="true"
      xmlValidation="false" xmlNamespaceAware="false">
```

The appBase attribute defines where Tomcat will look for web applications, and that is where you will place the expanded files, as shown in Listing 6-31. You'll return to unpackWARs in the next section.

Listing 6-31. *Deploying the Expanded Web Application*

```
<!-- ################################# -->
<!-- Deploy the web application      -->
<!-- ################################# -->

<!-- 1. Copy the expanded web application -->
<target name="deploy-copy-files" depends="copy-web"
        description="Deploy the application by copying it to Tomcat">
  <echo message="Copying the expanded web application to CATALINA_HOME"/>
  <property environment="env"/>
  <copy todir="${build.web.web-inf}" file="${src.web.conf}/web.xml"/>
  <copy todir="${env.CATALINA_HOME}/webapps/${appName}">
    <fileset dir="${build.web.root}"/>
  </copy>
</target>
```

Note that you have to copy the web.xml file into the web application's directory structure because you didn't do that when you created the WAR file in Chapter 5. If you have Tomcat running and autoDeploy set to true, the web application will become available after a few seconds.

Copying the WAR File

Copying a WAR file to Tomcat's webapps directory is an alternative to copying the expanded files. This is a much neater way of doing things and takes up less network bandwidth because compressed WARs are usually smaller than the expanded web application. If you have unpackWARs set to true, Tomcat will expand the WAR and deploy it, assuming autoDeploy is set to `true`. If you set `unpackWARs` to `false`, Tomcat will run the web application from the WAR, meaning slightly slower performance, but in this case Tomcat will not require write access to the server. See the previous section if you're unsure about this.

Listing 6-32 shows the copy operation.

Listing 6-32. *Deploying the Web Application As a WAR*

```
<!-- 2. Copy the WAR -->
<target name="deploy-copy-war" depends="package-web"
        description="Deploy the WAR by copying it to Tomcat">
  <echo message="Copying the WAR to CATALINA_HOME"/>
  <property environment="env"/>
  <copy file="${appName.war}" todir="${env.CATALINA_HOME}/webapps"/>
</target>
```

Deploying Using a Context XML File

If you have a context XML file for your application, you can copy that to Tomcat to deploy your web application. This means you do not have to copy the entire application onto the server. If you are not familiar with context XML files, Listing 6-33 shows a simple example called `antBook.xml` that uses the `build/web` directory of your project as the location for the web application.

Listing 6-33. *A Sample Context XML File Called* `antBook.xml`

```
<Context path="/antBook" docBase="C:/AntBook/ch06/build/web"
         debug="0" reloadable="true" />
```

If you were to drop this file into the `CATALINA_HOME/conf/[engine_name]/[host_name]` directory, then Tomcat would deploy the application at `C:/AntBook/ch06/build/web` (if `autoDeploy` is set to `true` in Tomcat). See the earlier "Copying the Expanded Web Application" section if you're unsure about this. With this knowledge, you can use Ant to automate this form of deployment, as shown in Listing 6-34.

Listing 6-34. *Deploying a Web Application by Copying Its Context XML File*

```
<!-- 3. Deploy the web application using a context XML file -->
<target name="deploy-context" depends="copy-web"
        description="Deploy the web application using a context XML file">
  <echo message="Deploying the web application using a context XML file"/>
  <property environment="env"/>
  <copy todir="${build.web.web-inf}" file="${src.web.conf}/web.xml"/>
  <copy todir="${env.CATALINA_HOME}/conf/Catalina/localhost"
        file="${src.web.conf}/${appName}.xml"/>
</target>
```

In this case, you are taking advantage of previous targets that prepare code in the `build/web` directory and so have to finish the job by copying the `web.xml` file into this directory. If you were using this approach to deployment, a better solution would be to assemble the web application in a folder outside the project's build directory and ensure it is suitably protected with operating-system security measures. You will then need to change the docBase attribute in the context XML file.

Deploying with the Manager Application

The final method of deploying the web application is using Tomcat's manager web application. This is a servlet that deals with all the deployment for you. To set up the manager application, make sure the following entries are in CATALINA_HOME/conf/tomcat-users.xml (or the equivalent authentication realm):

```
<?xml version='1.0' encoding='utf-8'?>
<tomcat-users>
  <role rolename="manager"/>
  <user username="antBook" password="antBOOk" roles="manager"/>
</tomcat-users>
```

This is the username and password you will use to work with the manager application. There's a lot more to Tomcat password security than this, but that's too much for this chapter. To find out more, go to jakarta.apache.org/tomcat/tomcat-5.5-doc/realm-howto.html.

The next stage is to make the Tomcat custom deployment tasks available to Ant. To do so, copy CATALINA_HOME/server/lib/catalina-ant.jar to ANT_HOME/lib, and add the following task definition to your build file (Chapter 10 covers task definitions in detail):

```
  <!-- The deploy task for web applications on Tomcat -->
  <taskdef name="deploy" classname="org.apache.catalina.ant.DeployTask"/>
```

You will need to set properties in build.properties, as follows, to keep the URL of the manager application out of build.xml:

```
# The location of the Tomcat server
tomcat.host=localhost
tomcat.port=8080
manager.url=http://${tomcat.host}:${tomcat.port}/manager
```

The last task to perform is to write the deployment target, as shown in Listing 6-35. Again, you'll use command-line properties for the username and password.

Listing 6-35. *Writing the Deployment Target*

```
  <!-- 4. Deploy the WAR using the manager application -->
  <target name="deploy" depends="package-web"
          description="Hot deploy the application">
    <echo message="Deploying the WAR to Tomcat"/>
    <deploy url="${manager.url}"
            username="${manager.user}"
            password="${manager.password}"
            path="/${appName}"
            war="file:${appName.war}"
            update="true"/>
  </target>
```

To deploy the application using the manager application, all you have to do is run the following:

```
> ant -Dmanager.user=antBook -Dmanager.password=antB00k deploy
```

If you want to remove the application from the server at any time, you can define an <undeploy> task and use it as in Listing 6-36.

Listing 6-36. *Undeploying the Web Application*

```
<!-- The undeploy task for web applications on Tomcat -->
<taskdef name="undeploy" classname="org.apache.catalina.ant.UndeployTask"/>

<!-- Undeploy the web application -->
<target name="undeploy" description="Undeploy the application">
  <echo message="Undeploying the WAR"/>
  <undeploy url="${manager.url}"
            username="${manager.user}"
            password="${manager.password}"
            path="/${appName}"/>
</target>
```

Summary

This chapter took you from the end of the compilation stage to the final deployment. You looked at creating documentation bundles and Javadocs, which are slightly problematic when compared to Ant's excellent ability to sense when a file has changed. In the case of Javadocs, you have to do this check for yourself if you are worried about this having a knock-on effect.

The <zip> and <tar> tasks are similar to the <jar> and <war> tasks that you saw in the previous chapter, but have extended functionality in line with their specialist remits. The <zip> task is more powerful than the <tar> task and can process large batches of files at once, though <tar> suits distributions for Unix/Linux systems much better.

You looked at three ways to distribute the application: FTP, e-mail, and web application deployment. These are all at the end of the build path and will typically be the only targets you invoke once an application has stabilized.

CHAPTER 7

Running an Application

Sometimes your build process needs more functionality than file manipulation, compilation, packaging, and distribution. Sometimes you need to run Java applications or external applications. This is particularly true if you want to set up the user environment once they have built the source code of your application. You could, for example, start a database and insert the initial data using SQL statements so that your application will run straightaway.

This chapter will cover the relevant Ant tasks so that you can run external applications from within your build process.

Using SQL

If you want to ensure that your database application is ready to run after you or the user has built it, you can use Ant's `<sql>` task. This task allows you to run batches of SQL scripts, which means you can create and populate a database in one database connection. It is important to remember that a single `<sql>` task represents one connection to the database, so multiple `<sql>` tasks mean multiple connections to the database, which may affect performance if you have other applications using the database as well.

One advantage of this task is that you can use it to read lines of SQL from multiple files. Therefore, you can package the final SQL files for your database with the application and use them in your build. By grouping all your SQL files under one `<sql>` task, you also limit the number of connections that Ant needs to make.

You can also take advantage of the fact that Ant's property files share the format of Java properties files. In other words, if you have placed database-specific information in a Java properties file, you can also use the properties in this file for Ant's `<sql>` task. This is how the example application is set up.

You can specify SQL in a number of ways:

- You can read it in from a file using the `src` attribute of the `<sql>` task (as described in Table 7-1).
- You can specify nested file sets. In this case, Ant will execute the SQL contained in every file of the file set in its own transaction. This technique allows you to process batches of SQL files quickly and efficiently. The drawback is that Ant doesn't guarantee the order of execution, so you cannot mix database and table creation statements with inserts.

- You can nest `<transaction>` elements that read SQL in from files. You have to specify each file individually, but you can control the order of execution.
- You can place SQL statements in the body of the `<sql>` tag.

If you need to specify a classpath, you can use the `classpath` attribute or nest a `<classpath>` element in the usual way.

Table 7-1. *The <sql> Task's Attributes*

Attribute	Description
append	Sets whether to append the output to the end of a file or overwrite the contents of the file (used in conjunction with output). The default is false.
autocommit	Sets the autocommit flag of this <sql> task's database connection. If you set this to true, every SQL statement will be committed when it is sent to the database. The default is false, meaning each SQL file is executed in a transaction, and the SQL statements will be committed when the entire transaction has completed.
caching	Tells Ant whether to cache loaders and the driver. The default is true.
classpath	The classpath to use when searching for the database driver. The default is the system classpath.
classpathref	The reference ID of a classpath defined earlier in the build. The default is blank.
delimiter	The string that separates the SQL commands. The default is ;.
delimitertype	Sets whether the delimiter should be on a line by itself (a value of row). The default is normal, meaning the delimiter can appear anywhere on a line.
driver	The fully qualified class name of the JDBC database driver. This attribute is required.
encoding	The encoding of the SQL files that you are reading. The default is your JVM's encoding.
escapeprocessing	Sets whether the java.sql.Statement objects produced by this task will perform escape substitution before sending the SQL to the database. The default is true.
keepformat	Sets whether Ant keeps the format of the SQL. The default is false.
onerror	The action to perform if an error occurs when executing a statement. This can be continue, which displays the error and carries on with the process; stop, which stops execution and commits the current transaction; and abort, which stops execution, aborts the transaction, and fails the task. The default is abort.
output	The file to which you want to redirect output. The default is standard out.
password	The password that Ant will use when connecting to the database. This attribute is required.
print	Sets whether to display the result sets that are returned from the database. The default is false.
rdbms	Tells Ant to run this task only if the database it's using matches the value of this attribute. The default is no restriction.

Table 7-1. *The <sql> Task's Attributes*

Attribute	Description
showheaders	Sets whether to display the headers from the result sets returned from the database. The default is true.
src	The file that contains the SQL statements you want to run. This attribute is required unless you nest <fileset> or <transaction> elements or place SQL between the opening and closing <sql> tags. It is ignored if you do any of these things.
url	The JDBC URL of the database. This attribute is required.
userid	The username that Ant will use when connecting to the database. This attribute is required.
version	Tells Ant to run this task only if the version of the database it's using matches the value of this attribute. The default is no restriction.

The example will use MySQL as the database, so you need to tell Ant about the relevant URL and driver. This information is shared with the application, so you'll store it in the common database.properties file, as shown in Listing 7-1. You'll also store details of the SQL files here.

Listing 7-1. *The database.properties File*

```
database.root=jdbc:mysql://localhost:3306/
driver.name=com.mysql.jdbc.Driver

drop.sql=SQL/drop.sql
create.sql=SQL/create.sql
insert.sql=SQL/insert.sql
```

Listing 7-2 shows the target that uses this information to connect to the database and execute the SQL statements contained in the SQL files drop.sql, create.sql, and insert.sql.

Listing 7-2. *The Target That Prepares the Database*

```
<!-- ##################################### -->
<!-- Targets that set up the environment -->
<!-- ##################################### -->

<!-- Prepare the database by creating it and inserting data -->
<target name="database"
        description="Prepare the database by creating it and inserting data">
  <echo message="Preparing the database by creating it and inserting data"/>

  <property file="${database.properties}"/>
```

```
    <sql driver="${driver.name}"
         url="${database.root}"
         userid="${database.user}"
         password="${database.password}">
      <classpath refid="build.classpath"/>
      <transaction src="${src.shared.conf}/${drop.sql}"/>
      <transaction src="${src.shared.conf}/${create.sql}"/>
      <transaction src="${src.shared.conf}/${insert.sql}"/>
    </sql>
  </target>
```

In this case, the `drop.sql` file contains a `DROP DATABASE IF EXISTS` statement to ensure that the database is clean before you create and insert the data. The `<transaction>` nested elements take only the `src` attribute, which behaves in the same way as the `src` attribute of the `<sql>` task. You can also place SQL in the body of a `<transaction>` element, in which case the `src` attribute is ignored.

The `<sql>` task will run the SQL statements from the files in the order they have been specified. This ensures that any `DROP` and `CREATE` statements operate in the correct order. The `<classpath>` element adds the MySQL connector that you use elsewhere in the build to the classpath.

■ **Note** You should not run this kind of task during every build. SQL tasks are ideal parts of a configuration target, but they can slow a build if included every time. Besides, you want the data to change naturally in response to user actions and not renew every time you run Ant. You should also be aware that production environments may already have the data installed in secure configurations that deny access to the Ant process. Systems administrators may not take kindly to you repeatedly inserting data and dropping and creating tables.

Running Java Applications

As always, Ant gives you the full power of the JVM to use in your build files, with the added power of Ant's properties and file sets. The example application comes with a command-line Java client that accesses the database and displays the results of the query. I'll show how to run the client with Ant for the purposes of demonstration, but it's usually better to provide a script to run a Java client. Lay users are more comfortable with a script because it encapsulates all the messy command-line options that set the classpath, and so on. Letting them loose with Ant can also mean prying eyes on your build file, which you may not want.

Table 7-2 shows the attributes of the `<java>` task. Deprecated attributes have been omitted.

Table 7-2. *The <java> Task's Attributes*

Attribute	Description
`append`	Sets whether to append the output to the end of a file or overwrite the contents of the file (used in conjunction with `output`). The default is `false`.
`classname`	The name of the class you want to execute. This attribute is required if you do not specify a value for `jar`.
`classpath`	The classpath for this Java invocation. The default is the system classpath.
`classpathref`	The reference ID of a classpath defined earlier in the build. The default is blank.
`dir`	The directory from where the JVM will be run. Ant ignores this attribute if `fork` is `false`. The default is `null`.
`error`	The file to which you want to redirect error messages. The default is the setting in `output`.
`errorproperty`	The property where Ant will store error messages. The default is blank.
`failonerror`	Tells Ant whether to stop the build if the command exits with a return code other than `0`. The default is `false`.
`fork`	Tells Ant to run the classes in an external JVM. The default is `false`.
`input`	The name of a file that will be the input to this command. You can only specify one of `input` and `inputstring`. The default is standard input from the console. In addition, you cannot obtain standard input if you set `spawn` to `true`.
`inputstring`	A string that will be the input to this command. You can only specify one of `input` and `inputstring`. The default is standard input from the console. In addition, you cannot obtain standard input if you set `spawn` to `true`.
`jar`	The name of the JAR file you want to execute. For this to work you must specify a `Main-Class` entry in the manifest and set `fork` to `true`. This attribute is required if you do not specify a value for `classname`.
`jvm`	The command that will run the JVM. Ant ignores this attribute if `fork` is set to `false`. The default is `java`.
`logError`	Tells Ant to write error messages to the Ant log files. The error messages will not appear in any output location that you have set. Ant ignores this attribute if you set `error` or `errorproperty`. The default is `false`.
`maxmemory`	The maximum amount of memory that Ant should allocate to a forked JVM. Ant ignores this attribute if `fork` is set to `false`. The default is your JVM's default.
`newenvironment`	Tells the JVM to ignore old environment variables if it is running as a separate process and new ones are specified. Ant ignores this attribute if you set `fork` to `false`. The default is `false`.
`output`	The file to which you want to redirect output. The default is standard `out`.
`outputproperty`	The property where Ant will store the output of this command (including error messages unless otherwise redirected). The default is blank.
`resultproperty`	The property where Ant will store the return code of this command. You can use this attribute only if `failonerror` is `false` and `fork` is `true` (the details follow this table). The default is blank.

Table 7-2. *The <java> Task's Attributes (Continued)*

Attribute	Description
spawn	Tells Ant to start a process that will live after the Ant process has finished. To use this you have to set fork to true and can't use error, input, output, result, or timeout. The default is false.
timeout	The time in milliseconds that Ant should wait before stopping this command. You should use this only if you set fork to true. The default is null.

Return codes are governed by a simple set of rules:

- If failonerror is true, then 0 is the only legal return code you can capture in a property. Other return codes ensure that the task fails.
- If failonerror is false and fork is false, then 0 is the only legal return code you can capture in a property. Other return codes ensure that the task fails because the build's JVM exits on an error return code.
- If failonerror is false and fork is true, then you can capture the return code.

You can nest a number of elements in the <java> task; some replace attributes, some apply only to forked JVMs, and some pass arguments to the JVM. I'll discuss the latter first.

You can nest <arg> elements to send arguments to the class you are running or nested <jvmarg> elements to send arguments to a forked JVM. They both take the same attributes (see Table 7-3). You can specify only one at a time.

Table 7-3. *The <arg> and <jvmarg> Elements' Attributes*

Attribute	Description
file	The name of a file to pass on the command line. This will be converted to an absolute filename.
line	A list of command-line arguments, separated by spaces. Ant cannot guarantee that the list you supply will be the same as the list it gives to the java command. Ant splits the line before passing it, which may not be the way you intended it to be split.
path	A pathlike string to pass on the command line. You can use : and ; as separators, though Ant will convert them to the system's default convention.
pathref	A reference ID to a path defined earlier in the build. Ant treats this path in the same way as the value of the path attribute.
value	A single command-line argument that can contain spaces.

These are other nested elements:

- <assertions>, which enables Java 1.4 assertions
- <bootclasspath>, which specifies the boot classpath for this command
- <classpath>, which specifies the classpath for this command

- <env>, which passes environment variables to the forked JVM
- <permissions>, which sets security permissions
- <redirector>, which redirects output
- <sysproperty>, which allows you to specify system properties for this command
- <syspropertyset>, which allows you to specify system properties using a property set (see Chapter 4)

You'll use the <classpath> element here to specify the JAR file that contains your client and the JAR file of the MySQL connector.

Running the Stand-Alone Client

One of the drawbacks of the <java> task is that you have to send a set number of arguments to the java command. This is fine if you have a constant number of values you want to use, but it is not so good if you have variable numbers of arguments to pass. For example, if you always run the target Java class with the same arguments, you do not have a problem. However, say you want to run it with two arguments sometimes and three arguments at other times. In this case, you could use two targets, one for the two-argument run and one for the three-argument run. Another option is to use properties to vary the arguments sent to the application.

Properties, however, make the situation more complicated, because if a property is not set, Ant will write the string you used to include the property. Usage checks will always fail in this case because they will read the argument as ${propertyName} instead of being empty, as would be the case if you ran the application at the command line. One way around this is to set defaults for every property you want to use as a command-line argument, as shown in Listing 7-3.

Listing 7-3. *Setting Defaults for Command-Line Arguments*

```
<!-- Set the argument defaults -->
<!-- The Java execution and the script use them -->
<target name="set-argument-defaults" depends="stand-alone"
        description="Set the defaults for the command-line arguments">
  <echo message="Setting the defaults for the command-line arguments"/>

  <!-- Set a default for the first argument -->
  <condition property="arg0" value="">
    <not>
      <isset property="${arg0}"/>
    </not>
  </condition>

  <!-- Set a default for the second argument -->
  <condition property="arg1" value="">
    <not>
      <isset property="${arg1}"/>
    </not>
  </condition>
</target>
```

Here you set the value of arg0 and arg1 to an empty string if they are not already set. Ant will send these values to the Java application, which can handle them if necessary. Listing 7-4 shows this in action. In this case, you are assuming the user has the latest binaries and so doesn't need to compile them. Adding the package-stand-alone target to the depends attribute would ensure the latest source is compiled before the user runs the code.

Listing 7-4. *Running the Client*

```
<!-- This first target is a Java invocation -->
<target name="run-stand-alone-java" depends="set-argument-defaults"
        description="Run the stand-alone application">
  <echo message="Running the stand-alone application"/>

  <java classname="org.mwrm.client.Client">
    <arg value="${arg0}"/>
    <arg value="${arg1}"/>
    <classpath refid="build.classpath"/>
  </java>
</target>
```

Redirecting Output

The stand-alone client returns a set of results to users, which they will see on their screens as part of the Ant build. With large data sets, this is not ideal, because to make sense of the data they will have to copy the data from the screen and into a file. In fact, they may only want to save the results for use later. One way to do this would be to use the output redirector (>) or pipe (|) at the command line. However, this would capture the entire output of the build, which is not what you or the user wants.

Ant can offer you more flexibility than this through its own <redirector> components. You can nest them inside certain tasks to redirect the output from that task and that task only. This allows you to capture only the output you are interested in and not the entire output of an Ant build. The stand-alone client is a perfect candidate for an Ant <redirector> because you want to save its output to a file.

The <redirector> component can also function as an input redirector, just like <. It has a number of attributes as listed in Table 7-4, and you can nest it in the <java>, <exec>, and <apply> tasks, though only one redirector is allowed per task.

Table 7-4. *The Attributes of the <redirector> Component*

Attribute	Description
alwayslog	Tells Ant whether to send data to the log in addition to any other destination. The default is false.
append	Tells Ant whether to append error or output messages to the files specified in error and output. The default is false.
createemptyfiles	Tells Ant whether to create the output files, even if they are to be empty. The default is true.

Table 7-4. *The Attributes of the <redirector> Component*

Attribute	Description
`error`	The name of the file where you want to place error messages for this task. If you don't specify a value, Ant will use standard `out`. The default is `null`.
`errorencoding`	The encoding for the error output. The default is the platform's default encoding.
`errorproperty`	The name of the property that will contain the error output of the task. The default is `null`.
`input`	The name of the file that contains the input stream for this task. You cannot specify `input` and `inputstring` together. The default is `null`.
`inputencoding`	The encoding for the input. The default is the platform's default encoding.
`inputstring`	A string that will be treated as the input of this task. You cannot specify `input` and `inputstring` together. The default is `null`.
`logError`	Tells Ant whether to send error messages to the Ant log. If you set this attribute to `true`, Ant will not write the error messages to the file named in `output` or the property set in `outputproperty`. However, this attribute has no effect if you use `error`/`errorproperty`. The default is `false`.
`output`	The name of the file where you want to place the output of this task. If you don't specify a value, Ant will use standard `out`. The default is `null`.
`outputencoding`	The encoding for the output. The default is the platform's default encoding.
`outputproperty`	The name of the property that will contain the output of the task. The default is `null`.

As you can see, the single redirector in each executable-style task acts as both an input redirector and an output redirector. You can nest mappers to match groups of files with the following nested elements: `<inputmapper>`, `<outputmapper>`, and `<errormapper>`. These are simple file mappers, the details of which appear in Chapter 11. You can filter the data with `<inputfilterchain>`, `<outputfilterchain>`, and `<errorfilterchain>` filters, which you'll also see in Chapter 11.

You'll just be using a simple output redirector to store the results of your client's query in a text file. However, you don't want to overwrite previous results with new results, and you don't want to continually append the results to the end of the same file. This could potentially lead to massive files, and the user would have to sift through the data to find the section they wanted. The solution is to add a timestamp to the result file's filename.

To do so, you'll use the `<tstamp>` task, which sets the values of the `TSTAMP`, `DSTAMP`, and `TODAY` properties. They have the following default formats:

- `TSTAMP`: `hhmm`
- `DSTAMP`: `yyyyMMdd`
- `TODAY`: `MMMM dd yyyy`

You can change these defaults if you want. This task has only one attribute, described in Table 7-5, and nested <format> elements, described after the table.

Table 7-5. *The Attribute of the <format> Element*

Attribute	Description
prefix	The prefix to add to the properties set by this task. The default is no prefix.

If you want to use a custom format for the timestamp or if you want to store the timestamp in a property other than TSTAMP, DSTAMP, and TODAY, then you have to use a nested <format> element for each new format or property. Table 7-6 shows the details of the <format> element's attributes.

Table 7-6. *The Attributes of the <format> Element*

Attribute	Description
locale	The locale to use when formatting the timestamp. The default is the user's locale.
offset	The number of units to use when offsetting the timestamp. You must define the unit type with the unit attribute; if you don't, the offset attribute has no effect. The default is zero.
pattern	The custom pattern for the timestamp stored in property. This attribute is required.
property	The name of the property that will contain the timestamp. This attribute is required.
timezone	The time zone to use, which will be displayed as part of the timestamp. The default is the user's local time zone.
unit	The unit type to use with the offset attribute. Units can be millisecond, second, minute, hour, day, week, month, or year. The default is null.

You have to put the output redirector and the timestamp together, so let's rewrite the run-stand-alone target, as shown in Listing 7-5.

Listing 7-5. *Saving the Results in a File with a Timestamp*

```
<target name="run-stand-alone-java"
        depends="set-argument-defaults, package-stand-alone"
        description="Run the stand-alone application">
  <echo message="Running the stand-alone application"/>

  <!-- We want to make a file for each set of results -->
  <property name="results.file" value="results.txt"/>
  <!-- The timestamp will uniquely identify the file -->
  <tstamp/>
```

```
  <java classname="org.mwrm.plants.client.PlantClient">
    <arg value="${arg0}"/>
    <arg value="${arg1}"/>
    <classpath refid="build.classpath"/>
    <redirector output="${DSTAMP}-${TSTAMP}-${results.file}"/>
  </java>
</target>
```

If you run this target, Ant will package the stand-alone client into its JAR file and then run the client. Ant will place any output from the `<java>` task in a file called `yyyyMMdd-hhmm-results.txt`. While this is useful, you may have problems if the build is set up to run 24 hours a day because the `hhmm` format of `TSTAMP` means you could have two files with the same name if the build runs exactly 12 hours after a previous run. To solve this, specify a `<format>` nested element and set the format of `TSTAMP` explicitly, like so:

```
<tstamp>
  <format property="TSTAMP" pattern="HHmm"/>
</tstamp>
```

Now Ant will add a 24-hour time to the timestamp.

Running Native Programs

Ant, while extremely powerful and flexible, can't always offer everything you want to do. If this is the case, you can use the <exec> task, which can run any command-line program. You can, for example, run scripts that prepare the environment for your application. The <exec> task's attributes are a lot like the `<java>` task's attributes (see Table 7-7).

By default, the JVM will launch the command itself rather than invoking the underlying shell. This has implications on Windows, for instance, because the JVM will search only for files with the `.exe` extension if you don't specify an extension, which means it won't find scripts and batch files. You have two ways around this: set the `vmlauncher` attribute to `false`, or supply the full name of the batch file, including extension.

Table 7-7. *The <exec> Task's Attributes*

Attribute	Description
`append`	Sets whether to append the output to the end of a file or overwrite the contents of the file (used in conjunction with `output`). The default is `false`.
`dir`	The directory from where the program will be run. The default is `null`.
`error`	The file to which you want to redirect error messages. The default is the setting in `output`.
`errorproperty`	The property where Ant will store error messages. The default is blank.
`executable`	The command you want to execute. This should be the name of the command and should not be accompanied by any arguments. You specify them with nested <arg> elements. This attribute is required.

Table 7-7. *The <exec> Task's Attributes (Continued)*

Attribute	Description
`failifexecutionfails`	Tells Ant whether to stop the build if the command fails to start at all. The default is `true`.
`failonerror`	Tells Ant whether to stop the build if the command exits with a return code other than `0`. The default is `false`.
`input`	The name of a file that will be the input to this command. You can specify only one of `input` and `inputstring`. The default is standard input from the console. In addition, you cannot obtain standard input if you set `spawn` to `true`.
`inputstring`	A string that will be the input to this command. You can specify only one of `input` and `inputstring`. The default is standard input from the console. In addition, you cannot obtain standard input if you set `spawn` to `true`.
`logError`	Tells Ant to write error messages to the Ant log files. The error messages will not appear in any output location that you have set. Ant ignores this attribute if you set `error` or `errorproperty`. The default is `false`.
`newenvironment`	Tells the program to ignore old environment variables if new ones are specified. The default is `false`.
`os`	Ant will execute the command only if it is running on an operating system in this list. Ant uses `String.indexOf() < 0` to see whether the operating system matches anything in this list, so you can specify the operating systems in any format you like, even a continuous string with no separators. The default is to always run the command.
`output`	The file to which you want to redirect output. The default is standard `out`.
`outputproperty`	The property where Ant will store the output of this command (including error messages unless otherwise redirected). The default is blank.
`resolveexecutable`	Tells Ant to locate the executable in the project's base directory or the directory specified by `dir`. The default is `false` (use the user's current path).
`resultproperty`	The property where Ant will store the return code of this command. You can use this attribute only if `failonerror` is `false` (you'll find details about this after the table). The default is blank.
`searchpath`	Tells Ant to use the system `PATH` environment variable to find the command. The default is `false`.
`spawn`	Tells Ant to start a process that will live after the Ant process has finished. You can't use `error`, `input`, `output`, or `result`. The default is `false`.
`timeout`	The time in milliseconds that Ant should wait before stopping this command. The default is `null`.
`vmlauncher`	Tells Ant whether to use the JVM's execution functionality instead of the operating system's shell. The default is `true`.

Starting Tomcat with Ant

To demonstrate the <exec> task, let's add a target that starts Tomcat in anticipation of deploying the web application. The Tomcat startup script is in CATALINA_HOME/bin and is called startup.bat on Windows and startup.sh on other systems. You need to check that Tomcat is not running before trying to start it, which means you have to see whether a process is running on the Tomcat server's computer on the Tomcat port.

You'll set a property called tomcat.running if Ant finds a process running on localhost at port 8080 (you set these properties in Chapter 6). For this you'll use a <condition> element with a nested <socket> element. Listing 7-6 shows this target.

Listing 7-6. *Checking That Tomcat Is Running*

```
<!-- Check whether Tomcat is running -->
<target name="check-port" description="Check whether Tomcat is running">
  <echo message="Checking whether Tomcat is running"/>
  <condition property="tomcat.running">
    <socket server="${tomcat.host}" port="${tomcat.port}"/>
  </condition>
</target>
```

If this property is set, you don't want to start Tomcat. Therefore, you need to use an unless attribute in the next target to check the tomcat.running property. You'll also set the name of the executable depending on the operating system you're running Ant on, though you'll see a different approach afterward.

For now, add the following property to the project's build file:

```
# The name of the Tomcat start script
tomcat.executableName=startup
```

This is the name of Tomcat's startup script. Listing 7-7 contains the target that starts Tomcat if it is not running already.

Listing 7-7. *Starting Tomcat*

```
<!-- Start Tomcat if it isn't running -->
<target name="start-tomcat" depends="check-port"
        description="Start Tomcat if it isn't running" unless="tomcat.running">
  <echo message="Starting Tomcat"/>

  <!-- Set the executable property according to OS -->
  <condition property="executable" value="${tomcat.executableName}.bat">
    <os family="windows"/>
  </condition>
```

```
    <condition property="executable" value="${tomcat.executableName}.sh">
      <os family="unix"/>
    </condition>

    <property environment="env"/>

    <exec executable="${env.CATALINA_HOME}/bin/${executable}" spawn="true"/>
  </target>
```

You set the spawn attribute of <exec> to true because you want to continue with the build while Tomcat starts, mainly because Tomcat doesn't stop running until you tell it to stop. In other words, it doesn't send a return code if it starts successfully. Theoretically, it's a never-ending process. You are using the default value for the vmlauncher attribute, which is true. This means the JVM will use its own execution mechanism, and you therefore have to check the OS type because the JVM needs the whole filename of the Tomcat script, including its extension. The OS, on the other hand, knows that a .bat or .sh file is executable and so doesn't need the file extension, as shown next.

If you wanted to run Tomcat before deploying the web application, you would have to add the start-tomcat target to the depends attributes of the deployment targets, as follows:

```
  <target name="deploy-copy-files" depends="copy-web,start-tomcat"
          description="Deploy the application by copying it to Tomcat">

  <target name="deploy-copy-war" depends="package-web,start-tomcat"
          description="Deploy the WAR by copying it to Tomcat">

  <target name="deploy" depends="package-web,start-tomcat"
          description="Hot-deploy the application">
```

To dispense with the checks to determine the operating system, you can set the <exec> task's vmlauncher attribute to false, as shown in Listing 7-8.

Listing 7-8. *Using the Operating System's Shell to Run the Command*

```
  <!-- Start Tomcat if it isn't running -->
  <target name="start-tomcat" depends="check-port"
          description="Start Tomcat if it isn't running" unless="tomcat.running">
    <echo message="Starting Tomcat"/>

    <property environment="env"/>

    <exec executable="${env.CATALINA_HOME}/bin/${tomcat.executableName}"
          spawn="true" vmlauncher="false"/>
    <sleep seconds="15"/>
  </target>
```

The <sleep> task waits for the specified amount of time before it returns control to Ant, which will give Tomcat enough time to start before another task tries to interact with it.

You can specify the hours, minutes, seconds, and milliseconds attributes, which are cumulative and accept negative numbers. Take the following example:

```
<sleep minutes="1" seconds="10" milliseconds="-900"/>
```

This will cause Ant to sleep for one minute and one second because that is the sum of all the attributes. The values are not precise because the OS can round them up or down as its abilities require. Very small values may even be ignored.

Creating PGP Hashes with Ant

You may recall from Chapter 6 that you created MD5 and SHA1 hashes for the distributions of your application. The third method for creating a hash that you looked at was Pretty Good Privacy (PGP), though you didn't actually generate the hash because you want to use the pgp executable to do so. Here's an example of the command line you want to replicate:

```
> pgp -s -b -o ./build/antBook-bin.zip.asc -z pgpP@ss ./dist/antBook-bin.zip
```

You've already seen the -s option that tells PGP you want to sign something. -b tells PGP to keep the hash signature separate from the file, and -o is the file where PGP will place the resulting hash. -z specifies the password you set when you first created your key ring (see Chapter 2 for more on this). In this case, you'll place the file in the build folder because PGP creates temporary files in the output directory during the hash generation and doesn't remove them if it fails to generate a hash. This means the distribution directory would contain these temporary files if something goes wrong with the process. To avoid this, you'll copy the hash file into the distribution file if the process succeeds. If it does not succeed, you can use the MD5 and SHA1 hashes in the meantime.

To start with, move all your hash-generation tasks into a single target so that you can use it from any target you want. You'll pass it the name of the file to hash so you can base the PGP hash's name on it in the new target. (The <checksum> task does this automatically.) All you need to do to generate the hashes is place an <antcall> task in each of the packaging targets, as shown in Listing 7-9.

Listing 7-9. *An <antcall> Task Calls the Hash-Generation Target*

```
<!-- Zip the documentation -->
<target name="zip-docs" depends="docs" description="Zip the documentation">
  <echo message="Zipping the documentation"/>
  <zip destfile="${dist}/${appName}-${package.docs}.zip">
    <!-- Include the documentation -->
    <fileset dir="${docs.all.dir}">
      <patternset refid="docs.all"/>
    </fileset>
    <!-- Include the license and the README -->
    <fileset dir="${docs.misc.dir}">
      <patternset refid="docs.misc"/>
    </fileset>
  </zip>
```

```
    <antcall target="generate-hashes">
      <param name="file" value="${appName}-${package.docs}.zip"/>
    </antcall>
  </target>
```

This calls the hash-generation target and adds the `file` property to the build for the duration of `generate-hashes`.

The start of `generate-hashes` is a slight rewrite of the two `<checksum>` tasks from Chapter 6, to take into account the more dynamic nature of the file to hash. In this case, you are assuming the files are in the distribution directory because that's how the project works; you wouldn't be hashing anything that isn't in the distribution directory. Another reason for this assumption is that it's easier to build the PGP hash if you separate the filename from the directory, as you'll see after Listing 7-10. If you wanted to make this target more general, you could pass a `dir` attribute to it from the calling target.

Listing 7-10. *The Hash-Generation Target*

```
<!-- Generate the hashes for a package -->
<target name="generate-hashes" description="Generate the hashes for a package">
  <echo message="Generating the hashes for ${file}"/>
  <checksum file="${dist}/${file}" forceOverwrite="true"/>
  <checksum file="${dist}/${file}" forceOverwrite="true" algorithm="SHA1"/>

  <!-- We want a fresh file -->
  <delete failonerror="false">
    <fileset dir="." includes="**/${file}.asc"/>
  </delete>

  <!-- PGP creates a temporary file if it fails,
       so we use the scratch directory -->
  <exec executable="pgp" spawn="false" vmlauncher="false">
    <arg value="+force"/>
    <arg value="+batchmode"/>
    <arg value="-s"/>
    <arg value="-b"/>
    <arg value="-o"/>
    <arg value="${build}/${file}.asc"/>
    <arg value="-z"/>
    <arg value="${pgp.password}"/>
    <arg value="${dist}/${file}"/>
  </exec>

  <!-- Copy the file to the distribution directory -->
  <copy file="${build}/${file}.asc" todir="${dist}" failonerror="false"/>
</target>
```

The <exec> task used in Listing 7-10 takes a little bit of explaining. First, the way Ant passes arguments to PGP means that the space before the filename in, for example, -o ${build}/${file}.asc will cause PGP to try to make a file called ' build/antBook-docs.zip.asc', including the spaces, which can't be done. To get around this, you have split the argument in two and send it to PGP one after the other. This means that order is important here. An alternative would be to do the following and eliminate the space:

```
<arg value="-o${build}/${file}.asc"/>
```

The +force and +batchmode command-line options are designed for situations where automatic or unattended processes try to generate hashes, which is exactly what you are doing here. The first one suppresses confirmation questions such as, "Are you sure you want to overwrite this file?" The second removes, among other things, the prompt for a password if you forget to supply one or supply the wrong one. You'd probably rather continue with the build in this case than have it hang waiting for a response. You won't get a PGP hash, but you will get MD5 and SHA1 hashes.

When you run the packaging targets now, don't forget to set the -Dpgp.password option at the command line should you not want to place the pgp.password property in the build file (and you probably shouldn't).

Note If you want to fail the build if PGP couldn't generate a hash, it's as simple as setting the <exec> task's failonerror attribute to true. If you do this, you may want to remove the <copy> task's failonerror attribute because it would be redundant.

Summary

This chapter introduced some ways to run commands, whether they are SQL inserts into a database, Java programs, or native applications. The latter two are similar and share a number of attributes. The approach you should take with them is also similar as a result. Passing arguments to these tasks can lead to problems, so you need to think about variable numbers of arguments carefully.

Native programs can help you set up the environment prior to running other Ant targets, and this chapter showed how to ensure that a web server is running before deploying an application to it.

CHAPTER 8

Testing an Application

Testing your application is a vital part of the software development process and one that you skimp on at your peril. Not testing properly can cost time, money, and effort when you could have removed bugs much earlier in the process and saved all the heartache. One important technique for testing is unit testing, which is the main way you can use Ant for testing your application.

In this chapter, you'll look at the JUnit testing framework and how to integrate it into Ant. Ant can then run the test cases you write, save their output, and display this output in a number of ways, depending on your needs. I won't cover how to write test cases or the theory behind unit testing, just as I didn't cover the theory behind object-oriented programming or writing Java web applications. If you are not already unit testing, you may want to explore the JUnit web site (`www.junit.org`) or read *Test-Driven Development: By Example*, by Kent Beck (Addison-Wesley, 2002), for an introduction.

You'll also look at code conventions and how to test them with Ant using the Checkstyle framework.

Before you look at JUnit, I'll discuss why you would want to use JUnit with Ant, rather than other techniques.

Testing by Instantiation

One way to test an application is to create a `main()` method in the object you are testing so that you can instantiate the class at the command line. If the class already has a `main()` method, you would use that as the basis of your test. The principal goal of testing is to observe the object's interface to other objects or the user, so giving you some output in the former case tells you whatever you want to know about the object's state. The latter case shows you what the user will experience. In both cases, you would use Ant's `<java>` task to run the test.

This approach has many problems:

- The testing code is combined with the source code, which means you must remove it or ensure it is switched off before you deploy the final application. This adds one more degree of complexity to a build. Ideally, Ant would test the code and then, if it passes the tests, deploy it automatically. Using the `main()` method means you have to intervene to either remove the test code and recompile or incorporate a test source tree that mirrors the real source tree.

- The only way to tell whether the application has failed a test is to look at the output and decide whether it has failed. Nothing is automatic about this, thus defeating the purpose of using Ant.
- You should be testing the application's interface, not how you've laid out its internals. In other words, the `main()` method can check `private` and `protected` components, which isn't what you want, though it's sometimes easy to slip a `private` or `protected` test into the testing regime.
- If you want to save the results or display them in a better way than through `System.out.println()`, you have to write custom code to capture output. This code would change for every object you want to test.
- If you hand the project on to someone else, they may not necessarily know the details of these custom testing plans. Writing code that passes or fails depending on a user's say-so means you will slow down any future maintenance efforts while the new maintainer learns the testing regime. Remember, the new maintainer could be you.

These problems will soon become insurmountable in even small projects. JUnit, however, does not suffer from any of these problems and is an invaluable tool during application development.

Testing with JUnit

JUnit (`www.junit.org`) is the standard unit-testing framework for Java development. It is incredibly useful and easy to extend, so you can use many, many extensions for your application, two of which are HttpUnit (`httpunit.sourceforge.net`) and DbUnit (`dbunit.sourceforge.net`). These extensions are specially designed to work with web applications and database-driven applications, respectively.

■ **Note** One point to remember when reading this chapter is the distinction between a JUnit error and a JUnit failure. An *error* is an unexpected problem with the class, such as an internal server error or `NullPointerException`. A *failure* indicates application behavior at odds with what you expect as indicated by the failure of an assertion. They are both as important as each other during a build but are fixed in different ways.

Installing the Testing Frameworks

The JUnit tasks are optional Ant tasks, so before Ant can use any of the testing frameworks, you must make sure the classes are on its classpath. This means you have to place the `junit.jar` file from the JUnit download into `ANT_HOME/lib` or supply the path to it with the `-lib` command-line option as follows:

```
> ant -lib C:\junit\junit.jar test
```

The extension classes are required to be part of only the build classpath and not the Ant classpath. In other words, Ant does not require them to instantiate the JUnit tasks. It requires them only if a test class uses them as part of a test. For this reason, you need to add the extension classes only to a project's classpath using a path set.

■ **Note** The extensions will come with their own copies of the JUnit classes. Bear this in mind when assigning classpaths.

Organizing the Test File Structure

Your test classes should not be part of your application's source tree because they are not part of your application. The usual technique is to place them in a separate directory structure that mirrors the packages of the main application, which associates the tests with the objects they are testing. This situation is as follows:

```
src/
  shared/
         conf/
              database.properties
         java/
              org/
                  mwrm/
                       shared Java classes
  stand-alone/
              java/
                   org/
                       mwrm/
                            stand-alone client
  web/
      conf/
           web.xml
      images/
      java/
           org/
               mwrm/
                    servlet classes
      pages/
            HTML pages
            JSP pages
      tags/
           tag files

test/
     org/
         mwrm/
              test classes
```

The test directory is at the same level as the src directory and contains the same package structure. When you build the test classes, you will place them in the main build directory because they will not interfere with the main application there, and this makes the clean task operate on test classes too.

Listing 8-1 shows the properties you will be using in this chapter.

Listing 8-1. *The Properties for the Test Targets*

```
# The test directory
test.src=test
test.build=${build}/test
test.junit.reports=${test.build}/reports/junit
test.junit.data=${test.build}/data/junit
test.junit.style=${test.src}/style/junit

httpunit.home=C:/httpunit
httpunit.jar=${httpunit.home}/lib/httpunit.jar
```

Initializing the Testing Environment

As you run the tests, you'll want to have fresh data and reports for analysis. However, the JUnit tasks do not keep track of the reports and data they generate, so they don't remove old data. This means if you remove or rename a test, the results of the old test will persist and appear in subsequent reports if you are not careful. One way to solve this is to remove the data and reports before each test run, as shown in Listing 8-2.

Listing 8-2. *Initializing the Testing Environment*

```
  <!-- ################################### -->
  <!-- Testing targets                     -->
  <!-- ################################### -->

  <!-- Prepare the test directories -->
  <target name="test-init" description="Prepare the test directories">
    <echo message="Preparing the test directories"/>
    <delete dir="${test.junit.reports}"/>
    <delete dir="${test.junit.data}"/>
    <mkdir dir="${test.build}"/>
    <mkdir dir="${test.junit.reports}"/>
    <mkdir dir="${test.junit.data}"/>
  </target>
```

Here you remove the old reports and data so that you have a clean start to the testing process.

Compiling the Test Classes

Before you can use the test classes to test your application, you have to compile them successfully. As you saw previously, you will keep the test source in the `test` directory and use the same packages as the main application.

The `<javac>` task that compiles the test classes will have to use the extensions' classes, so you build a testing classpath, as shown in Listing 8-3. Notice how you exclude the `junit.jar` file of the HttpUnit distribution so that Ant uses the master `junit.jar` file that is on its classpath. This avoids clashes in the classpath that can lead to unexpected results.

Listing 8-3. *The Test Classpath*

```
<!-- #################################### -->
<!-- The test build classpath             -->
<!-- #################################### -->

<path id="test.classpath">
  <path refid="build.classpath"/>
  <fileset dir="${httpunit.home}/jars">
    <include name="*.jar"/>
    <exclude name="junit.jar"/>
  </fileset>
  <pathelement location="${httpunit.jar}"/>
  <pathelement location="${test.build}"/>
</path>
```

Now that you have the classpath, you can compile the classes. In this case, the target needs the most up-to-date versions of the code to test, so you'll compile the tests only if the application compiles. Listing 8-4 shows the target.

Listing 8-4. *The Target to Compile the Test Classes*

```
<!-- Compile the test classes -->
<target name="compile-tests"
        depends="package-stand-alone,deploy-copy-war,test-init"
        description="Compile the test classes">
  <echo message="Compiling the test classes"/>
  <javac destdir="${test.build}"
         srcdir="${test.src}">
    <classpath refid="test.classpath"/>
  </javac>
</target>
```

This is a straightforward `<javac>` command that takes a classpath and compiles some Java source to a specified destination directory. You create a JAR file in the `dist` directory because that makes it easier to distribute the test classes should you want to send them to someone else.

Testing the Application

You are now ready to run some tests. The main JUnit task is called `<junit>`; Table 8-1 lists its attributes.

Table 8-1. *The <junit> Task's Attributes*

Attribute	Description
`dir`	The directory in which to invoke the forked JVM, so this setting is ignored if `fork` is set to `false`. The default is the current directory.
`errorproperty`	The name of the property to set if there is a JUnit error. The default is `null`.
`failureproperty`	The name of the property to set if there is a JUnit failure or error. The default is `null`.
`filtertrace`	Sets whether to filter out JUnit and Ant stack traces from error and failure stack traces. The default is `true`.
`fork`	Tells Ant to run the tests in a separate JVM. The default is `false`.
`forkmode`	If you are running forked tests, this setting controls how Ant handles the fork. If you set it to `once`, a single forked JVM will handle all the tests; if you set it to `perBatch`, a new JVM will handle each batch of tests (as set by the `<batchtest>` element, which you'll learn more about later in this section); and if you set it to `perTest`, a new JVM will handle each test. A single JVM can run tests with the same values only for `errorproperty`, `failureproperty`, `filtertrace`, `haltonerror`, and `haltonfailure`, so more than one JVM may be required even if you set this attribute to `once`. The default is `perTest`.
`haltonerror`	Sets whether Ant should stop the build if a JUnit error occurs. The default is `false`.
`haltonfailure`	Sets whether Ant should stop the build if a JUnit failure or error occurs. The default is `false`.
`includeantruntime`	Sets whether the forked JVM should have the Ant classes in its classpath, so this setting is ignored if `fork` is set to `false`. The default is `true`.
`jvm`	The executable to use when forking a JVM, so this setting is ignored if `fork` is set to `false`. The default is `java`.
`maxmemory`	The maximum amount of memory that Ant will assign to the forked JVM, so this setting is ignored if `fork` is set to `false`. The default is no limit.
`newenvironment`	Sets whether a forked JVM will ignore old environment variables when new ones are specified, so this setting is ignored if `fork` is set to `false`. The default is `false`.
`printsummary`	Tells Ant to display simple statistics for each test. The values are `true`, `false`, and `withOutAndErr`. When testing, Ant usually swallows calls to `System.out` and `System.err`, but it won't if you use `withOutAndErr`. The default is `false`.
`reloading`	Sets whether the forked JVM should use a new classloader for every test, so this setting is ignored if `fork` is set to `false`. The default is `true`.

Table 8-1. *The <junit> Task's Attributes*

Attribute	Description
showoutput	Tells Ant to send output to its logs as well as the formatters specified (formatters are covered in the "Improving the Test with Better Output and Build Failure" section). The default is false (use only formatters).
tempdir	The temporary file that Ant will use. The default is this project's base directory.
timeout	Cancels any tests that take longer than this setting, which is measured in milliseconds. Ant ignores this attribute if fork is set to false. The default is to not time out.

The <junit> task also takes a number of nested elements, some of which you'll use in this example. For others, particularly those that work with forked JVMs, you should consult the Ant documentation.

You'll start by looking at the <classpath> and <test> nested elements because they are the basic elements and are the ones you'll use in every build. Listing 8-5 shows basic testing using a single test case.

Listing 8-5. *A Single Test Using the Test Classpath*

```
<target name="test" depends="compile-tests" description="Test the application">
  <echo message="Testing the application"/>
  <junit>
    <classpath refid="test.classpath"/>
    <test name="org.mwrm.WebTest"/>
  </junit>
</target>
```

The <classpath> attribute references the test classpath that you built in Listing 8-3. The <test> element's name attribute takes a fully qualified class name, which in this case is org.mwrm.WebTest. This class will run a test against the web application. To specify more tests, simply add more <test> elements, though I'll discuss the shortcomings of this in the "Using XML to Store Test Data" section.

If you were to run the test and it failed (as it should when you first write it), you'd see something like the following:

```
test:
   [echo] Testing the application
  [junit] Test org.mwrm.WebTest FAILED

BUILD SUCCESSFUL
```

The test case failed, but which test in the test case was it? This output is not very informative and won't help you diagnose which area of functionality failed the test. Therefore, the test is useless and might as well not have been run. Another odd thing about this result is that the build was successful, despite the test failure.

Improving the Test with Better Output and Build Failure

You can solve the problems of sparse output and erroneous build success easily by using two of the `<junit>` task's attributes, as shown in Table 8-1. Specifically, you can improve the sparse output by setting `printsummary` to `true`, and you can fail the build on a test failure by setting `haltonfailure` to `true`. Listing 8-6 shows this new setup.

Listing 8-6. *Improving the Output and Failing the Build When a Test Fails*

```
<target name="test" depends="compile-tests" description="Test the application">
  <echo message="Testing the application"/>
  <junit haltonfailure="true" printsummary="true">
    <classpath refid="test.classpath"/>
    <test name="org.mwrm.WebTest"/>
  </junit>
</target>
```

Now if you run this test, you get the following:

```
test:
   [echo] Testing the application
  [junit] Running org.mwrm.WebTest
  [junit] Tests run: 2, Failures: 1, Errors: 0, Time elapsed: 6.189 sec

BUILD FAILED
```

This is much better because the build now fails, and you can see that it was one out of two tests that failed. Note, however, that you still don't know which of the two tests failed. To further increase the functionality, you can add a formatter using the nested `<formatter>` element.

A formatter adds more information over and above the summary shown previously, and you can specify what format you want to use. The three choices are `brief`, `plain`, and `xml`. `brief` is a less verbose version of `plain`, which in turn displays a fair amount of information about the tests and what failures occurred. In this example, you'll use a plain formatter and return to XML in a moment. Listing 8-7 shows how to use a formatter.

Listing 8-7. *Using a Formatter to Improve the Output*

```
<target name="test" depends="compile-tests" description="Test the application">
  <echo message="Testing the application"/>
  <junit haltonfailure="true" printsummary="false">
    <classpath refid="test.classpath"/>
    <formatter type="brief" usefile="false"/>
    <test name="org.mwrm.WebTest"/>
  </junit>
</target>
```

Note that you set usefile to false, which means that Ant will print the results to the console. You also set printsummary to false to ensure that only the formatter writes to the console. The summary tells you the same kind of things as the formatter anyway.

If you want to use a file to store the output, omit this attribute or set it to true. The name of the resultant file is determined by the name of the test class and in the case of this test will be TEST-org.mwrm.WebTest.txt. If you were to use the XML formatter, it would be TEST-org.mwrm.WebTest.xml. In other words, TEST- is used as a prefix to the class name and an appropriate extension is used.

If you were to run the new target, you would see something like the following:

```
test:
   [echo] Testing the application
  [junit] Testsuite: org.mwrm.WebTest
  [junit] Tests run: 2, Failures: 1, Errors: 0, Time elapsed: 3.886 sec

  [junit] Testcase: testSession(org.mwrm.WebTest):        FAILED
  [junit] Session not cancelled after empty results
  [junit] junit.framework.AssertionFailedError: Session not cancelled after
empty results
  [junit]     at org.mwrm.WebTest.testSession(Unknown Source)



BUILD FAILED
```

This output shows you what you want to know: which tests failed and why. While this is just about readable, better ways exist to deal with test data, which brings me to XML.

Using XML to Store Test Data

Rather than using the brief and plain formatters to save data as plain text that you'll have to wade though, you should save data as XML, which is easier to manipulate should you want to examine the data. To do so, set the type attribute of the <formatter> element to xml, as shown in Listing 8-8.

Listing 8-8. *Saving Test Data As XML*

```
<target name="test" depends="compile-tests" description="Test the application">
  <echo message="Testing the application"/>
  <junit haltonfailure="true" printsummary="false">
    <classpath refid="test.classpath"/>
    <formatter type="brief" usefile="false"/>
    <formatter type="xml"/>
    <test todir="${test.junit.data}" name="org.mwrm.WebTest"/>
  </junit>
</target>
```

More is going on here than just setting the type attribute. You leave the original formatter so that you can examine the output on the console, and you add the todir attribute to the <test> element. This attribute tells the <junit> task where to write its data to, should it have a nested formatter that saves its data in a file. In other words, this tells the formatter where to write its XML files.

The output on the console will be the same as before, but you'll also have an XML file in the test.junit.data directory. If you open it, you'll see that the root element is called <testsuite> and contains a <properties> element that in turn contains a huge number of <property> elements. These elements are the properties that Ant knew about when it ran the test. The most important child elements of <testsuite>, however, are the <testcase> elements, as shown in Listing 8-9.

Listing 8-9. *An Abridged Test Result's XML File*

```
<?xml version="1.0" encoding="UTF-8" ?>
<testsuite errors="0" failures="1" hostname="localhost"
           name="org.mwrm.WebTest" tests="2" time="14.2"
           timestamp="2005-07-17T21:52:15">

<properties>
  ...
</properties>

<testcase classname="org.mwrm.WebTest" name="testIsRunning"
          time="8.602"></testcase>

<testcase classname="org.mwrm.WebTest" name="testSession"
          time="0.531">

  <failure message="Session not cancelled after empty results"
           type="junit.framework.AssertionFailedError">
    junit.framework.AssertionFailedError: Session not cancelled after empty
    results at org.mwrm.WebTest.testSession(Unknown Source)
  </failure>

</testcase>
</testsuite>
```

This is slightly more readable than the previous formatter's output and much easier to manipulate programmatically.

You're now at a stage where you have meaningful test output and can store the results of your tests for future examination. However, you've been running only one test case up until now. To add more, you would have to add more and more <test> nested elements, which is a headache and something you should not let developers or users do, or you would have to run them in batches.

Running a Batch of Tests

The <junit> task allows you to run a batch of tests at once and uses a file set to group these tests together. This means you must have a strong naming convention for your test cases. The naming convention should allow you to include all test cases easily while ignoring abstract and helper classes. The usual method is to end the name of test cases with Test. Thus, you have WebTest or ClientTest, not TestWeb.

With this in mind, let's use the <batchtest> element to include all the test cases. Listing 8-10 shows you how.

Listing 8-10. *Running All the Tests in a Batch*

```
<target name="test" depends="compile-tests" description="Test the application">
  <echo message="Testing the application"/>
  <junit haltonfailure="true" printsummary="false">
    <classpath refid="test.classpath"/>
    <formatter type="brief" usefile="false"/>
    <formatter type="xml"/>
    <batchtest todir="${test.junit.data}">
      <fileset dir="${test.build}" includes="**/*Test.class"/>
    </batchtest>
  </junit>
</target>
```

The todir attribute here replicates the todir attribute of the <test> element from before, while the file set simply includes all the test classes.

Creating a Report

The entire testing process is now automated, but you can still make more improvements. For example, you have lots of XML data to work with, which means you have to write parsing code to extract the data should you want to get any meaning from it. Luckily, the <junitreport> optional task is a built-in report generator that may well provide what you need. This report generator takes the results of all the tests, aggregates them into a master XML results file, and transforms them into an HTML report. Listing 8-11 shows how to use the <junitreport> element to create such a report.

Listing 8-11. *Creating an HTML Report*

```
<target name="test" depends="compile-tests" description="Test the application">
  <echo message="Testing the application"/>
  <junit haltonfailure="true" printsummary="false">
    <classpath refid="test.classpath"/>
    <formatter type="brief" usefile="false"/>
    <formatter type="xml"/>
    <batchtest todir="${test.junit.data}">
      <fileset dir="${test.build}" includes="**/*Test.class"/>
    </batchtest>
  </junit>
```

```
    <junitreport todir="${test.junit.data}">
      <fileset dir="${test.junit.data}">
        <include name="TEST-*.xml"/>
      </fileset>
      <report format="frames" todir="${test.junit.reports}"/>
    </junitreport>
  </target>
```

The todir attribute tells the report generator to construct the master XML file in the specified directory (in this case the same one that contains the other XML files). The nested file set tells the generator which files to use as the basis for its master XML file, and the <report> element specifies where to write the report. The format attribute of this element can be noframes or frames (the default). For now you are using the default style sheets that are embedded in the ANT_HOME/lib/ant-junit.jar file.

This approach has some problems as it stands, however: if you run this task and a test fails, Ant doesn't generate the reports because the build fails along with the test. In other words, Ant doesn't get to the <junitreport> element. To solve this, you can use the errorProperty and failureProperty attributes (set to the same property) of the <junit> task to indicate a failure and allow the build to continue until you reach the stage where you want to create a report. Once you have done so, you can use the <fail> task to fail the build if the property specified in errorProperty and failureProperty is set. Listing 8-12 shows this technique and also launches a browser to view the results instantly.

Listing 8-12. *Using errorProperty and failureProperty to Indicate a Build Failure*

```
<target name="test" depends="compile-tests" description="Test the application">
  <echo message="Testing the application"/>
  <junit printsummary="false"
         errorProperty="test.failed"
         failureProperty="test.failed">
    <classpath refid="test.classpath"/>
    <formatter type="brief" usefile="false"/>
    <formatter type="xml"/>
    <batchtest todir="${test.junit.data}">
      <fileset dir="${test.build}" includes="**/*Test.class"/>
    </batchtest>
  </junit>

  <junitreport todir="${test.junit.data}">
    <fileset dir="${test.junit.data}">
      <include name="TEST-*.xml"/>
    </fileset>
    <report format="frames" todir="${test.junit.reports}"/>
  </junitreport>

  <fail message="One or more tests failed.Check the reports
                in ${basedir}/${test.junit.reports}/index.html."
        if="test.failed"/>
</target>
```

Here, if any test causes an error or failure, you set the `test.failed` property. In turn, you have removed the `haltonfailure` attribute and added an explicit build failure that depends on the `test.failed` property. Now the build will run until the end of the target, no matter how many tests fail.

One final point is that you can specify your own style sheet for the XSL transformation using the `styledir` attribute of the `<report>` element. The style sheet for the report that uses frames must be called `junit-frames.xsl` and should be present in the directory specified in the `styledir` attribute. The style sheet for the report that doesn't use frames should be called `junit-noframes.xsl` and should also be placed in this directory. Here's an example:

```
<report format="frames" todir="${test.junit.reports}"
        styledir="${test.junit.style"/>
```

Running a Single Test in a Batch

The final embellishment to this testing regime is running a single test case instead of the whole batch, while still leaving the option to run the batch. This is useful when you want to test only one piece of functionality quickly without running the entire test suite. To do so, you use the same property for the `if` attribute of the `<test>` element and the `unless` attributes of the `<batchtest>` element, which makes them mutually exclusive. So, if you specify said property, Ant runs the test specified with the `<test>` element and ignores the `<batchtest>` element. The property will be the name of a test class, so you use the property in the name of the attribute of the `<test>` element too. Listing 8-13 shows the final target.

Listing 8-13. *Running a Single Test in a Batch*

```
<target name="test" depends="compile-tests" description="Test the application">
  <echo message="Testing the application"/>
  <junit printsummary="false"
         errorProperty="test.failed"
         failureProperty="test.failed">
    <classpath refid="test.classpath"/>
    <formatter type="brief" usefile="false"/>
    <formatter type="xml"/>
    <test if="test.class" name="${test.class}" todir="${test.junit.data}"/>
    <batchtest unless="test.class" todir="${test.junit.data}">
      <fileset dir="${test.build}" includes="**/*Test.class"/>
    </batchtest>
  </junit>

  <junitreport todir="${test.junit.data}">
    <fileset dir="${test.junit.data}">
      <include name="TEST-*.xml"/>
    </fileset>
    <report format="frames" todir="${test.junit.reports}"/>
  </junitreport>
```

```
    <fail message="One or more tests failed. Check the reports
                  in ${basedir}/${test.junit.reports}/index.html."
          if="test.failed"/>
  </target>
```

So, when you want to test a single piece of functionality, you can pass the name of a test class at the command line, and it is used by itself. Otherwise, every test runs.

Adding Dependency Checking to a Test Run

You have all you need to do the testing, but you don't necessarily want to run the tests during every build. For example, if the test classes have changed since the last build, you would want to run the build, but not if you have just updated some documentation or are just running the client again after a database update.

To check whether Ant will run the tests, you will create a `<condition>` task that consists of a number of nested `<uptodate>` conditions. Each of these `<uptodate>` conditions will check a part of the application to see whether it is as up to date as the binaries. The first check is to see whether the application source files are newer than the binaries. In this case, source files include Java files, JSP pages, HTML pages in the web application, configuration files, and so on. They do not include documentation or SQL files. Listing 8-14 shows the first set of checks. The `<condition>` task sets the `tests.notRequired` property to `true` if all the files are up to date. You can then use this to skip the tests.

Listing 8-14. *Checking the Application's Source Files*

```
  <!-- Check whether the tests should run -->
  <target name="check-tests" depends="test-init"
          description="Check whether the tests should run">
    <echo message="Checking whether the tests should run"/>

    <fileset id="shared-check" dir="${src.shared.root}"
             excludes="docs/**,**/*.sql,**/package.html"/>

    <condition property="tests.notRequired">

      <and>

        <uptodate targetfile="${appName.jar}">
          <srcfiles refid="shared-check"/>
        </uptodate>

        <uptodate targetfile="${appName.jar}">
          <srcfiles dir="${src.stand-alone.java}" includes="**/*.java"/>
        </uptodate>

        <uptodate targetfile="${appName.war}">
          <srcfiles refid="shared-check"/>
        </uptodate>
```

```
<uptodate targetfile="${appName.war}">
  <srcfiles dir="${src.web.root}"
            excludes="docs/**,**/${appName}.xml,**/package.html"/>
</uptodate>
```

The main points to note here are the filenames you are checking against (appName.jar and appName.war for the stand-alone and web applications, respectively) and the exclude and include patterns. When checking the shared code, you don't want to check any documentation, any SQL files, or any package.html Javadocs files, because they don't affect any functionality in your application.

The only files in the stand-alone code base you are interested in are Java source files. Therefore, you can use a single include pattern, which will also exclude the documentation by default. The web application has similar requirements to the shared code, except it does not contain SQL files and does contain a context XML file for hot deployment on Tomcat. You don't want to check that this file is up to date because the WAR file does not include it, so if you change it, the WAR file will be out-of-date until you change another component. You'd constantly be testing the WAR file but won't have changed any of its code.

The next check is against the test code. If the test code's source is newer than the test code's binaries, you want to do some testing. Listing 8-15 shows the next check.

Listing 8-15. *Checking the Test Source*

```
<uptodate>
  <srcfiles dir="${test.src}" includes="**/*.java"/>
  <globmapper from="*.java" to="${basedir}/${test.build}/*.class"/>
</uptodate>
```

In this case, you check the file set of Java files contained in the test source directory against the file set of class files. The <globmapper> element maps values from the source file set to the target file set before the <uptodate> element checks them. You'll see more of mappers in Chapter 11.

You also need to know whether the last build failed. This is an important piece of information because even if you don't alter the application's source files or the test's source code, tests can fail. If a test failed, you want to run the tests again regardless of the state of the code. With this in mind, use a marker file to indicate whether a test failed, like so:

```
last.test.failed.file=failed.txt
```

This will be created as part of the test target, just before you call the <fail> task, but you need to add the check for it in the <condition> task, as shown in Listing 8-16.

Listing 8-16. *Checking Whether the Last Test Failed*

```
<not>
  <available file="${last.test.failed.file}"/>
</not>
```

You also face a problem if someone wants to run a single test, as described in the "Running a Single Test in a Batch" section. In this case, let's assume they want to run the test regardless of anything else. You therefore need to check for the presence of the command-line property that specified the test to run, as shown in Listing 8-17.

Listing 8-17. *Checking That a User Wants to Run a Single Test*

```
        <not>
          <isset property="test.class"/>
        </not>

      </and>
    </condition>
  </target>
```

That's the end of the checking target, so all that's left is to modify the test target discussed previously. Listing 8-18 shows the new and improved target.

Listing 8-18. *Running the Tests After Checking Whether You Should*

```
  <!-- Test the application -->
  <target name="test" depends="check-tests,compile-tests"
          unless="tests.notRequired"
          description="Test the application">
    <echo message="Testing the application"/>

    <junit printsummary="false"
           errorProperty="test.failed"
           failureProperty="test.failed">
      <classpath refid="test.classpath"/>
      <formatter type="brief" usefile="false"/>
      <formatter type="xml"/>
      <test name="${test.class}" todir="${test.junit.data}" if="test.class"/>
      <batchtest todir="${test.junit.data}" unless="test.class">
        <fileset dir="${test.build}" includes="**/*Test.class"/>
      </batchtest>
    </junit>

    <junitreport todir="${test.junit.data}">
      <fileset dir="${test.junit.data}">
        <include name="TEST-*.xml"/>
      </fileset>
      <report format="frames" todir="${test.junit.reports}"/>
    </junitreport>

    <echo message="The last test run failed."
          file="${last.test.failed.file}"/>
```

```
<fail message="One or more tests failed. Check the reports
              in ${basedir}/${test.junit.reports}/index.html."
      if="test.failed"/>

  <delete file="${last.test.failed.file}"/>
</target>
```

This time you run the target only if the checks were passed. After that, the target should be familiar until the second <echo> task. Here you create the file that indicates that the build failed. If the build fails, then you leave the file intact; if it doesn't, you delete it.

Using a JAR File for Batch Tests

Future versions of Ant (1.7 and greater) are likely to allow you to use JAR files as the basis of your batch test. Listing 8-19 shows how.

Listing 8-19. *Using a JAR As the Basis of a Batch Test*

```
<zipfileset id="jarbatch" src="${appName-test.jar}"
            includes="**/*Test.class" />

<junit printsummary="false"
       errorProperty="test.failed"
       failureProperty="test.failed">
  <classpath refid="test.classpath"/>
  <formatter type="brief" usefile="false"/>
  <formatter type="xml"/>
  <batchtest todir="${test.junit.data}">
    <fileset refid="jarbatch"/>
  </batchtest>
</junit>
```

The <zipfileset> element holds the contents of a JAR file as a file set, which you then use as you would any other file set. Versions of Ant prior to 1.7 do not replace the / file separator with . and thus throw `FileNotFoundException` when trying to create a file in the `test.junit.data` directory. In other words, Ant tries to place the data in a file called `TEST-org/mwrm/Test.xml` instead of a file called `TEST-org.mwrm.Test.xml`. The `org/mwrm` directory does not exist at run time, so Ant can't find it.

Testing Code Conventions

Unit testing is an important part of any project, but another aspect of testing is checking the code against code conventions. Code conventions certainly matter in large projects where many developers will be working on the code. Standardizing the layout and naming conventions means that it's easier for a developer to come to grips with a new piece of code written by someone else on the team. Standardizing code in small projects is equally important, because it allows for clear layout and allows you to come to grips with your code if you return to it after a gap in development. As you've seen a few times in this book, you may not be the sole maintainer of the piece of code in perpetuity.

You can choose from a number of code convention checkers, but I'll show you how to use Checkstyle (`checkstyle.sourceforge.net`) in this chapter. Its one big advantage as far as this chapter is concerned is that it comes with an Ant task. This makes it easy for you to insert convention checking into your testing regime. I won't go into how to configure Checkstyle because it comes with two excellent coding convention definitions written in XML, one of which is the Sun coding convention as used by the Ant project. You will use this definition.

Download the binary distribution, and extract it to your file system. The JAR file you will use is `checkstyle.jar`. This contains the Ant task, Checkstyle's main classes, and a task definition file. I haven't shown a task definition file before, so it will be a useful exercise to demonstrate how to implement it.

The `<checkstyle>` task is fairly similar to the JUnit tasks you saw previously, so the concepts in this section will be familiar to you. It has the attributes defined in Table 8-2.

Table 8-2. *The `<checkstyle>` Task's Attributes*

Attribute	Description
`classpath`	The classpath to use. The default is Ant's classpath.
`classpathref`	A reference to a path defined earlier in the build. The default is Ant's classpath.
`config`	The coding convention definition XML file. You must specify one of `config` or `configURL`.
`configURL`	The URL of the coding convention definition XML file. You must specify one of `config` or `configURL`.
`failOnViolation`	Tells Ant whether to fail the build if the code fails the check. The default is `true`, which is the opposite of the `<junit>` task's `haltonerror` attribute's default.
`failureProperty`	The name of a property to set if the check failed. The default is `null`.
`file`	The file on which to run the style check. You can also specify file sets with nested `<fileset>` elements. This is required unless you specify a file set.
`maxErrors`	The maximum number of errors that Checkstyle will tolerate before the check fails. The default is zero.
`maxWarnings`	The maximum number of warnings that Checkstyle will tolerate before the check fails. The default is `Integer.MAX_VALUE` (`2147483647`).
`packageNamesFile`	A file that contains package names for custom code-checking modules. The default is `null`.
`properties`	A properties file that contains property values to use in the convention XML file. Nested `<property>` elements and Ant properties override properties set in this file.

The <checkstyle> task takes four nested elements: <fileset>, <classpath>, <formatter>, and <property>. I'll cover the <formatter> element in the course of the example. The <property> element takes a mandatory key attribute and either a value attribute or a file attribute. The latter is a path relative to the build's base directory.

Using the <checkstyle> Task

The goal of this section is to replicate the JUnit test regime with your Checkstyle tests. In other words, you'll apply a structure to the Checkstyle test targets that is analogous to the JUnit test targets because their features are so similar.

Before you start the check, you need to specify the location of Checkstyle in the file system. This will allow you to use Checkstyle's coding convention files and its report-formatting files. You also need to define the location of your test report data and the report. Set the following properties in the build.properties file like so:

```
checkstyle.home=C:/checkstyle
test.checkstyle.reports=${test.build}/reports/checkstyle
test.checkstyle.data=${test.build}/data/checkstyle
```

You also need to treat the report directories in the same way as the JUnit report directories. In other words, you need fresh copies of the data and the report for each build. Listing 8-20 shows the modified test-init target.

Listing 8-20. *Initializing the Testing Environment*

```
<!-- Prepare the test directories -->
<target name="test-init" description="Prepare the test directories">
  <echo message="Preparing the test directories"/>
  <delete dir="${test.junit.reports}"/>
  <delete dir="${test.junit.data}"/>
  <delete dir="${test.checkstyle.reports}"/>
  <delete dir="${test.checkstyle.data}"/>
  <mkdir dir="${test.build}"/>
  <mkdir dir="${test.junit.reports}"/>
  <mkdir dir="${test.junit.data}"/>
  <mkdir dir="${test.checkstyle.reports}"/>
  <mkdir dir="${test.checkstyle.data}"/>
</target>
```

To use the <checkstyle> task, you'll have to include it in Ant's classpath by copying checkstyle-3.5.jar to ANT_HOME/lib or by pointing to it with the -lib command-line option. This JAR file contains a task definition file called checkstyletask.properties, which contains the following line:

```
checkstyle=com.puppycrawl.tools.checkstyle.CheckStyleTask
```

This defines the <checkstyle> task and tells Ant which class to use to represent the task in the build. To reference this file, you use the resource attribute of the <taskdef> task, as shown in Listing 8-21. You'll also use the Sun coding conventions as provided by Checkstyle.

Listing 8-21. *Defining and Using the <checkstyle> Task*

```
<taskdef resource="checkstyletask.properties"/>
<checkstyle config="${checkstyle.home}/sun_checks.xml"
            failOnViolation="false">
  <formatter type="xml"
             tofile="${test.checkstyle.data}/checkstyle_report.xml"/>
  <fileset refid="javadoc"/>
</checkstyle>
```

You want to check all the Java source files, so you use the javadoc file set from Chapter 6. This includes all the source directories and is a convenient collection to use for your tests. You set the <formatter> element's type attribute to xml, which creates an XML file of the results. This in turn allows you to use an XSLT style sheet (provided with Checkstyle) to create an HTML report of the check. To get to that stage, though, you have to set failOnViolation to false, which is analogous to the JUnit tests you ran previously.

Transforming XML to HTML

Ant's <xslt> core task is ideal for transforming your XML results file into an HTML report. As already mentioned, Checkstyle comes with XSLT style sheets. These are in the checkstyle.home/contrib directory and are also analogous to those provided by JUnit.

The <xslt> task has a huge number of attributes, so I won't cover all of them. Instead, I'll cover those pertinent to transforming your XML report into an HTML report. The in attribute specifies the source XML file, the out attribute is the file that results from the transformation, and the style attribute is the style sheet to use in the transformation. Listing 8-22 shows the transformation.

Listing 8-22. *Transforming an XML Report into an HTML Report*

```
<xslt in="${test.checkstyle.data}/checkstyle_report.xml"
      out="${test.checkstyle.reports}/checkstyle_report.html"
      style="${checkstyle.home}/contrib/checkstyle-noframes-sorted.xsl"/>
```

If you decided to use one of the frames-based style sheets provided by Checkstyle, the file specified in the out attribute will be empty, and you should view the index.html file in the reports directory instead.

You still have a discrepancy between your Checkstyle test and your JUnit test. If you recall from the previous discussion, your JUnit tests generate a report whether your code passes them or not, which is how your Checkstyle tests operate. However, in the case of the JUnit tests, Ant fails the build if your code fails the JUnit tests. To do that with your Checkstyle tests, you'll have to use the <fail> task and a property again. Listing 8-23 shows the final version of your Checkstyle test target.

Listing 8-23. *The Checkstyle Test Target*

```
<!-- Check the coding conventions -->
<target name="coding-style" depends="test-init"
        description="Check the coding conventions">
  <echo message="Checking the coding conventions"/>
  <taskdef resource="checkstyletask.properties"/>
  <checkstyle config="${checkstyle.home}/sun_checks.xml"
              failOnViolation="false"
              failureProperty="checkstyle.failed">
    <formatter type="xml"
               tofile="${test.checkstyle.data}/checkstyle_report.xml"/>
    <fileset refid="javadoc"/>
  </checkstyle>
  <xslt in="${test.checkstyle.data}/checkstyle_report.xml"
        out="${test.checkstyle.reports}/checkstyle_report.html"
        style="${checkstyle.home}/contrib/checkstyle-frames.xsl"/>

  <fail message="One or more Checkstyle checks failed.
                 Check the reports in ${basedir}/${test.checkstyle.reports}"
        if="checkstyle.failed"/>
</target>
```

So, now you have replicated the JUnit test regime with your Checkstyle tests.

Summary

This chapter ran through adding JUnit unit testing to Ant by progressively building a testing target. I covered how to install the testing frameworks and how to organize tests within the project's directory structure. This is important because you do not want to mix application code with testing code, though mirroring the application's package structure is a useful technique.

You saw how you should initialize the testing environment as carefully as the build environment. Ant's JUnit tasks do not check for old data or test results, so you must clear away old results yourself to ensure accurate analysis. Once you have done this, you compile the testing classes and run the tests.

The default settings for Ant's JUnit tasks are not enough for most purposes, so you added a great deal of functionality to your testing targets. You now have a fairly complex and powerful testing target suitable for most builds.

CHAPTER 9

Using Ant in Large Projects

One of the beauties of Ant is that it scales extremely well with your projects. As your projects get larger and more complicated, so will your build files. This means you need to have a better way of managing your projects than a single monolithic build file. The answer is to use a master build file to control the common elements of your build while placing build instructions for each part of your project into subordinate build files.

You have seen in previous chapters how the build file describes the structure of your build. Splitting a build into separate build files, with each representing a single part of your build, follows this methodology. In other words, your build is split so your build file (now files) reflect the structure of the build.

This chapter will take you through the issues you must consider when working with large, complex builds. The example application is split into two separate applications that share core utility classes. This is an ideal structure to demonstrate how to use subordinate build files that are controlled by a master build file.

In this kind of scenario, the master build file will control the entire build and will call subordinate build files at appropriate times to mimic a build where all the targets are in one file. This means you have to ensure that each subordinate build file encapsulates a discrete piece of the build. If it depends on another subordinate build, then it is up to the master build file to run the subordinate builds in the correct order. Allowing subordinate builds to call each other can lead to problems and maintenance issues. Therefore, the subordinate build files cannot operate on their own and must be part of a larger build.

If you are developing a major project that has a number of facets, then it is usual practice to split the whole project into separate components that reflect each of these facets. As you've already seen in earlier chapters, you can easily split a project into shared utility code, GUI code, stand-alone clients, web applications, and so on. Each of these facets can quite easily sit in its own directory structure, quite separate from the other facets.

This helps the development team in a number of ways and lets each developer work on their own section of the application without fear of interference from another developer. This also means that the conceptually separate parts are kept apart physically as well.

None of this is new to you, especially because I've discussed it all earlier in the book. However, so far you've handled this situation with a single build file and a single properties file for the entire example application. The application is sufficiently complicated that you could easily use a separate build file for each facet of it. This means the massive build file (which is 1,273 lines long in my version) will be easier to manage and maintain. Another advantage is that you can edit each subordinate build file without changing the master build file, giving you more control over the whole build.

Using Master Build Files and Ant Delegation

The master build file should contain all the information and targets that are shared by all subprojects. This may sound pretty intuitive, but it can lead to some interesting problems. For example, if many of your subproject targets depend on an initialization target to create scratch directories (much like the `dir` initialization target), when you move them you will not be able to use the `depends` attribute of your subprojects' `<target>` elements to refer to the master build file. This means you will have to either replicate the `dir` target in each subproject's build file or make sure every target in the master build file that can call a subproject has a `depends` attribute that points to the master `dir` target. You'll return to this kind of problem when you alter the example application's build process in the next section.

Another thing to remember is that subordinate builds should not normally call other subordinate builds. It is the job of the master build file to group many subordinate builds into a coherent build. If one subordinate build relies on another, it is up to the master build file to enforce this relationship, just as it controls the dependencies.

Let's look at the example application and identify areas where you can instigate subordinate build files. The most obvious areas are the stand-alone application and the web application. However, as Figure 9-1 shows, you can potentially create subordinate builds in a few more areas.

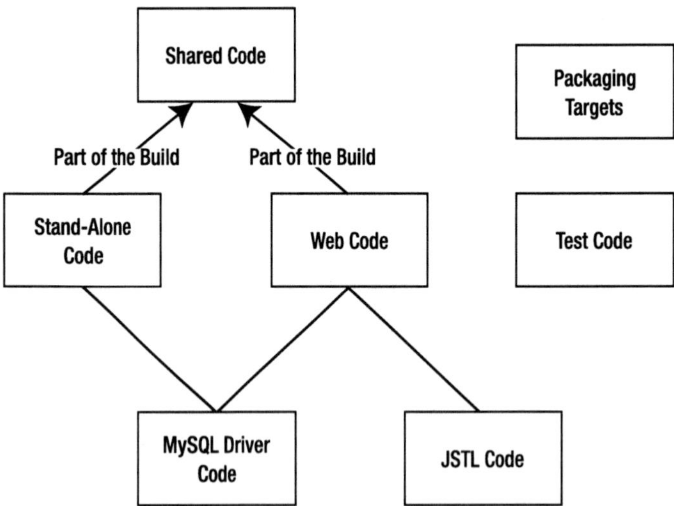

Figure 9-1. *The main portions of the example application's build*

Of the components listed in Figure 9-1, only the shared code is built as part of another component's build. In other words, the shared code is really a part of the build for the stand-alone code as well as being part of the build for the web application. This means ties exist between these two components and the final location of the compiled shared files. You can handle this with properties, so it should not cause any extra problems.

Every other component is completely separate from the others; therefore, those components are excellent candidates for subordinate builds.

Moving Ant Tasks to Subordinate Build Files

The first point to remember when moving targets to subordinate build files is that you cannot use the depends attribute of a <target> element to reference common targets. As you move targets into the new build file, you must note which targets it depends on and ensure that the master build file runs these targets before it calls the subordinate build file. A second, related issue is that the targets in the subordinate build file are no longer available to the master build file's depends attributes either, which means you must use the <ant> task (see Table 9-1) to call the subordinate build file if a master file depends on one of its targets. This can lead to a fair amount of spaghetti programming, but if your build file has definite endpoints that simply pull together the different build paths, your build will not be affected.

Table 9-1. *The <ant> Task's Attributes*

Attribute	Description
antfile	The name of the build file to use. This is a relative file path and uses the value of the dir attribute as the root of the path. The default is build.xml.
dir	Overrides the base directory for the project you are calling. The default is the current project's base directory, unless you set inheritAll to false, and then there is no default value, which means the base directory of the subordinate project is the value of its own basedir attribute.
inheritAll	Tells Ant whether to pass properties from the master build to the subordinate build. If set to false, Ant passes command-line properties only to the subordinate build. If set to true, Ant overrides any properties set in the subordinate build. The default is true.
inheritRefs	Tells Ant whether to pass references to the subordinate build. The default is false.
output	The file where you would like to store Ant's output. This is relative to the base directory of the subordinate build, which you can change with the dir attribute. The default is null.
target	The name of the target you want to run in the subordinate build. The default is the subordinate build's default target.

The <ant> task can also have nested <property>, <propertyset>, <reference>, and <target> elements. The <property> element is identical to the <property> task you saw in Chapter 3 and sets a property to pass to the new build. These properties are as powerful as those you set at the command line. Ant resolves any references in the master build before passing the property to the subordinate build. Chapter 3 described the <propertyset> element.

If you want to pass some references to the subordinate build only, you can set the inheritRefs attribute to false and specify those references you are interested in by using nested <reference> elements, like so:

```
<ant inheritRefs="false">
  <reference refid="build.classpath"/>
  <reference refid="javadoc" torefid="master.javadoc"/>
  <target name="build-both"/>
</ant>
```

The first element passes the build.classpath path to the subordinate build. The second passes the javadoc path to the subordinate build, but makes it available under the master.javadoc reference ID. The <target> element tells Ant to run the target specified in the name attribute. This is a useful element if you want to run a number of targets in the same subordinate build file. If you specify more than one target, Ant makes them depend on one another in the order you specify them.

Preparing for the Move

A useful technique when using subordinate builds is to leave a version of endpoint targets, such as package-web, in the master build file and use them to pull together the various subordinate builds as if these subordinate builds were called by the original target's depends attribute. In other words, some targets will produce the same results as before, but the tasks that do the work will be in subordinate build files. One useful side effect of this technique is that other types of targets, such as the packaging targets, usually depend on endpoint targets. By keeping these endpoint targets, you avoid breaking other parts of the build. Therefore, you keep the same external interface to other parts of the build while changing the location of the tasks. You'll see more of this as you go through this chapter.

Before you begin moving targets, you need a few properties in the properties file so that you have central control over the names of the subordinate files. Listing 9-1 shows the names of the files you'll be using.

Listing 9-1. *The Names of the Subordinate Build Files*

```
build.shared.xml=${src.shared.root}/build.xml
build.stand-alone.xml=${src.stand-alone.root}/build.xml
build.web.xml=${src.web.root}/build.xml
build.package.xml=build.package.xml
build.test.xml=${test.src}/build.xml

build.jstl.xml=build.jstl.xml
build.mysql.xml=build.mysql.xml
```

Moving the Third-Party Build Targets

The simplest moves are the targets that build the third-party libraries (JSTL and MySQL connector). They do not depend on anything but the dir target, which you will not be moving. However, you'll ensure that the dir target is called before any subordinate builds run. Create a file called build.mysql.xml, and place it in the example application's base directory. Listing 9-2 shows its contents. The one change from the master build file is in bold.

Listing 9-2. *The MySQL Connector Subordinate Build File*

```
<?xml version="1.0"?>

<project name="MySQL Connector Build"
         default="build-mysql-connector" basedir=".">

  <!-- CVSROOT for the MySQL connector -->
  <property name="mysql.cvsroot"
            value=":pserver:anonymous@cvs.sourceforge.net:/cvsroot/mmmysql" />

  <!-- Update or check out required sources from CVS for the MySQL connector -->
  <target name="checkout-mysql-connector"
          description="Update or check out required sources from CVS
                       for the MySQL connector">

    <echo message="Checking out the required sources from CVS
                   for the MySQL connector" />

    <cvs cvsroot="${mysql.cvsroot}" quiet="true"
         command="checkout" package="${mysql.build}"
         dest="${build}" compression="true" />
  </target>

  <!-- Build the MySQL connector from source -->
  <target name="build-mysql-connector" depends="checkout-mysql-connector"
          description="Build the MySQL connector from source">
    <echo message="Building the MySQL connector from source"/>

    <!-- The MySQL connector file needs this directory to exist -->
    <!-- Therefore we need to create it -->
    <mkdir dir="${build}/dist-mysql-jdbc"/>

    <ant antfile="build.xml" dir="${build}/${mysql.build}"/>

    <copy tofile="${mysql.jar}">
      <fileset dir="${build}/build-mysql-jdbc">
        <include name="mysql-connector*/*.jar"/>
      </fileset>
    </copy>
  </target>

</project>
```

The `build.jstl.xml` file is similarly straightforward, as shown in Listing 9-3.

Listing 9-3. *The JSTL Subordinate Build File*

```
<?xml version="1.0"?>

<project name="JSTL Build" default="build-jstl" basedir=".">

  <!-- ################################### -->
  <!-- CVS properties                      -->
  <!-- ################################### -->

  <!-- CVSROOT for the JSTL -->
  <property name="cvsroot"
            value=":pserver:anoncvs@cvs.apache.org:/home/cvspublic" />

  <!-- ################################################### -->
  <!-- CVS and build tasks for the JSTL and MySQL connector -->
  <!-- ################################################### -->

  <!-- Update or check out required sources from CVS for the JSTL -->
  <target name="checkout-jstl"
          description="Update or check out required sources from CVS
                       for the JSTL">

    <echo message="Checking out the required JSTL sources from CVS"/>

    <cvs cvsroot="${cvsroot}" quiet="true"
         command="checkout -P ${jstl.build}"
         dest="${build}" compression="true" />

  </target>

  <!-- Build the JSTL from source -->
  <target name="build-jstl" depends="checkout-jstl"
          description="Build the JSTL from source">
    <echo message="Building the JSTL from source"/>

    <ant antfile="build.xml" dir="${build}/${jstl.build}"/>

    <copy todir="${lib}">
      <fileset dir="${build}/${jstl.build}/${build}/lib">
        <include name="*.jar"/>
      </fileset>
    </copy>
  </target>

</project>
```

You can now call these targets from other build files using the `<ant>` task.

Moving the Shared Build Targets

Let's start to move the shared build into a build file in the shared source tree. This is a simple operation in this application because the shared build is completed by a <javac> command in the stand-alone build or the web build, as appropriate. As such, it depends only on the dir target, though the master build file will take care of that before calling either the stand-alone build or the web subordinate build. This in turn ensures that the shared code's dependency is covered.

Create a file called build.xml, and place it in the src/shared directory. Once you have done this, move the <javac> command from the master build file into it, as shown in Listing 9-4.

Listing 9-4. *The Shared Code's Subordinate Build File*

```
<?xml version="1.0"?>

<project name="Shared Code Build" default="compile-shared" basedir=".">

  <!-- Compile shared code -->
  <target name="compile-shared" description="Compile shared code">
    <echo message="Compiling the shared code"/>
    <javac srcdir="${src.shared.java}" destdir="${destination}"/>
  </target>

</project>
```

To make it compatible with the two main components of the application, you leave the destination as a property that the calling build file must set. This allows the stand-alone and web builds to control the position of their files independently.

Moving the Application-Specific Build Targets

Now you should move the stand-alone build's targets to a subordinate build file. (You'll get to the master build file once you've competed the subordinate files.) Create a file called build.xml, and place it in the src/stand-alone directory. The first stand-alone target in the master build file is compile-stand-alone. The two differences will be that it cannot depend on the dir target, and it cannot contain the shared code's <javac> task. The master build file will ensure that it runs the dir target and will call the shared subordinate build before calling the stand-alone subordinate build. Listing 9-5 shows the start of the stand-alone build's build file.

Listing 9-5. *The Beginning of the Stand-Alone Subordinate Build File*

```
<?xml version="1.0"?>

<project name="Example Application Build"
         default="package-stand-alone" basedir=".">

  <!-- ############################ -->
  <!-- The stand-alone application -->
  <!-- ############################ -->
```

```
<!-- Compile the stand-alone application -->
<target name="compile-stand-alone"
        description="Compile the stand-alone application">

  <echo message="Compiling the stand-alone application"/>
  <javac srcdir="${src.stand-alone.java}" destdir="${build.stand-alone.root}"/>
</target>
```

Listing 9-6 shows the other stand-alone target you are moving. The process of creating a JAR file of the stand-alone application does not change when you move it into the subordinate file, though you should consider some dependencies. Again, you'll use the `<ant>` task in the master build file to point to this target should it be necessary. Note that the `stand-alone-complete` target stays in the master build file because it needs to call other subordinate builds, such as the shared build and the MySQL connector build.

Listing 9-6. *Moving the Packaging Build*

```
<!-- Package the stand-alone application -->
<target name="package-stand-alone" depends="compile-stand-alone"
        description="Package the stand-alone application">
  <echo message="Creating the stand-alone JAR file"/>
  <copy file="${database.properties}" todir="${build.stand-alone.root}"/>
  <jar destfile="${appName.jar}" basedir="${build.stand-alone.root}"/>
</target>
```

You will still retain a `package-stand-alone` target in the master build file. This target will perform the same function as the old `package-stand-alone` target, but will use subordinate builds to do so. This allows you to maintain a number of dependencies, such as the one from `stand-alone-complete`.

You won't move the two targets that run the stand-alone application because they are really part of a master build.

That's it for the stand-alone application. You have moved all the stand-alone targets into a subordinate build file, and now you have to do the same for the web application. The process is similar, so there is no need to show it here.

Moving the Packaging Targets

The packaging targets, including those targets that build the documentation bundles, are large and complex enough that you can justify giving them their own subordinate build. The process for this is again quite simple. Copy all the packaging-related tasks into a file called `build.➥package.xml`, and remove any dependencies on `dir`, `package-stand-alone`, and `package-web`. Again, you'll call these targets from the master build file. You'll also add a new default target to run the `zip-all` and `tar-all` targets, as shown in Listing 9-7.

Listing 9-7. *The Zip and Tar Tasks' Subordinate Build*

```
<?xml version="1.0"?>

<project name="Example Application Package Build"
        default="package-all" basedir=".">

  <!-- ######################################## -->
  <!-- Packaging the distribution               -->
  <!-- ######################################## -->

  ...

  <!-- Zip the binary and source distributions -->
  <target name="zip-all" depends="zip-src,zip-bin"
          description="Zip the binary and source distributions">
    <echo message="Zipped the binary and source distributions"/>
  </target>

  <!-- Tar the binary and source distributions -->
  <target name="tar-all" depends="tar-src,tar-bin"
          description="Tar the binary and source distributions">
    <echo message="Tarred the binary and source distributions"/>
  </target>

  <!-- Create all the packages -->
  <target name="package-all" depends="zip-all,tar-all"
          description="Create all the packages">
    <echo message="Created all the packages"/>
  </target>

</project>
```

Leave `zip-all` and `tar-all` targets in the master build file. These targets will ensure that Ant builds the application before they call their namesakes in the subordinate build. As a consequence, the distribution targets will break, but I'll cover that in the "Changing the Master Build File" section.

Moving the Test Targets

Moving the test targets is easy. They largely depend on each other, though the `compile-tests` target depends on targets that compile both applications. You can easily solve this, however. First, place all the test targets in a file called `test/build.xml`. As you have done before, you leave a master build target that compiles both applications before running the JUnit tests. Second, you also leave a master build target that runs the Checkstyle tests. Listing 9-8 shows the skeleton of the testing build file.

Listing 9-8. *The <project> Element of the Test Subordinate Build File*

```
<?xml version="1.0"?>

<project name="Testing Build" default="test-all" basedir=".">

  ...

  <!-- Run all the tests -->
  <target name="test-all" depends="test,coding-style"
          description="Run all the tests">
    <echo message="All the tests have finished"/>
  </target>

</project>
```

Changing the Master Build File

The first change you'll make in the master build file is to exclude XML files from the Javadoc process. As things stand, the <javadoc> tasks will fail because the subordinate build XML files are included in their classpath and don't correspond to a Java file. To remedy this, you need to add a new <exclude> element to the Javadoc classpath, as shown in Listing 9-9. This is something to consider when building archives of binary files because you usually don't want to include the build files in a binary distribution. In this case, you are quite specific about the files to include in any archiving task, so there is no danger of including rogue subordinate build files.

Listing 9-9. *Excluding the Subordinate Build Files from the Javadoc Classpath*

```
  <!-- ################################### -->
  <!-- Javadoc file sets                   -->
  <!-- ################################### -->

  <fileset id="javadoc" dir="${src}">
    <exclude name="*/conf/**"/>
    <exclude name="*/docs/*"/>
    <exclude name="**/package.html"/>
    <exclude name="**/*.xml"/>
    <include name="shared/**"/>
    <include name="stand-alone/**"/>
    <include name="web/java/**"/>
  </fileset>
```

You remove some targets from the master build file and place them in subordinate build files. However, to maintain the structure of the master build, you need to call them as if they were in the master build file. In other words, the master build still has to contain a target that packages the stand-alone application. The difference is that all the implementation details are in the subordinate build. Listing 9-10 shows the two targets that deal with the stand-alone build.

Listing 9-10. *The Master Build Targets That Build the Stand-Alone Application*

```
<!-- ############################ -->
<!-- The stand-alone application -->
<!-- ############################ -->

<!-- Compile the stand-alone application -->
<target name="package-stand-alone" depends="dir"
        description="Compile stand-alone application">
  <echo message="Compiling the stand-alone application"/>
  <!-- First let's compile the shared code -->
  <property name="destination" value="${build.stand-alone.root}"/>
  <ant antfile="${build.shared.xml}" inheritRefs="true"/>
  <ant antfile="${build.stand-alone.xml}" inheritRefs="true"/>
</target>

<target name="stand-alone-complete" depends="dir"
        description="Compile stand-alone application,
        using CVS version of the MySQL connector">
  <echo message="Compiling stand-alone application,
                 using CVS versions of the MySQL connector"/>
  <ant antfile="${build.mysql.xml}" inheritRefs="true"/>
  <antcall target="package-stand-alone"/>
</target>
```

By maintaining a package-stand-alone target, you ensure that the tasks that rely on it (packaging and distribution tasks, for example) don't break. It is simply a placeholder for the appropriate subordinate builds. The same goes for stand-alone-complete.

Here you set the inheritRefs attribute of the <ant> task to true. This makes sure the subordinate builds have access to the build classpath and other necessary file sets. Without these references, you could not maintain a centralized master build file and would have to scatter build classpath definitions throughout the subordinate build files.

The final thing to note is that you use an <antcall> task to maintain the order of execution. In this case, you want Ant to build the MySQL connector before you compile the application and create its JAR file. The only way to ensure that a master target runs following a call to a subordinate build is to use an <antcall>.

The web application targets follow along the same lines, as shown in Listing 9-11.

Listing 9-11. *The Master Build Targets That Build the Web Application*

```
<!-- ############################ -->
<!-- The web application          -->
<!-- ############################ -->

<!-- Build the WAR file in one step -->
<target name="package-web" depends="dir"
        description="Build the WAR file in one step">
  <echo message="Building the WAR file in one step"/>
```

```
    <!-- First let's compile the shared code -->
    <property name="destination" value="${build.stand-alone.root}"/>
    <ant antfile="${build.shared.xml}" inheritRefs="true"/>
    <ant antfile="${build.web.xml}" inheritRefs="true"/>
  </target>

  <target name="web-complete"
          description="Compile web application,
                       using CVS versions of the MySQL connector and the JSTL">
    <echo message="Compiled web application,
                   using CVS versions of the MySQL connector and the JSTL"/>
    <ant antfile="${build.mysql.xml}" inheritRefs="true"/>
    <ant antfile="${build.jstl.xml}" inheritRefs="true"/>
    <antcall target="package-web"/>
  </target>
```

This time you use the web subordinate build in `package-web` and build the JSTL source in `web-complete`. This means the master build can still use `build-both` and `build-all` as before.

You also need to modify the master packaging targets, `zip-all` and `tar-all`. You'll also add a target that calls the default target in the package build, which is called `package-all`. All these targets ensure that Ant compiles the code before the packaging tasks run, as shown in Listing 9-12.

Listing 9-12. *The Master Build Targets That Package the Application*

```
  <!-- Zip the binary and source distributions -->
  <target name="zip-all" depends="package-stand-alone, package-web"
          description="Zip the binary and source distributions">
    <echo message="Zipping the binary and source distributions"/>
    <ant antfile="${build.package.xml}" target="zip-all" inheritRefs="true"/>
  </target>

  <!-- Tar the binary and source distributions -->
  <target name="tar-all" depends="package-stand-alone, package-web"
          description="Tar the binary and source distributions">
    <echo message="Tarring the binary and source distributions"/>
    <ant antfile="${build.package.xml}" target="tar-all" inheritRefs="true"/>
  </target>

  <!-- Create all the packages -->
  <target name="package-all" depends="package-stand-alone, package-web"
          description="Create all the packages">
    <echo message="Creating all the packages"/>
    <ant antfile="${build.package.xml}" inheritRefs="true"/>
  </target>
```

You'll have to change all the distribution targets because they depend on various packaging targets, all of which you have moved to a subordinate build. You have only three packaging targets to choose from now, and since the distribution targets deal with zip and tar files, you'll use package-all. This may be inefficient for the first run of the build because you'll package everything, regardless of what you want to distribute, but chances are you'll want to distribute everything at some point anyway.

Subsequent runs of the build will create only those distributions you have changed, so package-all acts as if it were, for example, zip-docs and tar-docs if the documentation is the only thing that has changed. Listing 9-13 shows one of the distribution targets as an example of the change.

Listing 9-13. *The Distribution Targets All Now Depend on package-all*

```
<!-- Place the documentation on FTP -->
<target name="ftp-docs" depends="package-all"
        description="Place the documentation on FTP">
  <echo message="Placing the documentation on FTP"/>
  <ftp server="${ftp.server}"
       userid="${ftp.user}"
       password="${ftp.password}"
       remotedir="${ftp.src.dir}"
       action="send"
       newer="true"
       timediffauto="true">
    <fileset dir="${dist}">
      <include name="${appName}-${package.docs}.*"/>
    </fileset>
  </ftp>
</target>
```

The targets that run the tests follow the same pattern as those that package the application. You maintain a test target as the entry point into the JUnit testing regime and a coding-style target as the entry point into the Checkstyle style-checking regime. You'll also add a master test target that runs both regimes by calling the default target in the test subordinate build file. Listing 9-14 shows these targets.

Listing 9-14. *The Master Build Targets That Test the Application*

```
<!-- ################################### -->
<!-- Testing targets                     -->
<!-- ################################### -->

<!-- Run the JUnit tests -->
<target name="test" depends="package-stand-alone, deploy-copy-war"
        description="Run the JUnit tests">
  <echo message="Running the JUnit tests"/>
  <ant antfile="${build.test.xml}" target="test" inheritRefs="true"/>
</target>
```

```
<!-- Check the coding conventions -->
<target name="coding-style" description="Check the coding conventions">
  <echo message="Checking the coding conventions"/>
  <ant antfile="${build.test.xml}" target="coding-style" inheritRefs="true"/>
</target>

<!-- Run all the tests -->
<target name="test-all" depends="package-stand-alone, deploy-copy-war"
        description="Run all the tests">
  <echo message="Running all the tests"/>
  <ant antfile="${build.test.xml}" inheritRefs="true"/>
</target>
```

These are the last alterations, but you have still to make some small additions. For example, you need a way to call individual targets in the subordinate build from the command line.

Running Individual Subordinate Targets

If you tried to run a target that was part of a subordinate build by specifying a file at the command line, you would get an error, as follows:

```
> ant -f src/web/build.xml compile-web
```

```
Buildfile: src\web\build.xml

compile-web:
     [echo] Compiling the web application

BUILD FAILED
C:\AntBook\ch09\src\web\build.xml:12: destination directory
"C:\AntBook\ch09\src\web\${build.web.root}" does not exist or is not a directory

Total time: 1 second
```

The value of the `build.web.root` property is not set, so Ant has used the `${build.web.root}` string as the value in the subordinate `compile-web` target. For example:

```
<javac destdir="${build.web.root}">
```

This means Ant tries to compile the classes into a directory called `${build.web.root}` and subsequently fails to do so. This kind of error occurs throughout the build. The diagnosis is simple: you haven't set any properties for this subordinate build (or any of the others). This is a side effect of centralizing classpaths and properties in the master build file. However, this is not a problem because you can easily write targets in the master build file that call individual targets in subordinate build files.

Listing 9-15 shows the targets that you can use to call targets in subordinate builds. You use command-line properties to set the name of the target to call, and the master build passes its references over, meaning you have access to all its properties and classpaths.

Listing 9-15. *Targets That Call Targets in Subordinate Builds*

```
<!-- #################### -->
<!-- Managing subprojects -->
<!-- #################### -->

<target name="stand-alone-target" depends="dir">
  <ant antfile="${build.stand-alone.xml}" target="${target}"
       inheritRefs="true"/>
</target>

<target name="web-target" depends="dir">
  <ant antfile="${build.web.xml}" target="${target}" inheritRefs="true"/>
</target>
```

Here's the example command line from before, which uses one of the new targets:

```
> ant -Dtarget=compile-web web-target
```

To run the tests, you would use a target as shown in Listing 9-16. It follows the same pattern as the targets I've just discussed, which means you can use it to pick individual targets in the test subordinate build. You also have to make sure that the code is up to date before you run the tests, so you use a depends attribute.

Listing 9-16. *A Target That Calls the Test Subordinate Build*

```
<!-- Run the tests -->
<target name="test-target" depends="package-stand-alone,deploy-copy-war">
  <ant antfile="${build.test.xml}" target="${target}" inheritRefs="true"/>
</target>
```

Really the only thing you need this target for is compiling the test classes without running a test, though you'd never get to the tests if the code failed to compile. This target is more for completeness than anything else.

Summary

This chapter ran through the process of using subordinate build files to encapsulate large, independent sections of a complex project. You took the monolithic master build file that you've built up over the past few chapters and split it into a number of smaller build files, each of which focuses on a certain fragment of the whole build.

The three sections of the application—that is, the shared code, the stand-alone code, and the web application code—lend themselves to this treatment. It is a straightforward way of dividing a large build. You split the master build file and placed the appropriate targets in the appropriate subordinate build files. You also moved the test targets into their own build file.

The final part of the chapter showed how to call individual targets in these subordinate build files so that the subordinate targets have access to references from the master build.

CHAPTER 10

Writing Custom Tasks

At this stage in the book, you have seen many of Ant's tasks; some of them are core to Ant, while others are optional because of their dependency on external libraries. During the course of the discussion, you also came across some limitations in the set of tasks provided with the Ant distribution. For example, you saw how the `<tar>` task is fairly cumbersome compared to its `<zip>` cousin. Another example is the `<javadoc>` task, which does not do any dependency checking when creating Javadocs. While you saw workarounds for these, this is no substitute for a task that does something cleanly and efficiently without any quirks.

The vast majority of Ant's tasks are excellent, and it is not often that you will find you need something more. However, one of the beauties of Ant is the ease with which you can write new tasks to scratch the itch you've had. The philosophy behind these custom tasks is similar to the reusability philosophy behind Ant (and object-oriented software as well). If you find yourself using clunky workarounds and `<exec>` tasks over and over again, it's time to write a custom task to automate and simplify the process.

In this chapter, you'll look at an Ant task's life cycle, its API, and some examples of custom tasks. These examples will also include some third-party custom tasks you may want to use in your builds. It's worth checking some of the third-party custom tasks listed at `http://ant.apache.org/external.html` to see whether someone has done the work for you.

Examining Custom Tasks

Before you actually write a serious custom task, you'll look at the life cycle of a task and how you can take advantage of the stages a task goes through during a project build. Many Java APIs, such as the JSP custom tag API, follow a similar pattern, so you may have come across something similar before. In the discussion on the custom task life cycle, you will inevitably dip into the API, but I'll leave most of the API discussion until after the life-cycle discussion.

As you've seen, every task you place in a build file as an XML element is represented by a Java class in Ant, and custom tasks are no exception. In fact, you saw a custom task in Chapter 6 when you defined the `<deploy>` task that places a web application onto a Tomcat server. Here's a reminder:

```
<taskdef name="deploy" classname="org.apache.catalina.ant.DeployTask"/>
```

Here the org.apache.catalina.ant.DeployTask class represents the <deploy> task when it appears in a build file. This class has class properties that correspond to the attributes of the <deploy> element, and this is how you interact with the class file. This class also runs certain operations at different points in the task's life cycle; you will learn more about this next.

Introducing the Custom Task Life Cycle

A custom task always follows the same path through the life of a project build. This means certain sections of your custom task's Java class must run at predefined points in a build, and Ant will expect to call certain methods at the appropriate time as specified by the task API. In other words, you need a guaranteed set of methods in the class that represents your task.

In common with other Java projects, the Ant API provides abstract classes with default methods for use as the basis of a custom task, the most important of which is org.apache.tools.ant.Task. This allows you to pick and choose which parts of the API to implement in any given custom task without worrying about the implementation of the other parts. The life cycle of the task is the major factor when deciding which code to place where and proceeds as follows:

1. Ant instantiates the class using its no-argument constructor.
2. Ant sets references to the project that contains the task and the location of its element in the build file. You can obtain this information using the inherited getProject() and getLocation() methods.
3. If you set an id attribute for the task's element, Ant registers a reference to this newly created task in the project object. However, the ID is not available to the task until later in its life cycle.
4. Ant sets a reference to the task's containing target. You can obtain this information using the inherited getOwningTarget() method later in the life cycle.
5. Ant calls the task's init() method. You should implement this method if you need to run any setup code before the task runs. This method does not have access to any of the task's attributes, including its id attribute.
6. If you have child elements for this task, Ant calls any addXXX(), addConfiguredXXX(), and createXXX() methods you have defined, one for each child element you have specified. XXX stands for the name of the child element. The type of method you choose depends on the type of nested element. You'll learn more about this later in the "Working with Nested Elements in Tasks" section.
7. Ant sets the attributes of this task using the appropriate setXXX() methods, where XXX stands for the name of the attribute. The task can now manipulate these attributes.
8. Ant calls the task's addText() method if you have defined it. This method adds the content character data sections inside the task's XML element.
9. Ant sets the attributes of all the task's child elements using the appropriate setXXX() methods.

10. Ant calls the child elements' `addText()` methods.
11. Ant calls the task's `execute()`. This is the only step that is repeated for a given task element. In other words, the same element's `execute()` method is called again and again by targets that depend on its containing target, but its other methods are not. This is because it is the same object as far as Ant is concerned. Another element of the same type will follow its own life cycle and will not be affected by the life cycle of the first task.

This is all well and good, but let's look at some examples that demonstrate the life cycle of a tag.

Introducing the Custom Task API

The first step in creating a custom task is to extend the `org.apache.tools.ant.Task` abstract class. This class gives you default implementations of the custom task API's methods, but you should always override the `execute()` method. This is where you will place the task's functionality, even though it is not mandatory for you to implement such a method. You'll return to this method in the "Writing an execute() Element" section.

The first custom task is a simple task that takes a name and displays it to the user via standard `out`. Here's an example of it in a build file:

```
<lifecycle name="Matthew"/>
```

You'll add a nested element in the "Working with Nested Elements in Tasks" section, but for now you'll use it as a single element with a mandatory `name` attribute. First I'll cover the constructor.

■ **Note** The Ant API contains other, more specialized abstract classes that you can extend should you need their particular specialism. They are `AbstractCvsTask`, `JDBCTask`, `MatchingTask`, `Pack`, and `Unpack` in the `org.apache.tools.ant.taskdefs` package. In this chapter, you'll use only `Task`. You can find more information at `http://ant.apache.org/manual/base_task_classes.html`.

Writing a Task's Constructor

Ant will call a task's constructor right at the beginning of a task's life cycle, and it should have no arguments. You cannot do an awful lot in the constructor if you want to implement it because so little information is available to the task at this stage. For example, Ant has not yet assigned it to the project object, which means it does not know which target it belongs to or where it is in the build file. Another consequence of not being a part of the project is that you cannot do any logging, to a file or to standard `out`, because the logger belongs to the project.

Listing 10-1 shows the first implementation of the demonstration task, with some `System.out.println()` calls to demonstrate the values of some important objects at this stage.

Listing 10-1. *The Example Task's Constructor*

```
package org.mwrm.ant.tasks;

import org.apache.tools.ant.Task;

// We'll need these objects in subsequent examples
import java.util.Hashtable;
import java.util.Enumeration;

import org.apache.tools.ant.Project;
import org.apache.tools.ant.BuildException;

import org.apache.tools.ant.UnknownElement;

public class LifeCycleTask extends Task {

    // The name attribute of this task
    private String name;

    // The body text of this task
    private String text;

    public LifeCycleTask() {
        System.out.println("---------------");
        System.out.println("Constructor called");
        System.out.println("Value of name attribute: " + name);
        System.out.println("Value of the body text: " + text);
        System.out.println("Project: " + getProject());
        System.out.println("Location: " + getLocation());
        System.out.println("Target: " + getOwningTarget());
        System.out.println("---------------");
    }
}
```

The methods you call in the constructor are inherited from the parent `org.apache.tools.ant.Task` class. The `getProject()` method returns an object that represents the parent project of this task (`org.apache.tools.ant.Project`), which allows you to access a number of useful pieces of information. (You'll learn more about this in the "Writing a Task's init() Method" section.) The `getLocation()` method returns an object that represents the location of this task within a build file (`org.apache.tools.ant.Location`), which has a `toString()` method that displays the location, including the line number. The `getOwningTarget()` method returns an object representing the target that this task belongs to (`org.apache.tools.ant.Target`), which also has a convenient `toString()` method that returns the name of the target.

To return some output, you have to use `System.out.println()` statements here, because the project's logger is unavailable. Should the logger be available, you will use it; this is the best way of returning output from a custom task because it is more flexible than `System.out.println()` statements.

Now that you have the code, you need to compile it. Listing 10-2 shows the properties you'll need before you set up a target to do the work for you. You'll use the same build file that you've been using throughout the book to take advantage of some of its properties and setup targets.

Listing 10-2. *The Properties for Compiling the Custom Tasks*

```
# Custom task properties
ant.tasks.src=ant
ant.tasks.build=${build}/ant
ant.tasks.jar=${dist}/${appName}-tasks.jar
```

You'll use this JAR file when running the custom task, so compile it as shown in Listing 10-3.

Listing 10-3. *Compiling the Custom Tasks*

```
<!-- ######################################## -->
<!-- Targets for demonstrating custom tasks -->
<!-- ######################################## -->

<!-- Compile the Ant tasks -->
<target name="compile-ant-tasks" depends="dir"
        description="Compile the Ant tasks">
  <echo message="Compiling the Ant tasks"/>
  <mkdir dir="${ant.tasks.build}"/>
  <javac srcdir="${ant.tasks.src}" destdir="${ant.tasks.build}"/>
  <jar destfile="${ant.tasks.jar}" basedir="${ant.tasks.build}"/>
</target>
```

To use a custom task, you must declare it with a <taskdef> element, an element you saw earlier in the chapter and in Chapter 6. You need to specify a name for the task and tell Ant which class to use when it encounters the task's element in a build file. The name you specify will be the name of the element. So, if you specify the name as a-task, the element would be <a-task>. Listing 10-4 shows how to declare a custom task and then use it.

Listing 10-4. *Declaring a Custom Task and Using It*

```
<!-- Demonstrate the life cycle of a task -->
<target name="lifecycle-target"
        description="Demonstrate the life cycle of a task">
  <echo message="Demonstrating the life cycle of a task"/>
  <taskdef name="lifecycle-task"
           classname="org.mwrm.ant.tasks.LifeCycleTask" />
  <lifecycle-task/>
</target>
```

You can declare the name of the task as lifecycle-task with the name attribute and then use it in the file as <lifecycle-task>. You've implemented only the constructor so far, so let's see what it does. Run the following:

```
> ant -lib dist/antBook-tasks.jar lifecycle-target
```

```
Buildfile: build.xml

lifecycle-target:
     [echo] Demonstrating the life cycle of a task
[lifecycle-task] ---------------
[lifecycle-task] Constructor called
[lifecycle-task] Value of name attribute: null
[lifecycle-task] Value of the body text: null
[lifecycle-task] Project: null
[lifecycle-task] Location:
[lifecycle-task] Target: null
[lifecycle-task] ---------------

BUILD SUCCESSFUL
```

Notice how any output from the task is prefixed with its name as you specified it. Note also the procession of null values that tells you this task is not attached to a project for the moment.

Place some text in the body of the task like so:

```
<lifecycle-task>
  The body text.
</lifecycle-task>
```

This will not make any difference to the task, because Ant has still not called the addText() method.

```
[lifecycle-task] Value of the body text: null
```

Writing a Task's init() Method

The init() method is the next stage in the life cycle of a task that you can influence. By the time a task reaches this stage, it has been through three more steps: it has a reference to the project that contains it and a reference to the location of its element in the build file, the project has a reference to it if you specified an id attribute, and it has a reference to its containing target.

To demonstrate what this means, you will implement the init() method for the custom task. It has the following signature:

```
public void init() throws BuildException
```

You have a number of new powers to use here, the most visible of which is the log() method. This is the best way to provide information to the user, and it simply calls the project logger's log() method. However, two versions are implemented in the task's parent class:

```
public void log(java.lang.String msg)
public void log(java.lang.String msg, int msgLevel)
```

The project's logger works with constants defined as part of the `Project` object, which define at what stage the message is displayed:

- `Project.MSG_DEBUG`
- `Project.MSG_VERBOSE`
- `Project.MSG_INFO`
- `Project.MSG_WARN`
- `Project.MSG_ERR`

The first two say that the message should be displayed only if the user runs Ant with the `-d` or `-v` command line, respectively. The other three are always displayed but define certain levels of urgency, though you can suppress messages at the `Project.MSG_INFO` level by setting the `-q` command-line option. The first version of `log()` logs the message at the level of `Project.MSG_INFO`.

You will display information at the level of `Project.MSG_VERBOSE` because you can turn it on by using the `-v` command-line option, while users will not see it during normal use of Ant. Listing 10-5 shows the central `logAll()` method that all the life-cycle methods will use. You couldn't use a central logging method for the constructor because most of the objects you are interested in weren't instantiated at that stage.

Listing 10-5. *The logAll() Method Displays This Task's Status*

```
public void logAll(String method) {
    log("---------------", Project.MSG_VERBOSE);
    log(method + " called", Project.MSG_VERBOSE);
    log("Value of name attribute: " + name, Project.MSG_VERBOSE);
    log("Value of the body text: " + text, Project.MSG_VERBOSE);
    log("Project: " + getProject().getName(), Project.MSG_VERBOSE);

    // Here we build some information on the location
    // within the build file
    String locationString = getLocation().getFileName();
    locationString = locationString + " at line "
        + getLocation().getLineNumber();

    // Location.getColumnNumber() is for Ant 1.7+
    // Comment it out if you are using Ant 1.6.x
    //locationString = locationString + " and column "
    //+ getLocation().getColumnNumber();

    log("Location: " + locationString, Project.MSG_VERBOSE);

    // We could use the Location.toString() method
    //log("Location: " + getLocation(), Project.MSG_VERBOSE);
```

```
        log("Target: " + getOwningTarget(), Project.MSG_VERBOSE);

        // referenceCheck() returns a string with information
        // on any references to custom tasks
        log(referenceCheck(), Project.MSG_VERBOSE);

        // If the configuration wrapper is null, we use its
        // run-time equivalent
        if (getWrapper() == null) {
            log("Reference id: "
                + getRuntimeConfigurableWrapper().getAttributeMap().get("id"),
                Project.MSG_VERBOSE);
        } else {
            // We use the protected getWrapper() method
            log("Reference id: " + getWrapper().getAttributeMap().get("id"),
            Project.MSG_VERBOSE);
        }

        log("---------------", Project.MSG_VERBOSE);
    }
```

You can now take advantage of the project object because this task gets a reference to it before the `init()` method, so you can obtain its name (`Project.getName()`), its description (`Project.getDescription()`), and its default target (`Project.getDefaultTarget()`), among other things. In this case, you'll display just its name to show the task has a reference to its project.

The task also knows its location within the build file, so you can get some information about it using the `Location` object's methods. This object also has a `toString()` method.

Listing 10-6 defines the `referenceCheck()` method, which searches through all the references that have been set in this project and checks to see whether they are tasks. After the `referenceCheck()` call, if you can't get a reference to the task's configuration wrapper (`org.apache.tools.ant.RuntimeConfigurable`) with the inherited `getWrapper()` method, you call the inherited `getRuntimeConfigurableWrapper()` method to obtain a `RuntimeConfigurable` object that represents a temporary run-time configuration. A task's `RuntimeConfigurable` object contains all its attributes, among other things, and is the only way to access its `id` attribute because there is no `getId()` method. Only one object may have a certain reference ID at any time, and you can use this information to find a specific task within the project. If you specify two tasks with the same `id` attribute, you'll see something similar to the following in Ant's output:

```
Overriding previous definition of reference to lifecycle-id
```

This means two tasks with a reference ID of `lifecycle-id` exist in the project, and Ant has used the second one in preference to the first. Note that the first task will still run before Ant overrides it, but it won't be a reference once Ant runs the second task.

You use the `RuntimeConfigurable.getAttributeMap().get()` method to show that even though the task has been added as a reference, it does not yet have any accessible attributes.

The final piece of code obtains the `id` attribute of the custom task you have found using its `RuntimeConfigurable` object. This object does have its attributes set, but Ant hasn't called any setter methods on the actual task.

Listing 10-6. *The referenceCheck() Method Looks for Custom Task References*

```
private String referenceCheck() {

    // The default setting
    String setString = "Reference not found.";

    // We need the references that have been set in this project
    Hashtable refs = getProject().getReferences();
    Enumeration e = refs.elements();

    // Let's iterate over them
    while (e.hasMoreElements()) {
        // We want to work with each object, so we'll instantiate an object
        Object obj = e.nextElement();

        // Check to see whether this object is a task
        // If it is, we'll build a string that contains its name and type
        if (obj.getClass().getName().
            equals("org.apache.tools.ant.UnknownElement")
            ||
            obj.getClass().getName().equals(this.getClass().getName())) {

            Task aTask = (Task)obj;
            setString =
                "Reference to " + aTask.getTaskName() + " found, of type "
                + aTask.getClass().getName() + ".";
            setString = setString + "Its id is "
            + aTask.getRuntimeConfigurableWrapper().
            getAttributeMap().get("id") + ".";
        }
    }
    return setString;
}
```

The `Project.getReferences()` method returns a `HashTable` of objects, each of which is an object placed as an Ant reference in the project. If an object is a task, you set the return string appropriately. A task is set as type `org.apache.tools.ant.UnknownElement` until the life cycle reaches the `execute()` method stage. Therefore, you have to check for this type as well as the actual class type of the task.

Listing 10-7 shows the `init()` method where you just call the output method.

Listing 10-7. *The Example Task's* `init()` *Method*

```
public void init() {
    logAll("init()");

}
```

Now, run the task as follows. Remember that the logging is set at the verbose level, but the following output has omitted the output in which you're not interested:

```
> ant -lib dist/antBook-tasks.jar -v lifecycle-target
```

```
Buildfile: build.xml

lifecycle-target:
     [echo] Demonstrating the life cycle of a task
[lifecycle-task] ---------------
[lifecycle-task] Constructor called
[lifecycle-task] Value of name attribute: null
[lifecycle-task] Value of the body text: null
[lifecycle-task] Project: null
[lifecycle-task] Location:
[lifecycle-task] Target: null
[lifecycle-task] ---------------
[lifecycle-task] ---------------
[lifecycle-task] init() called
[lifecycle-task] init() called
[lifecycle-task] Value of name attribute: null
[lifecycle-task] Value of the body text: null
[lifecycle-task] Project: Example Application Build
[lifecycle-task] Location: C:\AntBook\ch10\build.xml at line 1235 and column 38
[lifecycle-task] Target: lifecycle-target
[lifecycle-task] Reference not found.
[lifecycle-task] Reference id: null
[lifecycle-task] ---------------

BUILD SUCCESSFUL
```

You can see how you now have a value for the project's name and a name for the parent target. You also have information about the task's location in the build file. However, you haven't found any custom tasks set as references, and the `name` attribute and body text are still not set. To add a reference, change the task's entry in the build file to add an `id` attribute, as follows:

```
<lifecycle-task id="lifecycle-id"/>
```

Now run the same command:

```
> ant -lib dist/antBook-tasks.jar -v lifecycle-target
```

```
Buildfile: build.xml

lifecycle-target:
     [echo] Demonstrating the life cycle of a task
[lifecycle-task] ---------------
[lifecycle-task] Constructor called
[lifecycle-task] Value of name attribute: null
[lifecycle-task] Value of the body text: null
[lifecycle-task] Project: null
[lifecycle-task] Location:
[lifecycle-task] Target: null
[lifecycle-task] ---------------
[lifecycle-task] ---------------
[lifecycle-task] init() called
[lifecycle-task] Value of name attribute: null
[lifecycle-task] Value of the body text: null
[lifecycle-task] Project: Example Application Build
[lifecycle-task] Location: C:\AntBook\ch10\build.xml at line 1235 and column 55
[lifecycle-task] Target: lifecycle-target
[lifecycle-task] Reference to lifecycle-task found, of type org.apache.tools.ant
.UnknownElement. Its id is lifecycle-id.
[lifecycle-task] Reference id: null
[lifecycle-task] ---------------

BUILD SUCCESSFUL
```

Now you have a reference to a custom task in the project, though Ant has not set it to the correct type just yet. The reference object has an `id` attribute, but you can't get at it from the task itself still because no `setXXX()` methods have been called.

The next step in the life cycle is for Ant to call any `createXXX()` or `addXXX()` methods for nested elements. You don't have any of these in this example (though you will in the next section), so let's move on to the `setXXX()` methods.

Writing a setXXX() Method

The next step in the life cycle is when Ant calls a `setXXX()` method for each attribute set in the task's element, where `XXX` stands for the name of the attribute. This means that if you have ten `setXXX()` methods but set only one attribute, Ant will call only the one `setXXX()` element for the attribute you have set. In common with most Java mutator methods (for that is what these methods are), they must be `public void` and must take a single parameter. Ant can do some nifty conversions to change the value of the custom task's attributes into the type of this parameter, but you'll come to this later. For now you'll deal with strings.

As there are no steps in the life cycle between the `init()` method and this step, the objects in the project will not have changed. However, you now have access to the attribute values. Listing 10-8 shows the `setName()` method for the custom task.

Listing 10-8. *The setName() Method Sets the name Attribute*

```
public void setName(String name) {
    // The value of the name attribute
    this.name = name;
    logAll("setName()");
}
```

Here you set the name property of this custom task so you can use it elsewhere (that is, in the execute() method). You also need to add a name attribute to the custom task:

```
<lifecycle-task name="Matthew" id="lifecycle-id"/>
```

Now run Ant:

```
> ant -lib dist/antBook-tasks.jar -v lifecycle-target
```

```
Buildfile: build.xml

lifecycle-target:
     [echo] Demonstrating the life cycle of a task
[lifecycle-task] ---------------
[lifecycle-task] Constructor called
[lifecycle-task] Value of name attribute: null
[lifecycle-task] Value of the body text: null
[lifecycle-task] Project: null
[lifecycle-task] Location:
[lifecycle-task] Target: null
[lifecycle-task] ---------------
[lifecycle-task] ---------------
[lifecycle-task] init() called
[lifecycle-task] Value of name attribute: null
[lifecycle-task] Value of the body text: null
[lifecycle-task] Project: Example Application Build
[lifecycle-task] Location: C:\AntBook\ch10\build.xml at line 1235 and column 55
[lifecycle-task] Target: lifecycle-target
[lifecycle-task] Reference to lifecycle-task found, of type org.apache.tools.ant
.UnknownElement. Its id is lifecycle-id.
[lifecycle-task] Reference id: null
[lifecycle-task] ---------------
[lifecycle-task] ---------------
[lifecycle-task] setName() called
[lifecycle-task] Value of name attribute: Matthew
[lifecycle-task] Value of the body text: null
[lifecycle-task] Project: Example Application Build
[lifecycle-task] Location: C:\AntBook\ch10\build.xml:1235:
[lifecycle-task] Target: lifecycle-target
[lifecycle-task] Reference to lifecycle-task found, of type org.apache.tools.ant
.UnknownElement. Its id is lifecycle-id.
```

```
[lifecycle-task] Reference id: lifecycle-id
[lifecycle-task] ---------------

BUILD SUCCESSFUL
```

The only two things that are still not defined are the body text and the class type of the reference. Ant has called all the setXXX() methods and has set the value of the id attribute as well.

CONVERTING PARAMETER TYPES

Ant does not pass the value of a task's attribute directly to the appropriate setXXX() method. If it did, it couldn't expand any properties, and you'd have to do lots of getProject().getProperty("src.web") calls or similar. As it is, Ant will expand any properties before passing on the value. This is not the only trick it can pull, however, because it can convert the string value of the task's attribute into a number of different objects as the context demands.

This means you can write setXXX() methods with arguments other than strings and let Ant do all the conversion work for you. Here's the list of conversions that Ant does:

- If you have a boolean or Boolean argument, Ant will set it to true if the user specified "true," "yes," or "on" in the task's attribute. It will pass false if the user specified anything else ("false," "no," "off," "hello," and so on).
- If you have a char or Character argument, Ant passes only the first letter of the attribute's value.
- If you have an argument that is any other primitive type (or a wrapper for a primitive type), Ant attempts to convert the string into that type or wrapper. If it fails, it will throw a NumberFormatException, and the task won't run. If it succeeds, your method can be confident it has a number of the appropriate types with which to work.
- If you have an argument of type File, Ant will try to instantiate a File object with the attribute string as its file path. Ant can handle absolute and relative file paths. You'll see an example of this when you extend the <javadoc> task in the "Extending the <javadoc> Task" section.
- If you have an argument of type org.apache.tools.ant.types.Path, Ant will interpret the task's attribute as a string of tokens divided by : and ; separators. If the user specifies any relative paths, Ant uses the project's base directory as the reference point.
- If you have an argument that is a subclass of org.apache.tools.ant.types.EnumeratedAttribute, Ant calls its setValue() method with the value of the task's attribute. I won't cover this type in this chapter.
- If you have an argument of type java.lang.Class, Ant will take the task's argument to be a fully qualified classname and load a class of this type, as long as it can be found in the Ant classpath. The newly loaded class is then available in the task.
- If you have an argument of a type that has a constructor with a single argument of type String, such as java.lang.Locale, Ant will call that constructor with the value of the task's attribute and pass the new object to the setXXX() method.

Ant will always favor one of these more specialized methods over the plain string method, but you have no guarantee which specialized method it will call if you define more than one. Therefore, you should not rely too much on overloaded `setXXX()` methods.

Here's an example of the `java.lang.Class` flavor:

```
package org.mwrm.ant.tasks;

import org.apache.tools.ant.Project;
import org.apache.tools.ant.Task;
import org.apache.tools.ant.BuildException;

public class ClassSetTask extends Task {

    Class qualifiedName;

    public void execute() throws BuildException {
        log("qualifiedName: " + qualifiedName, Project.MSG_INFO);
    }

    public void setQualifiedName(Class qualifiedName) {
        if (qualifiedName.getName().equals("java.lang.Integer")
            ||
            qualifiedName.getName().equals("java.lang.String")) {
            log(qualifiedName.getName()+ " found.", Project.MSG_INFO);
        } else {

            String msg = "You can only specify java.lang.Integer "
                + "or java.lang.String in qualifiedName.";
            throw new BuildException(msg);
        }
        this.qualifiedName = qualifiedName;
    }
}
```

You can use it in the build file as follows:

```
  <target name="class-set-test">
    <taskdef name="class-set-test"
             classname="org.mwrm.ant.tasks.ClassSetTask" />
    <class-set-test qualifiedName="java.lang.Integer"/>
  </target>
```

Now invoke it:

```
> ant -lib dist/antBook-tasks.jar class-set-test
```

Writing an addText() Method

If you have defined an addText() method, Ant will call it after any setXXX() methods. It has the same signature as a standard mutator method with a single string parameter, though it is not defined as part of the parent Task's definition. This means the method has no default implementation, and therefore body text will not be added unless you implement this method.

Note You should be aware that indented elements and body text will contain a long string of whitespace and so won't be null. This means any usage checks that depend on the body text being null to succeed need to be rewritten; trimming the text doesn't help either because trimmed whitespace is still an empty string, which does not equal null. For example, a condition where you can't specify body text and nested elements together can't rely on the != null check to look for body text when you've indented nested elements and introduced whitespace as body text. The solution is to use the trim() method to trim all body text in the addText() method and set all subsequent empty strings to null. You can then do a null check.

Listing 10-9 shows the implementation. Ant will pass the body text to the addText() method as its string parameter. Once you have this data, you can do what you want with it.

Listing 10-9. *Implementing the addText() Method*

```
public void addText(String text) {
    // If the body text is just whitespace, it might as well be null
    if (text.trim().equals("")) {
        this.text = null;
    } else {
        this.text = text.trim();
    }
    logAll("addText()");
}
```

This acts just like a setXXX() method, so you proceed as you did in Listing 10-8. To display the text to the user, you trim the whitespace using String.trim().

Add some body text:

```
<lifecycle-task name="Matthew" id="lifecycle-id">
  The body text.
</lifecycle-task>
```

If you run the target as before, you can see the new body text and the execution of the addText() method:

```
> ant -lib dist/antBook-tasks.jar -v lifecycle-target
```

```
Buildfile: build.xml

lifecycle-target:
     [echo] Demonstrating the life cycle of a task
[lifecycle-task] ---------------
[lifecycle-task] Constructor called
[lifecycle-task] Value of name attribute: null
[lifecycle-task] Value of the body text: null
[lifecycle-task] Project: null
[lifecycle-task] Location:
[lifecycle-task] Target: null
[lifecycle-task] ---------------
[lifecycle-task] ---------------
[lifecycle-task] init() called
[lifecycle-task] Value of name attribute: null
[lifecycle-task] Value of the body text: null
[lifecycle-task] Project: Example Application Build
[lifecycle-task] Location: C:\AntBook\ch10\build.xml at line 1235 and column 54
[lifecycle-task] Target: lifecycle-target
[lifecycle-task] Reference to lifecycle-task found, of type org.apache.tools.ant
.UnknownElement. Its id is lifecycle-id.
[lifecycle-task] Reference id: null
[lifecycle-task] ---------------
[lifecycle-task] ---------------
[lifecycle-task] setName() called
[lifecycle-task] Value of name attribute: Matthew
[lifecycle-task] Value of the body text: null
[lifecycle-task] Project: Example Application Build
[lifecycle-task] Location: C:\AntBook\ch10\build.xml:1235:
[lifecycle-task] Target: lifecycle-target
[lifecycle-task] Reference to lifecycle-task found, of type org.apache.tools.ant
.UnknownElement. Its id is lifecycle-id.
[lifecycle-task] Reference id: lifecycle-id
[lifecycle-task] ---------------
[lifecycle-task] ---------------
[lifecycle-task] addText() called
[lifecycle-task] Value of name attribute: Matthew
[lifecycle-task] Value of the body text: The body text.
[lifecycle-task] Project: Example Application Build
[lifecycle-task] Location: C:\AntBook\ch10\build.xml:1235:
[lifecycle-task] Target: lifecycle-target
[lifecycle-task] Reference to lifecycle-task found, of type org.apache.tools.ant
.UnknownElement. Its id is lifecycle-id.
[lifecycle-task] Reference id: lifecycle-id
[lifecycle-task] ---------------

BUILD SUCCESSFUL
```

The only change here is that you have access to the body text. The reference is still an UnknownElement. The next two steps of the life cycle involve nested elements, so you'll come to them when you nest an element in the "Working with Nested Elements in Tasks" section.

Writing an execute() Element

The final step of the task's life cycle is the execute() method. It has the following signature:

```
public void execute() throws BuildException
```

By this stage in the life cycle, you have all the information you could possibly need and can now write the functionality of the task. One important point to consider in the execute() task is usage checking. You cannot rely on DTDs (as you saw in Chapter 3), so you must check the structure of the task yourself, and the execute() method is the best place to do so, simply because it is the end of the life cycle and you have a fully formed task. However, you should do usage checking at the most suitable time, which means you don't always have to do it in the execute() method.

You should also remember to write the functionality, because there's no other place to do so. Listing 10-10 shows the implementation of execute().

Listing 10-10. *The execute() Method Implements the Functionality of the Task*

```
public void execute() throws BuildException {
    // Check that the user set a name attribute
    if (name == null) {
        throw new BuildException("You must specify a name attribute in "
                                 + getTaskName() + ".");
    }
    logAll("execute()");
    // Write the name to output
    log(name, Project.MSG_INFO);
}
```

The usage check makes sure the user has used a name attribute and throws a BuildException should it be missing. This is the preferred way to signal to Ant that there was a problem of some kind. The task's functionality is implemented by the final log() method call. Here's the final run:

```
> ant -lib dist/antBook-tasks.jar -v lifecycle-target
```

```
Buildfile: build.xml

lifecycle-target:
...
[lifecycle-task] ---------------
[lifecycle-task] execute() called
[lifecycle-task] Value of name attribute: Matthew
[lifecycle-task] Value of the body text: The body text.
[lifecycle-task] Project: Example Application Build
[lifecycle-task] Location: C:\AntBook\ch10\build.xml:1235:
```

```
[lifecycle-task] Target: lifecycle-target
[lifecycle-task] Reference to lifecycle-task found, of type org.mwrm.ant.tasks
.LifeCycleTask. Its id is lifecycle-id.
[lifecycle-task] Reference id: lifecycle-id
[lifecycle-task] ---------------
[lifecycle-task] Matthew

BUILD SUCCESSFUL
```

The final items are filled in, and the task has performed its duty and shown the value of the name attribute. Let's run it without the -v option to see the results without the instructional information:

```
> ant -lib dist/antBook-tasks.jar lifecycle-target
```

```
Buildfile: build.xml

lifecycle-target:
     [echo] Demonstrating the life cycle of a task
[lifecycle-task] ---------------
[lifecycle-task] Constructor called
[lifecycle-task] Value of name attribute: null
[lifecycle-task] Value of the body text: null
[lifecycle-task] Project: null
[lifecycle-task] Location:
[lifecycle-task] Target: null
[lifecycle-task] ---------------
[lifecycle-task] Matthew

BUILD SUCCESSFUL
```

This shows the problem with placing System.out.println() calls in the constructor, and as you don't need them anymore, you should remove them and run the command again:

```
> ant -lib dist/antBook-tasks.jar lifecycle-target
```

```
Buildfile: build.xml

lifecycle-target:
     [echo] Demonstrating the life cycle of a task
[lifecycle-task] Matthew

BUILD SUCCESSFUL
```

It works as described, so let's introduce an error into the way you use the task by omitting the name attribute:

```
<lifecycle-task id="lifecycle-id">
  The body text.
</lifecycle-task>
```

Run the command to see the error message:

```
> ant -lib dist/antBook-tasks.jar lifecycle-target
```

```
Buildfile: build.xml

lifecycle-target:
     [echo] Demonstrating the life cycle of a task

BUILD FAILED
C:\AntBook\ch10\build.xml:1235: You must specify a name attribute in lifecycle-
task.
```

Working with Nested Elements in Tasks

Nested elements in tasks are slightly more complicated than attributes, though once you see how easy they are you'll be able to work with nested elements as a matter of course. You have three ways to implement a nested element and make its information available to your task. They are the `addXXX()`, `addConfiguredXXX()`, and `createXXX()` methods, and I'll discuss each as you go through this chapter.

The nested element is called `<name>`, and it has an optional attribute also called `name`. If you do not specify a `name` attribute, you must place text in the body of the nested tag, which will be added as if it were the value of a `name` attribute. You must specify either a `name` attribute or body text. In addition, you can't specify a `name` attribute in the parent task's element if you set nested tags, and you can't specify both. This usage information will become clearer as you work through the code.

Here's the example used throughout this section:

```
<lifecycle-nested-task id="lifecycle-id">
  <name name="Matthew"/>
  <name name="Laura"/>
  <name>Jones</name>
</lifecycle-nested-task>
```

Here's an example of an illegal setting:

```
<lifecycle-nested-task name="IllegalName" id="lifecycle-id">
  <name name="Matthew"/>
  <name name="Laura"/>
  <name>Jones</name>
</lifecycle-nested-task>
```

You set a `name` attribute as part of the parent task as well as nested `<name>` elements. Here's another illegal setting:

```
<lifecycle-nested-task id="lifecycle-id">
  <name name="Matthew"/>
  <name name="Laura"/>
  <name name="Miss">Jones</name>
</lifecycle-nested-task>
```

The third <name> element has a name attribute and body text, which you have decided is illegal.

These restrictions mean you have to modify the logAll() method slightly. If you use a name attribute, you want to display its value. On the other hand, if you use nested <name> elements, you don't want to display the name attribute's value (which will be null anyway). This means you have to wrap the offending line in an if check:

```
// If name is set, you have only one value to print
if (name != null) {
    log("Value of name attribute: " + this.name, Project.MSG_VERBOSE);
}
```

Each of the three methods for working with nested elements (addXXX(), addConfiguredXXX(), and createXXX()) works with a class that represents the nested elements, just as the task class represents the task's element. In the case of the addXXX() and addConfiguredXXX() methods, this class must have a constructor like one of the following signatures:

```
public NestedElement() {}
public NestedElement(Project project) {}
```

This class can be one you have written (as you'll do in this example) or any other class that has a constructor that fits one of the signatures (such as a file set, which you'll work with in the "Extending the <javadoc> Task" section). A createXXX() method does not have these restrictions. For now, let's write the class that represents the nested element by placing its definition in the custom task.

Listing 10-11 has the details of the new task.

Listing 10-11. *The Skeleton of the New Custom Class and Its Nested Element*

```
package org.mwrm.ant.tasks;

import java.util.Hashtable;
import java.util.Enumeration;
import java.util.Vector;

import org.apache.tools.ant.Project;
import org.apache.tools.ant.Task;
import org.apache.tools.ant.BuildException;

public class LifeCycleNestedTask extends Task {

    // The name attribute of this task
    private String name;
```

```
// The body text of this task
private String text;

// The collection of name elements
private Vector nameElements = new Vector();

public LifeCycleNestedTask() {...}

public void init() {...}

public void setName(String name) {...}

public void addText(String text) {...}

public void execute() throws BuildException {...}

private String referenceCheck() {...}

// The name element
public static class NameElement {

    // The name attribute of this element
    String name;

    public NameElement() {
        // Empty
    }

    // The mutator method for the name attribute
    public void setName(String name) {
        this.name = name;
    }

    // The accessor method for the name attribute
    public String getName() {
        return name;
    }

    // A method for dealing with body text
    public void addText(String text) {
        // Usage check
        if (name != null) {
            String msg = "You can't specify a name attribute "
                + "and nested text in <name> elements.";
            throw new BuildException(msg);
```

```
            } else {
                this.name = text.trim();
            }
        }
    }
}
```

This nested element follows the same rules as a task element in that it has a constructor that will be called first and then a setXXX() method that will be called before an addText() method. Referring to the task's life cycle, you will see that this process happens after Ant has called the parent task's addText() method and before it calls the parent task's execute() method.

You want to obtain information about the name to display, whether it is set in an attribute or in the body text. As such, you set the name property of the nested element to whichever value is provided. This is also the easiest place to check for this violation of the nested tag's usage because it concerns the nested tag only and doesn't rely on a taskwide condition. You'll check for taskwide violations as usual in the execute() method.

■ **Note** If this element were to have nested elements, you'd simply add the appropriate addXXX(), addConfiguredXXX(), or createXXX() method to its class definition and proceed as if this element were the outer element of the whole task. A containing element always follows the same format, no matter how deep it is in the structure itself. This simplicity of design makes it easy to nest as many elements as you want without tying yourself in knots.

You've got the class that implements the nested tag, so now you have to give the task some way of accessing its data. You'll start with the addName() method.

Writing an addXXX() Method

The first example will be the addName() method for the <name> nested element. When using addXXX() methods, Ant will create an instance of a nested element's class and pass it to the appropriate addXXX() method. Here's a general signature for an addXXX() method:

```
public void addXXX(XXXElement element)
```

In this case, the addName() method will be defined as follows:

```
public void addName(NameElement nameElement)
```

As you have already seen, if you are using an addXXX() method, the nested element's class must have a public, no-argument constructor or a public constructor that takes a Project class as a parameter. When Ant passes the instantiated class to the addXXX() method, it is not initialized, which means that none of its properties is set. This means that to use the values set by the user, you must make this instance available to the execute() method, where it will have its properties set. The usual way is to add it to a taskwide Vector of similar nested elements. In this task, you have set a Vector called nameElements to contain all the name elements.

Listing 10-12 shows the addName() method for the task.

Listing 10-12. *The addName() Element Adds <name> Elements to the Task*

```
public void addName(NameElement nameElement) {
    nameElements.add(nameElement);

    logAll("addName()");        log("Value of this name: "
    + nameElement.getName(), Project.MSG_VERBOSE);
}
```

Here's an example run:

```
> ant -lib dist/antBook-tasks.jar -v lifecycle-nested-target
```

```
Buildfile: build.xml

lifecycle-nested-target:
     [echo] Demonstrating the life cycle of a task
[lifecycle-nested-task] ---------------
[lifecycle-nested-task] Constructor called
...
[lifecycle-nested-task] ---------------
[lifecycle-nested-task] ---------------
[lifecycle-nested-task] init() called
...
[lifecycle-nested-task] ---------------
[lifecycle-nested-task] ---------------
[lifecycle-nested-task] addName() called

[lifecycle-nested-task] Value of the body text: null
[lifecycle-nested-task] Project: Example Application Build
[lifecycle-nested-task] Location: C:\AntBook\ch10\build.xml:1244:
[lifecycle-nested-task] Target: lifecycle-nested-target
[lifecycle-nested-task] Reference to lifecycle-nested-task found, of type org
.apache.tools.ant.UnknownElement. Its id is lifecycle-id.
[lifecycle-nested-task] Reference id: lifecycle-id
[lifecycle-nested-task] ---------------
[lifecycle-nested-task] Value of this name: null
[lifecycle-nested-task] ---------------
[lifecycle-nested-task] addName() called

[lifecycle-nested-task] Value of the body text: null
[lifecycle-nested-task] Project: Example Application Build
[lifecycle-nested-task] Location: C:\AntBook\ch10\build.xml:1244:
[lifecycle-nested-task] Target: lifecycle-nested-target
[lifecycle-nested-task] Reference to lifecycle-nested-task found, of type org
.apache.tools.ant.UnknownElement. Its id is lifecycle-id.
[lifecycle-nested-task] Reference id: lifecycle-id
[lifecycle-nested-task] ---------------
```

```
[lifecycle-nested-task] Value of this name: null
[lifecycle-nested-task] ---------------
[lifecycle-nested-task] addName() called

[lifecycle-nested-task] Value of the body text: null
[lifecycle-nested-task] Project: Example Application Build
[lifecycle-nested-task] Location: C:\AntBook\ch10\build.xml:1244:
[lifecycle-nested-task] Target: lifecycle-nested-target
[lifecycle-nested-task] Reference to lifecycle-nested-task found, of type org
.apache.tools.ant.UnknownElement. Its id is lifecycle-id.
[lifecycle-nested-task] Reference id: lifecycle-id
[lifecycle-nested-task] ---------------
[lifecycle-nested-task] Value of this name: null
[lifecycle-nested-task] ---------------
[lifecycle-nested-task] addText() called
...
[lifecycle-nested-task] ---------------
[lifecycle-nested-task] ---------------
[lifecycle-nested-task] execute() called
...
[lifecycle-nested-task] ---------------

BUILD SUCCESSFUL
```

Ant calls the addName() method three times—once for each <name> element in the example. In each case, you can't access the name value of the nested element, and it appears as null. To do so, you have to write a new execute() method, which will also include some usage tests. Listing 10-13 has the details.

Listing 10-13. *The execute() Method Checks Usage and Displays the Results*

```
public void execute() throws BuildException {
    if (name != null && nameElements.size() > 0) {
        String msg = "You can't specify a name attribute "
            + "and <name> elements.";
        throw new BuildException(msg);
    }
    if (name == null && nameElements.size() == 0) {
        String msg = "You must specify either a name attribute "
            + "or at least one <name> element.";
        throw new BuildException(msg);
    }
    if (nameElements.size() > 0 && text != null) {
        String msg = "You can't specify <name> elements "
            + "and body text.";
        throw new BuildException(msg);
    }
```

```
        logAll("execute()");
        // If name is not set, you want to check nested elements
        if (name == null) {
            // Get the name elements
            Enumeration e = nameElements.elements();

            // And then iterate over them
            while (e.hasMoreElements()) {
                NameElement nameElement = (NameElement)e.nextElement();

                // Usage check
                if (nameElement.getName() == null) {
                    String msg = "You must specify a name attribute "
                        + "or body text for a nested <name> element.";
                    throw new BuildException(msg);
                }
                log("Value of name element: " + nameElement.getName(),
                    Project.MSG_VERBOSE);
            }
        }

        log("---------------", Project.MSG_VERBOSE);
    }
```

The execute() method enforces the remaining usage information but defers checking that each <name> element has a name attribute until you iterate over the collection of <name> elements. (The name attribute here also means body text, if you recall the NameElement.addText() method.) This execute() method will be the same for the next two examples as well, because they both use NameElement classes.

Here's the result of this execute() method:

```
Buildfile: build.xml

lifecycle-nested-target:
     [echo] Demonstrating the life cycle of a task
...
[lifecycle-nested-task] ---------------
[lifecycle-nested-task] execute() called

[lifecycle-nested-task] Value of the body text: null
[lifecycle-nested-task] Project: Example Application Build
[lifecycle-nested-task] Location: C:\AntBook\ch10\build.xml:1244:
[lifecycle-nested-task] Target: lifecycle-nested-target
[lifecycle-nested-task] Reference to lifecycle-nested-task found, of type org
.mwrm.ant.tasks.LifeCycleNestedTask. Its id is lifecycle-id.
[lifecycle-nested-task] Reference id: lifecycle-id
[lifecycle-nested-task] ---------------
```

```
[lifecycle-nested-task] Value of name element: Matthew
[lifecycle-nested-task] Value of name element: Laura
[lifecycle-nested-task] Value of name element: Jones
[lifecycle-nested-task] ---------------

BUILD SUCCESSFUL
```

Writing an addConfiguredXXX() Method

The only difference between `addXXX()` methods and `addConfiguredXXX()` methods is that Ant sets all the properties of the nested element's class before it passes it to the `addConfiguredXXX()` method. This means you can gain access to the information set in the build file. Listing 10-14 shows the `addConfiguredName()` method. You should comment out the `addName()` method before you compile this version of the task because Ant can't guarantee which method it will call (it depends on your JVM).

Listing 10-14. *`addConfiguredName()` Gives You Access to the Nested Element's Properties*

```
public void addConfiguredName(NameElement nameElement) {
    nameElements.add(nameElement);

    logAll("addConfiguredName()");
    log("Value of this name: " + nameElement.getName(), Project.MSG_VERBOSE);

}
```

To compare the `addName()` method with the `addConfiguredName()` method, run the code again:

```
> ant -lib dist/antBook-tasks.jar -v lifecycle-nested-target
```

```
Buildfile: build.xml

[lifecycle-nested-task] ---------------
[lifecycle-nested-task] addConfiguredName() called

[lifecycle-nested-task] Value of the body text: null
[lifecycle-nested-task] Project: Example Application Build
[lifecycle-nested-task] Location: C:\AntBook\ch10\build.xml:1244:
[lifecycle-nested-task] Target: lifecycle-nested-target
[lifecycle-nested-task] Reference to lifecycle-nested-task found, of type org
.apache.tools.ant.UnknownElement. Its id is lifecycle-id.
[lifecycle-nested-task] Reference id: lifecycle-id
[lifecycle-nested-task] ---------------
[lifecycle-nested-task] Value of this name: Matthew
```

```
[lifecycle-nested-task] ---------------
[lifecycle-nested-task] addConfiguredName() called

[lifecycle-nested-task] Value of the body text: null
[lifecycle-nested-task] Project: Example Application Build
[lifecycle-nested-task] Location: C:\AntBook\ch10\build.xml:1244:
[lifecycle-nested-task] Target: lifecycle-nested-target
[lifecycle-nested-task] Reference to lifecycle-nested-task found, of type org
.apache.tools.ant.UnknownElement. Its id is lifecycle-id.
[lifecycle-nested-task] Reference id: lifecycle-id
[lifecycle-nested-task] ---------------
[lifecycle-nested-task] Value of this name: Laura
[lifecycle-nested-task] ---------------
[lifecycle-nested-task] addConfiguredName() called

[lifecycle-nested-task] Value of the body text: null
[lifecycle-nested-task] Project: Example Application Build
[lifecycle-nested-task] Location: C:\AntBook\ch10\build.xml:1244:
[lifecycle-nested-task] Target: lifecycle-nested-target
[lifecycle-nested-task] Reference to lifecycle-nested-task found, of type org
.apache.tools.ant.UnknownElement. Its id is lifecycle-id.
[lifecycle-nested-task] Reference id: lifecycle-id
[lifecycle-nested-task] ---------------
[lifecycle-nested-task] Value of this name: Jones
[lifecycle-nested-task] ---------------
[lifecycle-nested-task] execute() called

[lifecycle-nested-task] Value of the body text: null
[lifecycle-nested-task] Project: Example Application Build
[lifecycle-nested-task] Location: C:\AntBook\ch10\build.xml:1244:
[lifecycle-nested-task] Target: lifecycle-nested-target
[lifecycle-nested-task] Reference to lifecycle-nested-task found, of type org
.mwrm.ant.tasks.LifeCycleNestedTask. Its id is lifecycle-id.
[lifecycle-nested-task] Reference id: lifecycle-id
[lifecycle-nested-task] ---------------
[lifecycle-nested-task] Value of name element: Matthew
[lifecycle-nested-task] Value of name element: Laura
[lifecycle-nested-task] Value of name element: Jones
[lifecycle-nested-task] ---------------

BUILD SUCCESSFUL
```

This time you can display the values of the nested <name> elements before you reach the execute() method.

Writing a createXXX() Method

A `createXXX()` method differs from `addXXX()` and `addConfiguredXXX()` methods in that it can work with any kind of object as a nested element. You need to define a `createXXX()` method with a signature like the following:

```
public XXXElement createXXX()
```

The nested element is the `NameElement` class, which has an empty, no-argument instructor so it's not a special case. However, you'll add a new constructor and some extra logic, as shown in Listing 10-15.

Listing 10-15. *The `NameElement` Class Now Has an Overloaded Constructor*

```
// The name element
public static class NameElement {

    // The name attribute of this element
    String name;

    // Tells the class whether we've used the overridden constructor
    private boolean usedConstructor = false;

    public NameElement() {
        // Empty
    }

    // Used by the createName() method
    public NameElement(String text) {
        this.name = text;
        usedConstructor = true;
    }

    // The mutator method for the name attribute
    public void setName(String name) {
        this.name = name;
    }

    // The accessor method for the name attribute
    public String getName() {
        return name;
    }

    // A method for dealing with body text
    public void addText(String text) {
        // Usage check
        if (name != null && !usedConstructor) {
            throw new BuildException("You can't specify a name attribute
                                      and nested text in <name> elements.");
```

```
            } else {
                this.name = text.trim();
            }
        }
    }
```

You now have a constructor that takes a string as an argument and a usage check that takes this into account.

The most important thing to remember when using a createXXX() method is that you create the instance of the nested element's class and pass to it Ant with a return statement from the createXXX() method. Once you have returned it, Ant will configure it and set its properties, overriding any properties you have set if a user has set values for them in the build file. Listing 10-16 shows the createName() method.

Listing 10-16. *You Have to Do the Work in the createName() Method*

```
    public NameElement createName() {
        NameElement nameElement = new NameElement("Madeleine");

        nameElements.add(nameElement);

        logAll("createName()");
        log("Value of this name: " + nameElement.getName(), Project.MSG_VERBOSE);
        return nameElement;
    }
```

Before you compile and run this task, remember to comment out addConfiguredName().

If you run the following, you will see that the task sets the value of each nested element's name attribute in turn. After that, Ant overrides each one and uses the values from the build file:

```
> ant -lib dist/antBook-tasks.jar -v lifecycle-nested-target
```

```
Buildfile: build.xml

lifecycle-nested-target:
     [echo] Demonstrating the life cycle of a task
...
[lifecycle-nested-task] ---------------
[lifecycle-nested-task] createName() called

[lifecycle-nested-task] Value of the body text: null
[lifecycle-nested-task] Project: Example Application Build
[lifecycle-nested-task] Location: C:\AntBook\ch10\build.xml:1244:
[lifecycle-nested-task] Target: lifecycle-nested-target
[lifecycle-nested-task] Reference to lifecycle-nested-task found, of type org
.apache.tools.ant.UnknownElement. Its id is lifecycle-id.
[lifecycle-nested-task] Reference id: lifecycle-id
[lifecycle-nested-task] ---------------
```

```
[lifecycle-nested-task] Value of this name: Madeleine
[lifecycle-nested-task] ---------------
[lifecycle-nested-task] createName() called

[lifecycle-nested-task] Value of the body text: null
[lifecycle-nested-task] Project: Example Application Build
[lifecycle-nested-task] Location: C:\AntBook\ch10\build.xml:1244:
[lifecycle-nested-task] Target: lifecycle-nested-target
[lifecycle-nested-task] Reference to lifecycle-nested-task found, of type org
.apache.tools.ant.UnknownElement. Its id is lifecycle-id.
[lifecycle-nested-task] Reference id: lifecycle-id
[lifecycle-nested-task] ---------------
[lifecycle-nested-task] Value of this name: Madeleine
[lifecycle-nested-task] ---------------
[lifecycle-nested-task] createName() called

[lifecycle-nested-task] Value of the body text: null
[lifecycle-nested-task] Project: Example Application Build
[lifecycle-nested-task] Location: C:\AntBook\ch10\build.xml:1244:
[lifecycle-nested-task] Target: lifecycle-nested-target
[lifecycle-nested-task] Reference to lifecycle-nested-task found, of type org
.apache.tools.ant.UnknownElement. Its id is lifecycle-id.
[lifecycle-nested-task] Reference id: lifecycle-id
[lifecycle-nested-task] ---------------
[lifecycle-nested-task] Value of this name: Madeleine
[lifecycle-nested-task] ---------------
[lifecycle-nested-task] addText() called
...
[lifecycle-nested-task] ---------------
[lifecycle-nested-task] ---------------
[lifecycle-nested-task] execute() called

[lifecycle-nested-task] Value of the body text: null
[lifecycle-nested-task] Project: Example Application Build
[lifecycle-nested-task] Location: C:\JavaStuff\AntBook\ch10\build.xml:1244:
[lifecycle-nested-task] Target: lifecycle-nested-target
[lifecycle-nested-task] Reference to lifecycle-nested-task found, of type org
.mwrm.ant.tasks.LifeCycleNestedTask. Its id is lifecycle-id.
[lifecycle-nested-task] Reference id: lifecycle-id
[lifecycle-nested-task] ---------------
[lifecycle-nested-task] Value of name element: Matthew
[lifecycle-nested-task] Value of name element: Laura
[lifecycle-nested-task] Value of name element: Jones
[lifecycle-nested-task] ---------------

BUILD SUCCESSFUL
```

Choosing Which Method to Use

The first choice to make when looking at the three methods described previously is between createXXX() and addXXX()/addConfiguredXXX(). If the nested element's object has a constructor that takes more than one argument or an argument that isn't a Project object, then you must use createXXX(). If, however, it has no arguments or takes a single Project object as an argument, you should use one of addXXX() or addConfiguredXXX().

If you simply want to set defaults for a nested element's attributes, use addXXX(). Ant will override those that the user has set, and you don't have to worry about spoiling a user's settings. If you want to check and verify attribute values, use addConfiguredXXX(). You can then override or correct input. For example, you could strip out any whitespace if it was going to interfere with the task's workings.

Writing Example Custom Tasks

You have seen the details of a task's life cycle, so now you can write some more useful custom tasks than the instructional code in the rest of the chapter. You'll start by creating a task that displays usage information for the project. In other words, this task will mimic the -projecthelp Ant command-line option in a build file. You'll then use it as the default target of the build file so that the user knows which tasks do what when they run Ant with no target set.

The other example task is an extension of the <javadoc> task. If you recall Chapter 6, the main drawback of the <javadoc> task was the lack of a check to see whether the source files were newer than a destination file. This meant you had to use <uptodate> tasks to determine whether it was worth running a <javadoc> task. You'll now re-create the check-docs target from Chapter 6 as a custom task.

Providing Usage Information

The usual way to provide usage information in a build file is with <echo> tasks in the default target of the build. When the user runs Ant with no targets as arguments, the <echo> tasks display whatever information the writer of the build file has provided. The drawback to this method is a high maintenance cost. Build files can change quite fast when development is underway, and maintaining the usage information can sometimes fall by the wayside. Typos can easily creep into this method, especially if many similarly named targets appear in the build file. Neat formatting can also be a problem.

You'll solve all this by using Ant's own usage information mechanism. When you use the -projecthelp command-line option, Ant's org.apache.tools.ant.Main class uses its printDescription() and printTargets() methods to display the build's description and main targets. (See Chapter 3 for more about Ant's command-line options.) The Main class does all the work of generating target names and descriptions and formats them for display. This removes chances of typos and messy formatting while ensuring the list of targets is always up to date.

The task will have a single, optional element called buildfile, which points to the build file from which you want to obtain the usage data. If you want to use the task to display the current build's targets, you can use the ant.file built-in property, which refers to the current build file:

```
<projecthelp buildfile="${ant.file}"/>
```

However, this is the default setting in the task, so you have no need to do so. In other words, the buildfile attribute is optional. Listing 10-17 shows the source for this task.

Listing 10-17. *The ProjectHelpTask Displays Usage Information for a Build*

```
package org.mwrm.ant.tasks;

import org.apache.tools.ant.Task;
import org.apache.tools.ant.Main;
import org.apache.tools.ant.BuildException;

/**
 * <p>The <code>ProjectHelpTask</code> class displays usage information
 * for the current project. This is the same information as is displayed
 * by <code>-projecthelp</code>.</p>
 *
 */

public class ProjectHelpTask extends Task {

    // The location of the build file to use when obtaining usage information.
    String buildfile;

    /**
     * <p>Runs the task. It calls <code>org.apache.tools.ant.Main.main()</code>
     * with the <code>-projecthelp</code> parameter. It will also send
     * the current build file's filename via the <code>-f</code> parameter.</p>
     *
     * <p>The <code>buildfile</code> attribute is optional.
     * The default is the task's build file.</p>
     */
    public void execute() throws BuildException {
        // If the buildfile attribute is null, we'll use the task's build file
        if (buildfile == null) {
            buildfile = getLocation().getFileName();
        }

        // The arguments that we will pass to the Main class.
        // The buildfile attribute must follow the -f parameter.
        String[] args = {"-projecthelp", "-f", buildfile};

        // Call the Main Ant class with the arguments.
            Main.main(args);
        }
```

```
    /**
     * Setter method for the <code>buildfile</code> attribute.
     * @param buildfile The filename of the current build.
     *
     */
    public void setBuildfile(String buildfile) {
        this.buildfile = buildfile;
    }
}
```

In the execute() method, you first check to see whether the user has specified a buildfile attribute. If not, you set the current build file's filename as the value of buildfile. You then build the three command-line arguments you'll send to Ant's Main class, using the -projecthelp option to signify you want a list of targets and the -f option to specify the build file to use. You then run the Main class by calling its main() entry method. The beauty of this solution is that it uses Ant's own error-checking mechanisms to ensure that the file exists. If it does not, Ant's sensible error messages inform the user so you don't have to worry about anything.

To use this task in a build file, you have to declare it in a <taskdef> task, as shown in Listing 10-18.

Listing 10-18. *The Default Target Displays Usage Information for This Build*

```
<?xml version="1.0"?>

<project name="Example Application Build" default="default" basedir=".">
  ...

  <!-- ################# -->
  <!-- Usage information -->
  <!-- ################# -->

  <!-- Display a list of targets in this project -->
  <target name="default" description="Display a list of targets in this project">
    <echo message="Usage information for this project:"/>
    <taskdef name="projecthelp" classname="org.mwrm.ant.tasks.ProjectHelpTask" />
    <projecthelp/>
  </target>
</project>
```

Remember to compile the task and place its class file in Ant's classpath before running the build.

Extending the <javadoc> Task

To write a task that adds functionality to the <javadoc> task, you will extend the org.apache.tools.ant.taskdefs.Javadoc task. This gives you access to the methods and attributes of the <javadoc> task that are needed when carrying out its normal function. To implement the functionality that checks whether a set of target files is newer than a set of source files, you will use an internal <uptodate> task (org.apache.tools.ant.taskdefs.UpToDate) and use its eval() method to check the files.

■ **Note** You could have started from scratch and used the org.apache.tools.ant.taskdefs.MatchingTask class as the basis for your task because you will be pattern matching. However, you have no need to do this when you want the Javadoc-generation powers of the Javadoc class and the pattern-matching powers of the UpToDate class at your disposal.

The new task can have a single target file, specified by the task's target attribute, or a file set of target files, set with nested <targetfiles> elements. These two techniques are mutually exclusive, so you'll test to see whether a user has specified them together.

The setTarget() method has the following signature:

```
public void setTarget(File target)
```

Recall that Ant will convert string input into one of a number of types so that you can use it as effectively as possible. In this case, Ant converts the string filename specified in the target attribute in a File object representing that very file before passing it to the setTarget() method.

The file sets specified in <targetfiles> elements are compared as a logical AND, which means they all must be newer than the source files to suppress Javadoc creation. This is how you set things up in Chapter 6. The source files are specified by a file set represented by a <srcfiles> nested element.

You'll use addXXX() methods to add the nested elements because you don't need to do anything with them and they are just normal file sets. They have the following signatures:

```
public void addSrcfiles(FileSet fileset)
public void addTargetfiles(FileSet fileset)
```

FileSet objects have a no-argument constructor and are therefore suitable candidates for use in addXXX() methods. In this instance, you are simply renaming the <fileset> element <srcfiles> or <targetfiles>, as the case may be. You won't extend the <fileset> element's functionality, but of course this would be possible if you wanted to extend the FileSet class. You're renaming them so that it's clear what the function of each nested element is.

Listing 10-19 shows a valid example of the task.

Listing 10-19. *Using the Custom Javadoc Generator*

```
<!-- Generate Javadocs for the application -->
<target name="ext-javadocs" depends="dir"
        description="Generate Javadocs for the application"
        unless="docs.notRequired">
  <echo message="Generating Javadocs for the application"/>
  <taskdef name="ext-javadoc"
           classname="org.mwrm.ant.tasks.ExtendJavadocTask" />
  <ext-javadoc destdir="${docs}/api" windowtitle="${javadoc.windowtitle}"
               target="${dist}/${appName}-${package.docs}.tar.gz">
```

```
      <srcfiles dir="${src}" includes="**" excludes="ant/**"/>
      <fileset refid="javadoc"/>
      <doctitle>
        ${javadoc.doctitle}
      </doctitle>
      <classpath refid="build.classpath"/>
      <link href="http://java.sun.com/j2se/${javadoc.j2se.version}/docs/api"/>
      <link href="http://java.sun.com/j2ee/${javadoc.j2ee.version}/docs/api"/>
    </ext-javadoc>
  </target>
```

This will check to see whether the file set specified in the <srcfiles> element is newer than the file specified in the target attribute of <ext-javadocs>. If it is newer, then the <ext-javadocs> task generates Javadocs. Listing 10-20 shows an example with nested <targetfiles> elements.

Listing 10-20. *Using Nested <targetfiles> Elements with the <ext-javadoc> Task*

```
<ext-javadoc destdir="${docs}/api" windowtitle="${javadoc.windowtitle}">
  <targetfiles dir="." includes="${dist}/${appName}-${package.docs}.zip"/>
  <targetfiles dir="." includes="${dist}/${appName}-${package.docs}.tar.gz"/>
  <srcfiles dir="${src}" includes="**" excludes="ant/**"/>
  <fileset refid="javadoc"/>
  <doctitle>
    ${javadoc.doctitle}
  </doctitle>
  <classpath refid="build.classpath"/>
  <link href="http://java.sun.com/j2se/${javadoc.j2se.version}/docs/api"/>
  <link href="http://java.sun.com/j2ee/${javadoc.j2ee.version}/docs/api"/>
</ext-javadoc>
```

The main work of the task takes place in the internal <uptodate> task. You'll use its setTargetFile() method to specify the target file you want to check against. It has the following signature, so you can see why you need a File argument to setTarget() and FileSet objects to represent nested <targetfiles> elements:

```
public void setTargetFile(File file)
```

To specify the file set of source files, you'll use its addSrcfiles() method. Its signature is as follows:

```
public void addSrcfiles(FileSet fileset)
```

The real work takes place in the <uptodate> task's eval() method. It compares the target file and the source files and returns a result. Its signature is as follows:

```
public boolean eval()
```

You'll call this method once for every file in the target file sets. By doing so, you will find any files signaling you should generate some Javadocs. One thing to consider when using internal tasks like this is that you should always attach them to the current project. If you do not, Ant won't give them access to project-specific utilities, and you will get many NullPointerException stacks. In this case, the <uptodate> task uses a projectwide utility to scan directories for files and their modified times. If you didn't add it to the current project, it won't be able to obtain one.

Listing 10-21 shows the task in full.

Listing 10-21. *The ExtendJavadocTask Adds Checks for Up-to-Date Files to the <javadoc> Task*

```
package org.mwrm.ant.tasks;

import java.io.File;

import java.util.Enumeration;
import java.util.StringTokenizer;
import java.util.Vector;

import org.apache.tools.ant.Project;
import org.apache.tools.ant.BuildException;

import org.apache.tools.ant.taskdefs.Javadoc;
import org.apache.tools.ant.taskdefs.UpToDate;

import org.apache.tools.ant.types.FileSet;

/**
 * <p>The <code>ExtendJavadocTask</code> class
 * extends the <code>org.apache.tools.ant.taskdefs.Javadoc</code> task.
 * It checks whether a set of source files is newer than a set of target files
 * and if so, it generates Javadocs.</p>
 *
 */

public class ExtendJavadocTask extends Javadoc {

    // The attribute of the task element
    File target;

    // A set of file sets, each of which is provided by a nested file set
    private Vector targetFileSets  = new Vector();

    // The internal <uptodate> task
    private UpToDate utd;

    /**
     * <p>Creates a new instance of an internal
     * <code>&lt;uptodate&gt;</code> task
     * and adds it to the current project.</p>
     */
```

```
public void init() {
    // We need an instance of the <uptodate> task
    utd = new UpToDate();
    // We need to add the task to this project
    utd.setProject(this.getProject());
}

/**
 * <p>Checks whether Javadocs should be created and then calls
 * <code>super.execute()</code> if so.</p>
 * <p>This method does usage checks on the task's attributes
 * and its nested elements.
 * It will throw a <code>BuildException</code> if there is a violation.</p>
 */
public void execute() throws BuildException {
    // This is the usage information

    // We can't have a target attribute
    // and nested targetfiles elements
    if (target != null && targetFileSets.size() > 0) {
        String msg = "You can't specify a targetfile attribute "
            + "and <targetfiles> elements.";
        throw new BuildException(msg);
    }
    // We have to specify either a target attribute
    // or at least one nested targetfiles elements
    if (target == null && targetFileSets.size() == 0) {
        String msg = "You must specify either a targetfile attribute "
            + "or at least one <targetfiles> element.";
        throw new BuildException(msg);
    }

    // If this is false, the files aren't up to date
    // and we  have to run the Javadocs
    boolean eval = false;

    // If we've got to this point, we know the usage must be correct.
    // Let's check whether a single target attribute has been used.
    if (target != null) {
        // Get the results of the check
        eval = getResult(target);
    } else {
        // If a target attribute wasn't specified,
        // at least one nested targetfiles element was.

        // We first get all the file sets represented by the nested elements
        Enumeration e = targetFileSets.elements();
```

```
            // And then iterate over them
            while (e.hasMoreElements()) {

                // The next element is a file set, so we get its files
                // in a semicolon-separated list
                String files = e.nextElement().toString();
                // Next, we split the list into its filenames
                StringTokenizer st = new StringTokenizer(files, ";");
                // And iterate over them to test each one
                while (st.hasMoreTokens()) {
                    // We create a file from the current filename
                    // in the iteration
                    File tempTarget = new File(st.nextToken());
                    // Get the results of the check
                    eval = getResult(tempTarget);

                    // One false result is enough to fail the whole file set
                    if (eval == false) {
                        break;
                    }
                }
                // One false result is enough to fail the whole file set
                if (eval == false) {
                    break;
                }
            }
        }

        // If the test failed, we want to generate Javadocs
        if (eval == false) {
            super.execute();
        } else {
            log("Skipping Javadoc creation. The files are up to date.",
                Project.MSG_INFO);
        }
    }

    // Checks whether the files are up to date
    private boolean getResult(File file) {
        // Set the target property in the <uptodate> task
        utd.setTargetFile(file);
        // Evaluate the files
        return ((utd.eval() != false) ? true : false);
    }
```

```
    /**
     * <p>The setter method for the <code>target</code> attribute.</p>
     * @param target A file to check against
     */
    public void setTarget(File target) {
        this.target = target;
    }

    /**
     * <p>The setter method for the file set
     * contained in the nested <code>&lt;srcfiles&gt;</code> element.</p>
     * @param fileset A file set of source files
     */
    public void addSrcfiles(FileSet fileset) {
        utd.addSrcfiles(fileset);
    }

    /**
     * <p>The setter method for the file sets
     * contained in nested <code>&lt;targetfiles&gt;</code> elements.</p>
     * @param fileset A file set of target files
     */
    public void addTargetfiles(FileSet fileset) {
        targetFileSets.add(fileset);
    }
}
```

As you did earlier, you use a Vector to store multiple instances of nested elements, in this case <targetfiles>. When you want to test the files, you iterate over the Enumeration of this Vector and then iterate over each file set contained within it. For each of the files in a file set, you call the <uptodate> task's eval() method.

Using an antlib File

Up until now you have added your custom tasks to the build file with <taskdef> tasks. However, if your project uses a lot of custom tasks or a library of third-party tasks (as you will do later), you can include them in a batch in a better way. To do so, you must use an antlib file that contains the task definitions. An antlib file is an XML file with an <antlib> root element and a combination of <taskdef> and <typedef> elements. Once you have defined all the custom tasks you require in the antlib file, you include it in the build file as follows:

```
<typedef file="antlib.xml"/>
```

In effect, an antlib file acts as a properties file for task definitions with all the advantages that entails. For example, you have a central file that contains all your task definitions, which means they are easier to maintain. You can also copy this antlib file to another project and use its custom tasks with a single <typedef> statement instead of a whole collection of <taskdef> statements.

Note The <typedef> task is a more general version of the <taskdef> task, which you can use to add data types to an Ant project. The <taskdef> task is equivalent to <taskdef adapter="org.apache.tools.ant.TaskAdapter" adaptto="org.apache.tools.ant.Task"/>.

Moving all the custom and third-party tasks into an antlib file is as simple as wrapping them in an <antlib> element, as shown in Listing 10-22.

Listing 10-22. *The antlib.xml File Contains the Book's Task Definitions*

```
<?xml version="1.0"?>
<antlib>

  <!-- ######################################## -->
  <!-- The third-party tasks for the Ant book -->
  <!-- ######################################## -->

  <!-- The deploy task for web applications on Tomcat -->
  <taskdef name="deploy" classname="org.apache.catalina.ant.DeployTask"/>

  <!-- The undeploy task for web applications on Tomcat -->
  <taskdef name="undeploy" classname="org.apache.catalina.ant.UndeployTask"/>

  <!-- Checkstyle checks the code versus code conventions -->
  <taskdef resource="checkstyletask.properties"/>

  <!-- ################################### -->
  <!-- The custom tasks for the Ant book -->
  <!-- ################################### -->

  <!-- The first two demonstrate the life cycle of a task -->
  <taskdef name="lifecycle-task" classname="org.mwrm.ant.tasks.LifeCycleTask" />
  <taskdef name="lifecycle-nested-task"
           classname="org.mwrm.ant.tasks.LifeCycleNestedTask" />

  <!-- Extends the <javadoc> task -->
  <!-- It checks source file modification times vs. target file modifications -->
  <taskdef name="ext-javadoc" classname="org.mwrm.ant.tasks.ExtendJavadocTask" />

  <!-- Demonstrates converting parameters -->
  <taskdef name="class-set-test" classname="org.mwrm.ant.tasks.ClassSetTask" />

  <!-- Displays usage information generated from a build file -->
  <taskdef name="projecthelp" classname="org.mwrm.ant.tasks.ProjectHelpTask" />

</antlib>
```

Now if you import this file to a build file with a <typedef> element, all these tasks are available to Ant.

Another helpful way to use an antlib file is to package it with your custom tasks in a JAR file. By placing this JAR file in Ant's classpath, you can then reference it with a <typedef> task. For example, let's place the antlib.xml file in the org/mwrm/ant directory of a JAR in Ant's classpath. You'll use the properties shown in Listing 10-23.

Listing 10-23. *The Properties for Adding an antlib File to a JAR File*

```
ant.tasks.antlib.xml=antlib.xml
ant.tasks.antlib.package=org/mwrm/ant
ant.tasks.antlib.dir=${ant.tasks.build}/${ant.tasks.antlib.package}
```

To use these properties when building the JAR file, you'll add a <copy> task to the compile-ant-tasks target from earlier in the chapter. Listing 10-24 shows how this task copies the antlib file into the build directory of the JAR file and into the package specified in ant.tasks.antlib.package.

Listing 10-24. *Adding an antlib File to a JAR File*

```
<!-- Compile the Ant tasks -->
<target name="compile-ant-tasks" depends="dir"
        description="Compile the Ant tasks">
  <echo message="Compiling the Ant tasks"/>
  <mkdir dir="${ant.tasks.build}"/>
  <javac srcdir="${ant.tasks.src}" destdir="${ant.tasks.build}"/>
  <copy file="${ant.tasks.antlib.xml}" todir="${ant.tasks.antlib.dir}"/>
  <jar destfile="${ant.tasks.jar}" basedir="${ant.tasks.build}"/>
</target>
```

You could then use the custom tasks in a build file as follows, referencing its package and filename:

```
<typedef resource="${ant.tasks.antlib.package}/${ant.tasks.antlib.xml}"/>
```

This entry evaluates to the following:

```
<typedef resource="org/mwrm/ant/antlib.xml"/>
```

The final way to include an antlib file is to use the special antlib:package.name namespace URI. When Ant encounters an element within the defined namespace, it checks the classpath for a resource called antlib.xml and loads any tasks defined here. If you used this approach with the example, you'd define the namespace and tasks as shown in Listing 10-25.

Listing 10-25. *Defining the antlib Namespace*

```
<project name="Example Application Build" default="default" basedir="."
        xmlns:antBook="antlib:org.mwrm.ant">

  <!-- Display a list of targets in this project -->
  <target name="default" description="Display a list of targets in this project">
    <echo message="Usage information for this project:"/>
    <antBook:projecthelp/>
  </target>

</project>
```

The <project> element introduces the antBook namespace and tells Ant that its URI points to an antlib file in the org.mwrm.ant package. You then use the antBook namespace to identify a custom tag later in the file.

Using Third-Party Custom Tasks

A great place to start if you are looking for third-party Ant tasks is the Ant-Contrib project (http://ant-contrib.sourceforge.net). This collection of custom tasks includes a large number of logic tasks, an HTTP POST task, and some property-manipulation tasks, among others. It also includes an Ant performance-monitoring tool.

You've also already seen some product-specific Ant custom tasks for the Tomcat server and the Checkstyle tool. To this list you can add custom tasks for the Subversion source code versioning system (http://subclipse.tigris.org/svnant.html), which is an alternative to CVS, and major pieces of server software, such as BEA's WebLogic server (http://e-docs.bea.com/wls/docs90/).

As a demonstration, let's use one of the Ant-Contrib tasks to solve one of the problems running through this book: the <javadoc> task's lack of conditional functionality. You've already solved this problem twice. The first time you set up your own conditional checking with <uptodate> conditions in a separate target. The second time you wrote a custom task to include the conditional functionality. This time you'll wrap the <javadoc> task in an Ant-Contrib <if> task that will run it only if a nested condition is true. The general structure of the <if> task you will be using is as follows:

```
<if>
  <nested.condition/>
  <then>
    <task/>
    <task/>
  </then>
</if>
```

The <if> task accepts only one nested condition, but you can use <and> and <or> elements to include other checks. You already have the condition from Chapter 6, so you'll use that as shown in Listing 10-26, though you have to use a <not> element this time because of the <if> task's semantics. That is, without the <not> element, the <if> task will run the task if all the conditions nested within the <and> element are true. You want the opposite to happen, so you have to reverse the decision.

The <javadoc> task is the same as the one in Chapter 6. You can use only one <then> element in each <if> element (though you can also use one <then> element in each <elseif> element, as described next). To use the target shown in Listing 10-26, you must have the Ant-Contrib JAR file in Ant's classpath. The <typedef> task will then be able to find it and include its tasks in the build.

Listing 10-26. *Using the Ant-Contrib <if> Task*

```
<typedef resource="net/sf/antcontrib/antlib.xml"/>

<!-- Use antcontribs <if> to check if you should build the Javadocs -->
<target name="javadocs-antcontrib" depends="dir"
        description="Use antcontribs &lt;if&gt; to check the Javadocs">
  <echo message="Using antcontribs &lt;if&gt; to check the Javadocs"/>
  <if>
    <not>
      <and>
        <uptodate targetfile="${dist}/${appName}-${package.docs}.zip">
          <srcfiles dir="${src}" includes="**"/>
        </uptodate>
        <uptodate targetfile="${dist}/${appName}-${package.docs}.tar.gz">
          <srcfiles dir="${src}" includes="**"/>
        </uptodate>
      </and>
    </not>
    <then>
      <echo message="Generating Javadocs for the application"/>
        <javadoc destdir="${docs}/api" windowtitle="${javadoc.windowtitle}">
          <fileset refid="javadoc"/>
          <doctitle>
            ${javadoc.doctitle}
          </doctitle>
          <classpath refid="build.classpath"/>
          <link
          href="http://java.sun.com/j2se/${javadoc.j2se.version}/docs/api"/>
          <link
          href="http://java.sun.com/j2ee/${javadoc.j2ee.version}/docs/api"/>
        </javadoc>
    </then>
  </if>
</target>
```

In addition to the <then> nested element, you could have specified nested <elseif> elements or a single <else> element. The <elseif> element is the same as the <if> task, but it cannot contain an <else> element. The <else> element is a container for tasks just as the <then> element is.

Summary

In this chapter, you looked at how to write Ant custom tasks when the tasks that come with Ant just don't do what you want. You started by examining the custom task life cycle and what this means when you are writing a custom task. You moved on to the API and used various techniques to examine the life cycle in detail. This included examining the values of Ant objects at different stages of the life cycle.

You looked at nested elements, which to begin with can look quite complex but are really straightforward. The process for adding layers of nesting is the same as it is for one layer of nesting. I discussed the three different methods that Ant provides for setting nested elements and showed when to use each method.

Toward the end of the chapter, you learned how to write two useful custom tasks. The first prints usage information given a build file, and the second checks the freshness of files before creating Javadocs. The absence of this ability somewhat limits the built-in `<javadoc>` task.

You finished the chapter by looking at some third-party custom tasks.

CHAPTER 11

Extending Ant

Up until Chapter 10, I showed how to use Ant as it comes out of the box, with the odd addition to illustrate a point. However, Chapter 10 introduced custom tasks, which give you enormous power and flexibility if Ant does not provide what you want. This is not the end to Ant's extensions; I'll cover some of the others in this chapter, as well as some aspects of Ant you won't use during the normal course of a build but are useful nonetheless.

Specifically, you'll look at logging in Ant, which is not something you've really cared about until now. Ant comes with some simple logging mechanisms of its own, but you can expand on these greatly with frameworks such as JUnit. You'll also see how to write your own logging components using the Ant API.

Another component you'll look at in this chapter is mappers. Many tasks operate on files but can usually work with only one at a time. Mappers are a way of selecting groups of files for a task and so boost the efficiency of many Ant tasks.

Logging Ant Builds

Not all Ant builds are watched over and therefore are left to their own devices. Like every automatic process, however, it is useful to capture the results of an automatic build so that you can see the outcome. You could place these results on a web server, which means you could view them remotely and respond appropriately. Another reason to capture the results of a build is to analyze build times if the build is taking too long or is using up too many system resources.

Ant has two kinds of logging components: listeners and loggers. Ant informs listeners of various events that take place during a build:

- When a build starts
- When a build finishes
- When a target starts
- When a target finishes
- When a task starts
- When a task finishes
- When a message is logged

Ant provides the `org.apache.tools.ant.BuildListener` interface for you to implement should you want to create a custom listener. It defines seven methods that correspond to the events listed previously. Much like custom tasks, Ant calls the appropriate method at the appropriate point in the listener's life cycle.

A logger is a kind of listener that also has access to Ant's output and error streams, which listeners do not. However, you can use a logger from a listener via the project's `log()` method. You can also set a logger's global logging level and make its output suitable for use in emacs or similar systems. `org.apache.tools.ant.BuildLogger` is the interface that you must implement to create a custom logger.

■ **Note** While you can create custom listeners and loggers, Ant does provide its own implementations, which you'll look at first.

Ant's basic logging mechanism displays logging messages to standard `out` by default, which is how you've seen the log messages up to this point in the book. You also saw how to send log messages to the logging mechanism and the different logging levels in Chapter 10 when you used a custom task's `log()` method. If you wanted to save the results of an Ant build, you would use the `-logfile` command-line option as follows:

```
> ant -logfile ant.log dir
```

This produces a file like the one shown in Listing 11-1.

Listing 11-1. *The `ant.log` Log File Produced with the `-logfile` Option*

```
dir:
     [echo] Creating the working directories
    [mkdir] Created dir: C:\AntBook\ch11\build\stand-alone
    [mkdir] Created dir: C:\AntBook\ch11\build\web\WEB-INF\classes

BUILD SUCCESSFUL
Total time: 4 seconds
```

This is pretty much what you would see on the console, minus the name of the build file Ant is using. This is the case with all the forms of logging you will see in this chapter.

The default logger is called `org.apache.tools.ant.DefaultLogger`, and you can specify it with the `-logger` command-line option as follows:

```
> ant -logger org.apache.tools.ant.DefaultLogger dir
```

If you want to remove empty targets from the output, you can use the `org.apache.tools.ant.NoBannerLogger` implementation. This means any targets that don't produce output will not appear in the log, whether that be the console or a file.

■ **Note** You can set only one logger with the `-logger` command-line option. However, some of the loggers you'll see in this chapter can be called as listeners with the `-listener` option. This means you can have two loggers at once should you need the functionality.

Sending E-mail Confirmations

One way to make sure you see the results of a build is to set up an automatic e-mail notification service with Ant's mail logger. This logger uses a number of properties to configure the mail it sends and can vary the message depending on the success or failure of the build. Listing 11-2 shows an example properties file for this logger, which you should specify with a `<property>` task.

Listing 11-2. *Properties That Configure Ant's Mail Logger*

```
MailLogger.mailhost=smtp.mail.yahoo.co.uk
MailLogger.user=antBook
MailLogger.password=antB0Ok
MailLogger.from=ant.log@example.com
MailLogger.failure.to=ant.results@example.com
MailLogger.success.to=ant.results@example.com
MailLogger.failure.subject=Build failed
MailLogger.success.subject=Build succeeded
```

It would be a good idea to pass the username and password on the command line, but automated builds make this difficult because you still have to store them as plain text. To run the mail logger, use the following `-logger` option:

```
> ant -logger org.apache.tools.ant.listener.MailLogger compile-stand-alone
```

The e-mail will contain the results of the build as they appeared in the console or in the log file, should you specify that option. The mail logger still displays the output as if it were the default logger.

■ **Note** If you set the `MailLogger.success.notify` property to `false`, Ant will not send an e-mail if the build succeeds. Conversely, if you set `MailLogger.failure.notify` to `false`, Ant will not send an e-mail if the build fails.

Using XML Logs

Ant also supplies an XML logger that can display the results on the console as XML or save them in XML format. You can also specify a style sheet to attach to the XML file so that, for example, web browsers can transform it into HTML for a user. In this case, you can use the XML logger as a logger by using the `-logger` option or a listener by using the `-listener` option.

If you use it as a logger, it will supplant the default logger and will display the XML to the console unless you use the `-logfile` option to specify an output file. The listener version allows you to specify any logger you like. It will save the output to a file called `log.xml`, unless you use the `XmlLogger.file` property to specify an alternative filename.

Both these incarnations set a reference to an XSL style sheet. By default this is `log.xsl` in the current directory, but you can specify another filename with the `ant.XmlLogger.stylesheet.uri` property. Ant comes with an example XSL file, `ANT_HOME/etc/log.xsl`, which is an excellent place to start if you want to use this technique. If you find that it doesn't provide just what you want, then it's also a great basis for your own version.

Here is the XML logger in its different guises:

```
> ant -listener org.apache.tools.ant.XmlLogger compile-stand-alone
> ant -logger org.apache.tools.ant.XmlLogger -logfile log.xml compile-stand-alone
```

The first command will save the XML results in `log.xml` and will display the normal set of messages on the console. The second command will save the XML results in `log.xml` but won't display any results on the console.

Figure 11-1 shows the results of the XSL transformation of the XML file in a browser.

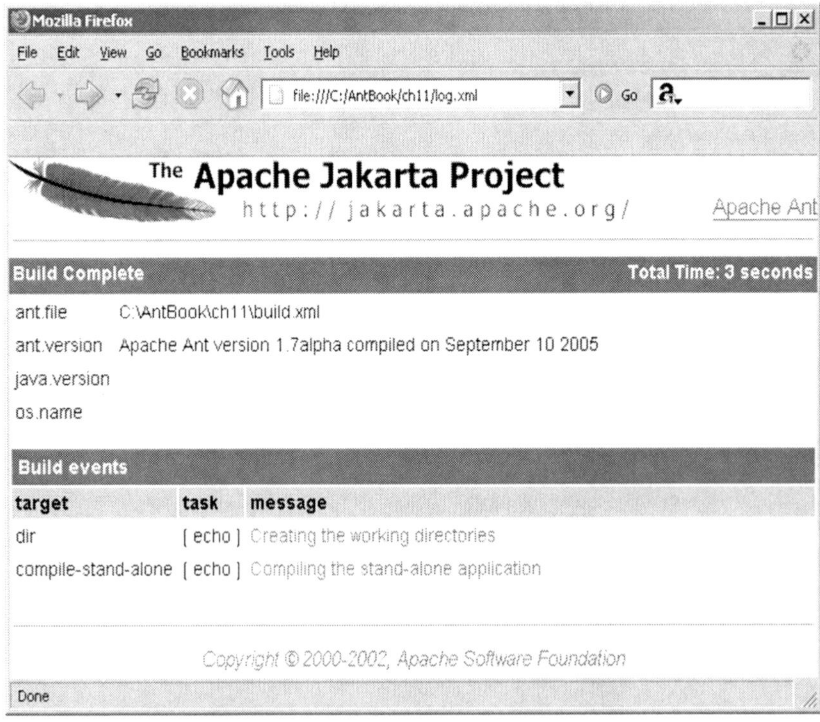

Figure 11-1. *The transformed output of the XML logger*

Using a Log4j Logger

The final logger you'll look at is the Log4j logger. (You won't look at another logger, called the ANSI color logger, here.) Log4j is the de facto logging framework for Java applications, so it's natural that Ant should include a logger that uses it. The Log4j logger is much more flexible than the previous options and has the advantage that you call it with the -listener command-line option so you can use it at the same time as the mail logger. I won't go into any detail as to how Log4j works except where it applies to Ant.

The first step is to download the Log4j classes from http://logging.apache.org/log4j/. Extract the files, and place LOG4J_HOME/dist/lib/log4j.jar in Ant's classpath. You can either put it in ANT_HOME/lib or use the -lib switch at the command line. The final step of configuration is to add a Log4j configuration file, as shown in Listing 11-3. Call this file log4j.properties, and place it in Ant's classpath as well. For the purposes of this chapter, you can leave it in the build's base directory if you want. Ant will find it there. Remember to change the path to the log file to suit your system.

Listing 11-3. *The log4j.properties File*

```
# Set the root logger for Ant
log4j.rootLogger=INFO, AntLogger

# Log to a file
log4j.appender.AntLogger=org.apache.log4j.FileAppender
log4j.appender.AntLogger.File=C:/TEMP/antBook/logs/ant.log

# Use the simple layout
log4j.appender.AntLogger.layout=org.apache.log4j.SimpleLayout
```

This is a simple configuration that sets the level of logging and the log file for Ant to use. The logging levels are, in ascending order of severity, as follows: ALL, DEBUG, INFO, WARN, ERROR, FATAL, and OFF. You should be careful to set the level of logging to the minimum you require because build times can increase significantly if you choose too low a level; at the same time, you may miss crucial information if you set the level too high.

To use the built-in Log4j logger, you have to specify it with the -listener option at the command line, like so:

```
> ant -listener org.apache.tools.ant.listener.Log4jListener -lib log4j.jar dir
```

Here the dir target serves as a simple example. Listing 11-4 shows the contents of the ant.log file, with the start and end of the build and the start and end of the target highlighted in bold.

Listing 11-4. *The ant.log Log File*

```
INFO - Build started.
INFO - Task "property" started.
INFO - Task "property" finished.
INFO - Task "property" started.
INFO - Task "property" finished.
INFO - Task "property" started.
INFO - Task "property" finished.
INFO - Task "path" started.
INFO - Task "path" finished.
...
```

```
INFO - Target "dir" started.
INFO - Task "echo" started.
WARN - Creating the working directories
INFO - Task "echo" finished.
...
INFO - Target "dir" finished.
INFO - Build finished.
```

If you compare these entries to what Ant displayed to the console, you will see the message on the screen that was sent by the <echo> task. Referring to the log file, you can see that the <echo> task sent this message at the level of WARN (defined by Project.MSG_WARN). You can set the level of the <echo> task's messages, but by default it logs only those messages of warning level and higher. Other tasks send messages at the information level. Now that you have the basics in place, you can create more complex logging setups.

Using Patterns in Log Files

Log4j doesn't limit you to using simple text files. For example, the previous log file has no dates or times. To change this, you can use a pattern layout, which uses pattern characters just as C does. Table 11-1 describes those characters relevant to Ant. See http://logging.apache.org/log4j/docs/api/org/apache/log4j/PatternLayout.html for more details on Log4j's logging patterns. To specify a pattern character in a log pattern, prefix it with %.

Table 11-1. *Pattern Layout Placeholders*

Pattern Character	Description
c	The category of the logging event. In Ant terms, this displays the project component that made the log entry. You can configure the precision of the category name by placing an integer in brackets after the character. In this case, only the corresponding number of the rightmost components of the category name will be printed. For example, for the category org.apache.tools.ant.Project, the pattern %c{1} will print Project. This is a useful pattern character when you want to find out where a certain log message has come from. You can then use this information to create more specific log files. I'll cover this in Chapter 12.
d	The date of this log entry, which may be followed by a date format enclosed between braces (for example, %d{HH:mm:ss} or %d{dd MMM yyyy HH:mm:ss}). If no format is given, then ISO 8601 format is used. For better results, you should use the Log4j date formatters. These are ABSOLUTE, DATE, and ISO8601, for specifying AbsoluteTimeDateFormat, DateTimeDateFormat, and ISO8601DateFormat, respectively (for example, %d{ISO8601} or %d{ABSOLUTE}). ABSOLUTE is HH:mm:ss,SSS. DATE is dd MMM YYYY HH:mm:ss,SSS. ISO8601 is YYYY-MM-dd HH:mm:ss,SSS.
F	The filename where the logging request was issued. This can be slow, so you should avoid using this option unless execution speed isn't an issue.

Table 11-1. *Pattern Layout Placeholders*

Pattern Character	Description
l	The location of the caller that generated the logging event. The location information depends on the JVM implementation but usually consists of the fully qualified name of the calling method, followed by the filename and line number between parentheses. Here's an example: `org.apache.tools.ant.listener.Log4jListener.buildStarted(Log4jListener.java:58)`. The location information can be useful, but obtaining it is extremely slow.
L	The line number where the logging request was issued. Obtaining caller location information is extremely slow.
m	The application-supplied message associated with the logging event.
M	The method name where the logging request was issued. Obtaining caller location information is extremely slow.
n	The platform-dependent line-separator character(s). This conversion character offers practically the same performance as using a line-separator string such as `\n` or `\r\n`. Thus, it's the preferred way of specifying a line separator.
p	Used to output the priority of the logging event.
r	Used to output the number of milliseconds elapsed since the start of the application until the creation of the logging event.
t	Used to output the name of the thread that generated the logging event.
%	The sequence `%%` outputs a single percent sign.

Listing 11-5 shows how to put these characters into action.

Listing 11-5. *Using Patterns in Log Entries*

```
# Set the root logger for Ant
log4j.rootLogger=INFO, AntLogger

# Log to a pattern file
log4j.appender.AntLogger=org.apache.log4j.FileAppender
log4j.appender.AntLogger.File=C:/TEMP/antBook/logs/ant.pattern.log

# Use a pattern layout
log4j.appender.AntLogger.layout=org.apache.log4j.PatternLayout
log4j.appender.AntLogger.layout.ConversionPattern=%d{ISO8601} : %p : %m %n
```

In this case, you're logging the date in ISO 8601 format, followed by the priority of the message (`%p`) and the message itself (`%m`). The line ends with a new-line character (`%n`). Run the same command as before:

```
> ant -listener org.apache.tools.ant.listener.Log4jListener -lib log4j.jar dir
```

It should look something like Listing 11-6.

Listing 11-6. *The `ant.pattern.log` Log File*

```
2005-09-09 22:47:45,849 : INFO : Build started.
2005-09-09 22:47:47,962 : INFO : Task "property" started.
2005-09-09 22:47:48,252 : INFO : Task "property" finished.
2005-09-09 22:47:48,252 : INFO : Task "property" started.
2005-09-09 22:47:48,252 : INFO : Task "property" finished.
2005-09-09 22:47:48,252 : INFO : Task "property" started.
2005-09-09 22:47:48,252 : INFO : Task "property" finished.
2005-09-09 22:47:48,252 : INFO : Task "path" started.
2005-09-09 22:47:49,384 : INFO : Task "path" finished.
...
2005-09-09 22:47:51,537 : INFO : Target "dir" started.
2005-09-09 22:47:51,537 : INFO : Task "echo" started.
2005-09-09 22:47:51,557 : WARN : Creating the working directories
2005-09-09 22:47:51,557 : INFO : Task "echo" finished.
...
2005-09-09 22:47:51,597 : INFO : Target "dir" finished.
2005-09-09 22:47:51,758 : INFO : Build finished.
```

Here you can see the pattern has been applied to each of the log entries.

Using HTML Log Files

If you want, you can also log entries to HTML log files. Listing 11-7 shows this configuration.

Listing 11-7. *Writing to an HTML Log File*

```
# Set the root logger for Ant
log4j.rootLogger=INFO, AntLogger

# Log to an HTML file
log4j.appender.AntLogger=org.apache.log4j.FileAppender
log4j.appender.AntLogger.File=C:/TEMP/antBook/logs/ant.log.html

# Set the layout to HTML, and specify a title
log4j.appender.AntLogger.layout=org.apache.log4j.HTMLLayout
log4j.appender.AntLogger.layout.Title=Apress Ant Log
```

Figure 11-2 shows the results.

Here you can see the default HTML layout, which shows the category that caused the logging event and the time from the start of the first logging event (the start of the build). It's interesting to note that logging at the start and end of tasks has a category of `org.apache.tools.ant.UnknownElement`. If you look at Figure 11-3, you can see that actual logging messages from inside a task have the implementing class's classname as their category.

You'll return to these categories in the "Logging Project Components" section.

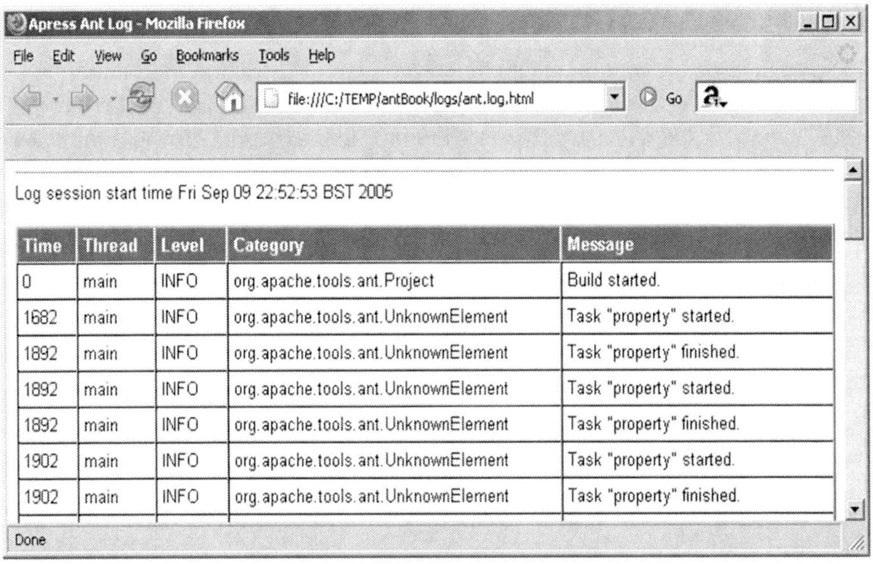

Log session start time Fri Sep 09 22:52:53 BST 2005

Time	Thread	Level	Category	Message
0	main	INFO	org.apache.tools.ant.Project	Build started.
1682	main	INFO	org.apache.tools.ant.UnknownElement	Task "property" started.
1892	main	INFO	org.apache.tools.ant.UnknownElement	Task "property" finished.
1892	main	INFO	org.apache.tools.ant.UnknownElement	Task "property" started.
1892	main	INFO	org.apache.tools.ant.UnknownElement	Task "property" finished.
1902	main	INFO	org.apache.tools.ant.UnknownElement	Task "property" started.
1902	main	INFO	org.apache.tools.ant.UnknownElement	Task "property" finished.

Figure 11-2. *The HTML layout log*

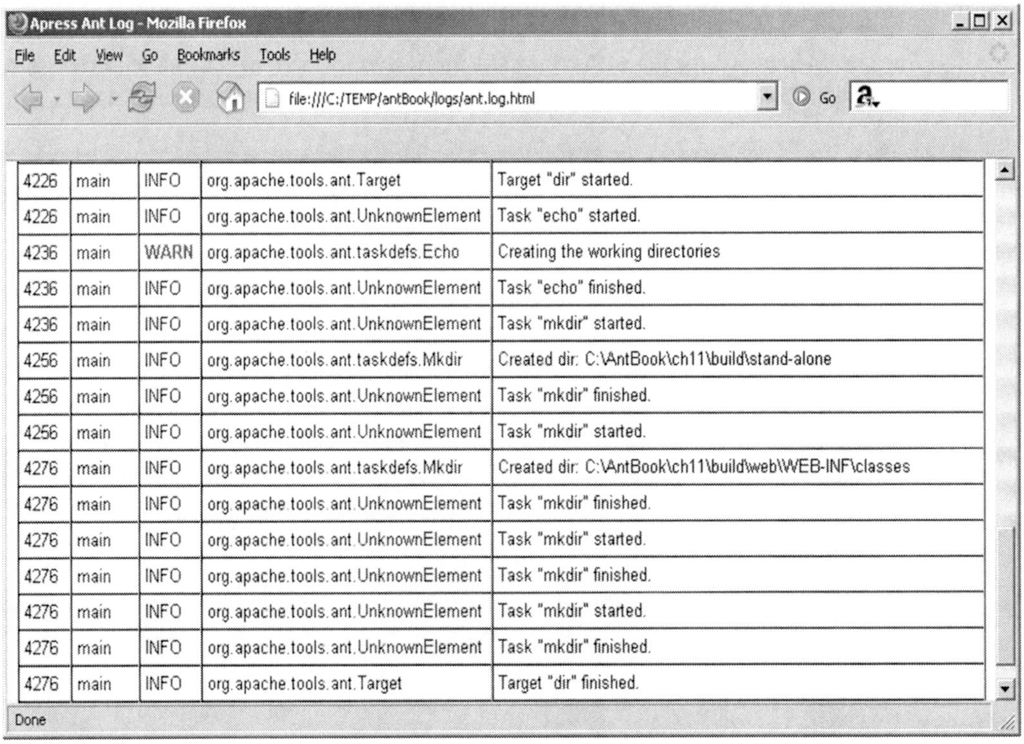

4226	main	INFO	org.apache.tools.ant.Target	Target "dir" started.
4226	main	INFO	org.apache.tools.ant.UnknownElement	Task "echo" started.
4236	main	WARN	org.apache.tools.ant.taskdefs.Echo	Creating the working directories
4236	main	INFO	org.apache.tools.ant.UnknownElement	Task "echo" finished.
4236	main	INFO	org.apache.tools.ant.UnknownElement	Task "mkdir" started.
4256	main	INFO	org.apache.tools.ant.taskdefs.Mkdir	Created dir: C:\AntBook\ch11\build\stand-alone
4256	main	INFO	org.apache.tools.ant.UnknownElement	Task "mkdir" finished.
4256	main	INFO	org.apache.tools.ant.UnknownElement	Task "mkdir" started.
4276	main	INFO	org.apache.tools.ant.taskdefs.Mkdir	Created dir: C:\AntBook\ch11\build\web\WEB-INF\classes
4276	main	INFO	org.apache.tools.ant.UnknownElement	Task "mkdir" finished.
4276	main	INFO	org.apache.tools.ant.UnknownElement	Task "mkdir" started.
4276	main	INFO	org.apache.tools.ant.UnknownElement	Task "mkdir" finished.
4276	main	INFO	org.apache.tools.ant.UnknownElement	Task "mkdir" started.
4276	main	INFO	org.apache.tools.ant.UnknownElement	Task "mkdir" finished.
4276	main	INFO	org.apache.tools.ant.Target	Target "dir" finished.

Figure 11-3. *The messages from within a task are given a specific category.*

Using the Console to Display Log Messages

Ant already logs to the console window at different levels depending on the command-line options (-q for quiet, -v for verbose, or -d for debug). The advantage of using Log4j is that you can use custom layouts, and Ant doesn't display everything to the console. However, Ant overrides any custom layout if it would have displayed the message anyway. Listing 11-8 shows how to log to the console.

Listing 11-8. *Logging to the Console*

```
# Set the root logger for Ant
log4j.rootLogger=INFO, AntLogger

# Log to the console
log4j.appender.AntLogger=org.apache.log4j.ConsoleAppender
log4j.appender.AntLogger.Target=System.out

# Set a custom layout level
log4j.appender.AntLogger.layout=org.apache.log4j.PatternLayout
log4j.appender.AntLogger.layout.ConversionPattern=%d{ISO8601} : %p : %m %n
```

The pattern here is the same as that for the pattern layout file, so the output to the console will be identical. To illustrate how Ant overrides this logging, refer to the following output:

```
dir:
2005-09-09 23:17:34,211 : INFO : Target "dir" started.
     [echo] 2005-09-09 23:17:34,221 : INFO : Task "echo" started.
     [echo] Creating the working directories
2005-09-09 23:17:34,241 : INFO : Task "echo" finished.
```

Notice how the message from the <echo> task is displayed as normal and is not filtered through Log4j and converted into your pattern. A better way of putting it is that Ant didn't allow the Log4j message through.

Logging to Different Destinations

Now that you know how to log to different media, you can send different levels of messages to different destinations. In the example shown in Listing 11-9, all messages of level INFO and higher are logged to a log file, and those of ERROR and higher are logged to a web page.

Listing 11-9. *Sending Logging Messages to Two Destinations*

```
# Send all INFO messages and higher to a file and
# all ERROR messages and higher to the console
log4j.rootLogger=INFO, AntINFO, AntERROR
```

```
# Use a pattern file for the INFO messages
log4j.appender.AntINFO=org.apache.log4j.FileAppender
log4j.appender.AntINFO.File=C:/TEMP/antBook/logs/ant.pattern.log
log4j.appender.AntINFO.layout=org.apache.log4j.PatternLayout
log4j.appender.AntINFO.layout.ConversionPattern=%d{ISO8601} : %r : %p : %m %n

# Use an HTML file for ERROR messages
log4j.appender.AntERROR=org.apache.log4j.FileAppender
log4j.appender.AntERROR.File=C:/apache/htdocs/logs/ant.log.html
log4j.appender.AntERROR.layout=org.apache.log4j.HTMLLayout
log4j.appender.AntERROR.layout.Title=Apress Error Log
log4j.appender.AntERROR.Threshold=ERROR
```

This time you include the time from the start of the first logging event (the start of the build) with the %r pattern. This means you can analyze build times if you want and if it's important to you. Figure 11-2 shows an example of this time setting. You also send serious problems to a web page on your Apache server, where you can check on the progress of automated builds.

You can use a huge number of variations with Log4j, such as using the Windows system log and Unix syslog, though such exhaustive treatment is beyond the scope of this chapter.

Logging Project Components

So far you have seen how to log messages, no matter where they originated, to one or more destinations. However, you can log messages from different locations to different files. For example, you may want to monitor the project start and finish times in one file but want to see messages from a particular class in another. This means you could see what was occurring in each component. To replicate this, you must assign a component's Log4j logger to an appender. The configuration is then the same as before.

To assign a logger to an appender, use the following convention:

```
log4j.logger.CATEGORY_NAME=[LOGGING_LEVEL],APPENDER_NAME
```

The CATEGORY_NAME is usually the fully qualified classname of the component you want to log. You've already seen a bit of this in the "Using HTML Log Files" section, but here's a brief list of the options:

- When the project starts and ends, CATEGORY_NAME is org.apache.tools.ant.Project.
- When a target starts and ends, CATEGORY_NAME is org.apache.tools.ant.Target.
- When a task starts and ends, CATEGORY_NAME is org.apache.tools.ant.UnknownElement.
- When a logging message originates from within a task, CATEGORY_NAME is the fully qualified classname of the task's implementing class.
- CATEGORY_NAME can also be a generalized package name. For example, a CATEGORY_NAME of org.apache.tools.ant will log message from the project logger and the target logger. org.apache.tools.ant.taskdefs will log all messages from within tasks.

Messages that indicate the start of a project component are always logged at INFO level. However, messages that indicate the end of a project component are logged at INFO if the project component finished successfully or ERROR if not. This means that task and target failures are logged at ERROR.

Listing 11-10 shows a log4j.properties file that sets a master log file that will log everything and a log file that logs only messages from the project, from the target, and from inside tasks. In other words, it ignores all task start and end events and replicates the usual Ant console output.

Listing 11-10. *A log4j.properties File That Logs Context-Specific Messages*

```
# Use individual loggers for different components
log4j.rootLogger=INFO, AntLogger

# Log to a file
log4j.appender.AntLogger=org.apache.log4j.FileAppender
log4j.appender.AntLogger.File=C:/TEMP/antBook/logs/ant.log

# Use the simple layout
log4j.appender.AntLogger.layout=org.apache.log4j.SimpleLayout

# Set a logger for project components
log4j.logger.org.apache.tools.ant.Project=INFO,AntComponentLogger
log4j.logger.org.apache.tools.ant.Target=INFO,AntComponentLogger
log4j.logger.org.apache.tools.ant.taskdefs=INFO,AntComponentLogger

log4j.appender.AntComponentLogger=org.apache.log4j.FileAppender
log4j.appender.AntComponentLogger.File=C:/TEMP/antBook/logs/ant.pattern.log
log4j.appender.AntComponentLogger.layout=org.apache.log4j.PatternLayout
log4j.appender.AntComponentLogger.layout.ConversionPattern=%p: %m: %d{ISO8601} %n
log4j.appender.AntComponentLogger.Threshold=INFO
```

You saw an example of the AntLogger logger's output in Listing 11-4. You can therefore compare it to the output of the AntComponentLogger logger, as shown in Listing 11-11. This is pretty similar to Ant's normal output.

Listing 11-11. *A Log That Captures Messages Only from the Project, from Targets, and from Inside Tasks*

```
INFO: Build started.: 00:26:59,770
INFO: Target "dir" started.: 00:27:03,195
WARN: Creating the working directories: 00:27:03,215
INFO: Created dir: C:\AntBook\ch11\build\stand-alone: 00:27:03,245
INFO: Created dir: C:\AntBook\ch11\build\web\WEB-INF\classes: 00:27:03,265
INFO: Target "dir" finished.: 00:27:03,265
INFO: Build finished.: 00:27:03,325
```

The one slight drawback of this approach is that you repeat the logging activity if you set the same levels of logging for the two log files. In the previous example, all messages at INFO and higher, including those from the project, from targets, and from inside tasks, are logged to the ant.log file. The logging messages from the project, from targets, and from inside tasks are also logged to the ant.pattern.log file, which means your server will be working hard to log double the amount of log messages.

Note The root logger will log messages from all other loggers, regardless of its level of logging. For example, if you set AntLogger to ERROR and AntComponentLogger to INFO, AntLogger will still log all the INFO messages logged by AntComponentLogger.

Writing Your Own Listener

A custom build listener must implement the org.apache.tools.ant.BuildListener interface. This interface defines the following seven methods, each corresponding to a build event:

- void buildStarted(BuildEvent event)
- void buildFinished(BuildEvent event)
- void targetStarted(BuildEvent event)
- void targetFinished(BuildEvent event)
- void taskStarted(BuildEvent event)
- void taskFinished(BuildEvent event)
- void messageLogged(BuildEvent event)

Each of these takes an org.apache.tools.ant.BuildEvent object as a parameter, which represents the build event that has taken place. This object provides information about the calling project component (project, target, or task), any exception associated with it, and the log priority of any message associated with it.

Note When writing a custom logger or listener, you should not write to standard out because Ant swallows these calls and then displays them using its own display mechanism. This can lead to potential infinite loops because Ant could feasibly pass the message back to the listener or logger, and so on. You should use the logger's output stream instead of standard out.

Listing 11-12 shows a simple implementation of a custom listener.

Listing 11-12. *The* `BuildEventListener` *Class Receives Notification of Build Events*

```
package org.mwrm.ant.listeners;

import org.apache.tools.ant.Project;
import org.apache.tools.ant.BuildListener;
import org.apache.tools.ant.BuildEvent;

public class BuildEventListener implements BuildListener {

    public void buildStarted (BuildEvent start) {
        start.getProject().log("buildStarted() called.", Project.MSG_ERR);
    }

    public void buildFinished (BuildEvent finish) {
        finish.getProject().log("buildFinished() called.", Project.MSG_ERR);
    }

    public void targetStarted (BuildEvent start) {
        start.getProject().log("Target [" + start.getTarget().getName()
                               + "] started.", Project.MSG_ERR);
    }

    public void targetFinished (BuildEvent finish) {
        finish.getProject().log("Target [" + finish.getTarget().getName()
                                + "] finished.", Project.MSG_ERR);
    }

    public void taskStarted (BuildEvent start) {
        start.getProject().log("Task [" + start.getTask().getTaskName()
                               + "] started.", Project.MSG_ERR);
    }

    public void taskFinished (BuildEvent finish) {
        finish.getProject().log("Task [" + finish.getTask().getTaskName()
                                + "] finished.", Project.MSG_ERR);
    }

    public void messageLogged (BuildEvent event) {
        // empty
    }
}
```

Here you simply print to the log when an event happens. You can't use the log in `messageLogged()` because any logger assigned to this project takes responsibility for logging messages from this event. However, you can perform other tasks, such as writing the messages to a file, in `messageLogged()`. To obtain the message, call `event.getMessage()`. Only the `messageLogged()` method has access to the message.

If you compile this class, you can assign it as a listener as follows:

```
> ant -listener org.mwrm.ant.listeners.BuildEventListener
```

Now each event will be enclosed in statements from your custom listener.

Writing Your Own Logger

Custom loggers have to implement the `org.apache.tools.ant.BuildLogger` interface, which extends `org.apache.tools.ant.BuildListener`. This means you have to implement the seven methods from the previous section, though you also have to implement the following:

- `void setEmacsMode(boolean emacsMode)`
- `void setErrorPrintStream(java.io.PrintStream err)`
- `void setMessageOutputLevel(int level)`
- `void setOutputPrintStream(java.io.PrintStream output)`

The final three of these are the most important, because they govern Ant's output for the current build. The two `setXXXPrintStream()` methods define where the output will end up, and you use them to gain access to standard `out` or another output stream if you want. If you do not set an output stream, Ant swallows its output, and users will not see anything. You can use the `setMessageOutputLevel()` method to define the whole logger's message threshold. Therefore, you can set the logger to disregard debugging messages, even if the user specifies `-d` at the command line, and so on.

This example ignores the `-d` option and Ant's default logging level (information) and logs messages only at the warning level or higher. To do so, leave the `setMessageOutputLevel()` method empty, and use a class member variable to set the logger's logging level. Listing 11-13 shows the logger's class.

Listing 11-13. *The `BuildEventLogger` Class Receives Notification of Build Events*

```
package org.mwrm.ant.loggers;

import java.io.PrintStream;

import org.apache.tools.ant.Project;
import org.apache.tools.ant.BuildLogger;
import org.apache.tools.ant.BuildEvent;

public class BuildEventLogger implements BuildLogger {

    // The PrintStream to write nonerror messages to
    protected PrintStream out;

    // The PrintStream to write error messages to
    protected PrintStream err;
```

```
    // Sets whether to tailor output for emacs, etc
    protected boolean emacsMode = false;

    // We'll set this logger to log only warnings and above
    protected int msgOutputLevel = Project.MSG_WARN;

    // We've seen these in the listener example
    public void buildStarted (BuildEvent start) {
        // empty
    }

    public void buildFinished (BuildEvent finish) {
        // empty
    }

    public void targetStarted (BuildEvent start) {
        // empty
    }

    public void targetFinished (BuildEvent finish) {
        // empty
    }

    public void taskStarted (BuildEvent start) {
        // empty
    }

    public void taskFinished (BuildEvent finish) {
        // empty
    }

    // When a message is sent to this logger,
    // Ant calls this method
    public void messageLogged (BuildEvent event) {
        // We need to determine how important this message is
        int priority = event.getPriority();

        // If it's as important as our log level, we display it
        if (priority <= msgOutputLevel) {
            out.println(event.getMessage());
        }
    }

    // Ant will pass the output stream to this logger
    public void setOutputPrintStream(PrintStream output) {
        this.out = new PrintStream(output, true);
    }
```

```
    // Ant will pass the error stream to this logger
    public void setErrorPrintStream(PrintStream err) {
        this.err = new PrintStream(err, true);
    }

    // Sets the display mode
    public void setEmacsMode(boolean emacsMode) {
        this.emacsMode = emacsMode;
    }

    public void setMessageOutputLevel(int level) {
        // We will leave this empty to use the default level,
        // which we set above
    }

}
```

The messageLogged() method is the key to loggers and listeners. Whenever a log() call is made, whether it is in a task, a project, a listener, or a logger, Ant will call this logger's messageLogged() method, so you must deal with log messages here. If you do not print them to the output stream, the user will not see them. Ant treats log() calls from within this logger in the same way. To see how this works, make the following changes:

```
    public void buildStarted (BuildEvent start) {
        start.getProject().log("Message from buildStarted().", Project.MSG_ERR);
    }
    ...
    public void messageLogged (BuildEvent event) {
        // We need to determine how important this message is
        int priority = event.getPriority();

        // If it's as important as our log level, we display it
        if (priority <= msgOutputLevel) {
            out.println("messageLogged: " + event.getMessage());
        }
    }
```

If you run a build, you should see the following:

```
> ant -logger org.mwrm.ant.loggers.BuildEventLogger -d
```

```
messageLogged: Message from buildStarted().
```

The log() call in buildStarted() is passed to messageLogged() where you build the new string. The message will not appear anywhere else. Notice also that Ant will not display the normal ream of debugging messages even though you used the -d option.

Using the Ant-Contrib Performance Listener

The Ant-Contrib project that you learned about in the previous chapter provides a listener with which you can monitor your build's performance. To use it, simply specify it at the command line, assuming the Ant-Contrib files are in your classpath:

```
> ant -listener net.sf.antcontrib.perf.AntPerformanceListener compile-stand-alone
```

```
Buildfile: build.xml

...results omitted...

BUILD SUCCESSFUL
Total time: 39 seconds

Statistics:
-------------- Target Results ---------------------
Example Application Build.dir: 0.080 sec
Example Application Build.compile-stand-alone: 35.331 sec

-------------- Task Results -----------------------
Example Application Build..property: 0.000 sec
Example Application Build.compile-stand-alone.echo: 0.010 sec
Example Application Build..fileset: 0.020 sec
Example Application Build.dir.mkdir: 0.030 sec
Example Application Build..patternset: 0.050 sec
Example Application Build..patternset: 0.051 sec
Example Application Build..taskdef: 0.060 sec
Example Application Build..patternset: 0.070 sec
Example Application Build..path: 0.211 sec
Example Application Build..property: 0.220 sec
Example Application Build..path: 1.001 sec
Example Application Build..patternset: 1.041 sec
Example Application Build.compile-stand-alone.javac: 1.162 sec
Example Application Build.compile-stand-alone.javac: 34.149 sec

-------------- Totals ----------------------------
Start time: Sun, 18 Sep 2005 10:27:33.349
Stop time: Sun, 18 Sep 2005 10:28:13.046
Total time: 39.697 sec
```

From these results, you can see which tasks and targets take the longest and work on them should they be problematic. Unsurprisingly, the previous results show that the <javac> tasks and the compile-stand-alone target take by far the longest, while the <mkdir> tasks and the dir target are quick.

Using Mappers

Mappers are Ant's way of converting a batch of file paths into another batch of file paths. This is a useful extension of several tasks that allow them to operate on groups of files rather than a single file at a time. Examples of tasks that use mappers are <copy>, <pathconvert>, and <uptodate>, which you have already seen. These tasks take a file set of source files and produce a file set of target files that have been converted by the mapper. In the case of <uptodate>, the file set of target files is used in the comparison. <uptodate> is actually a bit of an exception to the mapper rules, but I'll get to that in the "Using Glob Mappers" section.

You specify mappers with either a <mapper type="mapper_type"> declaration or a <mappermapper_type> element. This chapter will use the second method. To demonstrate mappers, I'll show the <pathconvert> task because it uses mappers to form the result of its conversion.

Using Identity Mappers

Identity mappers map a set of file paths to another, identical set of file paths. You specify an identity mapper with an <identitymapper> element as follows:

```
<pathconvert property="converted">
  <path>
    <fileset dir="${src.shared.java}" includes="**/*.java"/>
  </path>
  <identitymapper/>
</pathconvert>
<echo>${converted}</echo>
```

Here's the result:

```
    [echo] C:\AntBook\ch11\src\shared\java\org\mwrm\Constants.java;C:\AntBook\
ch11\src\shared\java\org\mwrm\PropertiesLoader.java;C:\AntBook\ch11\src\shared\
java\org\mwrm\SelectData.java
```

This set of files is identical to the original set as defined by the pattern in the <fileset> element.

Using Flatten Mappers

Flatten mappers take a set of file paths and strip away everything but the actual filename. You specify a file mapper with a <flattenmapper> element as follows:

```
<pathconvert property="converted">
  <path>
    <fileset dir="${src.shared.java}" includes="**/*.java"/>
  </path>
  <flattenmapper/>
</pathconvert>
<echo>${converted}</echo>
```

Here's the result:

```
[echo] Constants.java;PropertiesLoader.java;SelectData.java
```

This time the mapper has taken away any directory paths from the file set.

Using Merge Mappers

Merge mappers take a set of file paths and map it to a constant filename. This means every file in the source set will map to the same filename. You specify a merge mapper with a `<mergemapper>` element as follows:

```
<pathconvert property="converted">
  <path>
    <fileset dir="${src.shared.java}" includes="**/*.java"/>
  </path>
  <mergemapper to="${appName.jar}"/>
</pathconvert>
<echo>${converted}</echo>
```

Here's the result:

```
[echo] dist/antBook.jar;dist/antBook.jar;dist/antBook.jar
```

In this case, the merge mapper has mapped each source file to the target filename.

Using Glob Mappers

Glob mappers are more complicated than the other mappers you've seen so far. To start with, you specify a pattern that will match a set of files, using up to one * wildcard character. This wildcard represents a string that will be substituted in the target set of file paths. You then specify a target pattern that includes a * wildcard. Ant will replace the * wildcard in the target pattern with the string represented by the * wildcard in the source files.

For example, apply the pattern `C:/*/ch11` to `C:/AntBook/ch11`. In this case, the * wildcard will represent `AntBook` in any replacement pattern. Now specify a target pattern of `C:/TEMP/*/logs`. This will evaluate to `C:/TEMP/AntBook/logs` because the * wildcard in the target is replaced by the string matched in the source pattern.

You specify a glob mapper with a `<globmapper>` element. Here you'll replace `.java` with `.class`, where it appears at the end of a file path:

```
<pathconvert property="converted">
  <path>
    <fileset dir="${src.shared.java}" includes="**/*.java"/>
  </path>
  <globmapper from="*.java" to="*.class"/>
```

```
</pathconvert>
<echo>${converted}</echo>
```

Here's the result:

```
    [echo] C:\AntBook\ch11\src\shared\java\org\mwrm\Constants.class;
C:\AntBook\ch11\src\shared\java\org\mwrm\PropertiesLoader.class;
C:\AntBook\ch11\src\shared\java\org\mwrm\SelectData.class
```

In this case, everything before the string ".java" has been selected by the * wildcard. When you then place a * wildcard before the string ".class", Ant places the file paths from the source selection into the target file paths. One thing omitted from this example is the <globmapper> element's handledirsep attribute, which causes Ant to ignore the difference between / and \. You'll use it in the next example.

■ Note This last operation is that the <javac> task selects the names of its output files. By using a mapper behind the scenes, it can quickly and efficiently create a list of target files.

The next example shows a situation where you want to add directories to the middle of the file paths:

```
<pathconvert property="converted">
  <path>
    <fileset dir="${test.src}" includes="**/*.java"/>
  </path>
  <globmapper from="${basedir}/${test.src}/*.java"
              to="${basedir}/${test.build}/*.class"
              handledirsep="true"/>
</pathconvert>
<echo>${converted}</echo>
```

Here's the result:

```
    [echo] C:\AntBook\ch11/build/test/org\mwrm\WebTest.class
```

Let's step through this example. Set the file set, which happens to be a single file:

```
C:\AntBook\ch11\test\org\mwrm\WebTest.java
```

The * wildcard matches the org\mwrm\WebTest section of this, so Ant saves this for when it needs to create target file paths. To build the target file path, Ant adds the project's base directory (C:\AntBook\ch11) onto the value of the test.build property (build/test), followed by the saved value of * (org\mwrm\WebTest) and .java. The resultant file path is what you see in the previous result listing.

This is your chance to examine the <uptodate> task again, because it gives different results when using a glob mapper. Here's an example from Chapter 8:

```
<uptodate>
  <srcfiles dir="${test.src}" includes="**/*.java"/>
  <globmapper from="*.java" to="${basedir}/${test.build}/*.class"/>
</uptodate>
```

This glob mapper performs the same operation as the one from the previous example but uses a different from pattern. This is because the <srcfiles> element maintains the source files as a relative path and will treat the target files as such unless you specify an absolute path.

Using Regexp Mappers

A *regexp* mapper works on similar principles to the glob mapper but uses regular expressions to map files. You specify the regular expression in the from attribute of the <regexpmapper> element, and you can then refer to it in the to attribute. If you want to match the results of the entire regular expression, you use the \0 back reference, as shown here:

```
<pathconvert property="converted">
  <path>
    <fileset dir="${test.src}" includes="**/*.java"/>
  </path>
  <regexpmapper from="^(.*)\.java$$" to="\0"/>
</pathconvert>
<echo>${converted}</echo>
```

Here's the result:

```
[echo] C:\AntBook\ch11\test\org\mwrm\plants\PlantWebTest.java
```

If you want to refer to just part of the expression, you can use subexpressions, such as the previous (.*) expression. You can then refer to them with \1, \2, \3, and so on, where \1 refers to the first subexpression, \2 refers to the second subexpression, and so on. Let's change the example a little bit:

```
<pathconvert property="converted">
  <path>
    <fileset dir="${test.src}" includes="**/*.java"/>
  </path>
  <regexpmapper from="^(.*)\.java$$" to="\1.class"/>
</pathconvert>
<echo>${converted}</echo>
```

This time the result is as follows:

```
[echo] C:\AntBook\ch11\test\org\mwrm\plants\PlantWebTest.class
```

You've matched everything up to the `.java` extension and then referred to it with `\1` and added a `.class` extension to it.

Using Chained Mappers

The final type of mapper is a *chained* mapper, which you can use to contain two or more of the mappers described. In this case, the chained mapper applies the first mapper and then applies the next mapper to the results of this operation, and so on, until it has used all the mappers it contains. This all means the order in which you specify the nested mappers matters.

You specify a chained mapper with the `<chainedmapper>` element. Let's combine two of the previous examples with a chained mapper:

```
<pathconvert property="converted">
  <path>
    <fileset dir="${src.shared.java}" includes="**/*.java"/>
  </path>
  <chainedmapper>
    <flattenmapper/>
    <globmapper from="*.java" to="*.class"/>
  </chainedmapper>
</pathconvert>
<echo>${converted}</echo>
```

Here's the result:

```
[echo] Constants.class;PropertiesLoader.class;SelectData.class
```

Here you can see the chained mapper has applied the flatten mapper like before and has removed the path information from each filename. The chained mapper has then taken these results and applied a glob mapper to map `*.java` files to `*.class` files.

Summary

In this chapter, you saw how to set up and use logging in Ant. Ant comes with some default logging mechanisms that are useful for attended builds because they display output to the console, though one can e-mail the results to ensure you see what is happening. If you want more flexible options, then you have to turn to Log4j or write a custom logger or listener. You saw the interfaces and methods involved in this and worked through some examples.

You also looked at mappers and how they can extend the functionality of those Ant tasks that work with files. Of the mappers you looked at, the glob mapper is the most complicated, but, as is the case with most things, it is the most powerful. You will find that you use this type of mapper more than any other.

CHAPTER 12

Using the Ant API

You are coming to the end of the book and have seen what Ant can do. You have built your application in many different ways; packaged it in zip and tar files; and distributed it via e-mail, FTP, and hot deployments. These functions are all part of Ant's normal setup and show its remarkable capabilities. However, one of Ant's most valuable features is its open nature, which allows you to add extensions and new features.

The previous two chapters showed ways to do just that. Custom tasks can build on existing tasks in a number of ways. First, you can add functions to an existing task, just as you did when you extended the `<javadoc>` task to add checks for up-to-date files. Second, if Ant does not provide a task for a certain action you want to perform, then you can write one yourself. For example, you wrote a task that displays usage information based on the build file that contains the task. Third-party tasks fall into this category and are useful resources. The previous chapter looked at other components that extend Ant.

The common theme here is that you are using the Ant API to extend Ant. You can take this further by removing the need for a build file and running an Ant build programmatically. This is what Ant does anyway; it just needs a build file for configuration. In this chapter, I'll show how to build command-line classes with a `main()` method. These classes will use the Ant API to simplify tasks that can be tedious to implement.

Designing a Class to Use the Ant API

The Ant API contains a lot of useful functionality that your Java programs could quite easily harness. This functionality has been used and abused by many Ant users and maintainers, so you can be confident of its ability to perform its work robustly and efficiently. Another feature of the Ant API is that it has been used and tested on many platforms, so you can be sure the functionality imported from the API will be as portable as Ant.

When you want to use the Ant API, you'll probably be using a specific task to perform the work. After all, it is the tasks that do the real work in a normal Ant build, so you'll have to use them in your stand-alone class. The first stage in the process is selecting the Ant task you want to replicate in a programmatic build. Once you have chosen the task, you have then to look at its element from the build file.

A task's element is important because it gives you insight into the member attributes of the underlying class. While you have access to the Ant source code, you shouldn't need to dig around in it because all the attributes map easily to a `setXXX()` method in the class. This is how you built a custom class in Chapter 10. You should check which of these attributes are required and which are optional and then tailor your checks on the command-line arguments as appropriate. You should also decide which of the attributes you are supporting and which of them you will let users set on the command line.

A great way to start, therefore, is to choose the task you want to use and then write the usage check. Once you have this in place, you can move on to working with the task. Quite often you will find that the usage check is the largest part of your class because the Ant task's class encapsulates so much of the work.

Working with the Task Life Cycle

When using the Ant API, you approximate a task's life cycle in your code. The first step is to instantiate a new instance of the task class by calling its constructor, which is how a task starts life in a project. In most cases, you can call the `execute()` method once you've set some member variables with `setXXX()` methods, omitting the `init()` method. However, some tasks have an `init()` method that you must call before using that task in an application. If you are unsure, add a call to `init()` just in case or check the Javadocs for the task you are using.

Choosing a Task

In this chapter, I'll show how to write a class that deploys WAR files to a running Tomcat server and undeploys web applications. This example will use the third-party `<deploy>` and `<undeploy>` tasks that come with Tomcat as an example to show that using the Ant API is the same whether you are using core tasks or third-party ones.

Listing 12-1 shows how you used these tasks in your example build, which is how you will use these tasks in a stand-alone class.

Listing 12-1. *The <deploy> and <undeploy> Tasks You Will Use*

```
<deploy url="${manager.url}"
        username="${manager.user}"
        password="${manager.password}"
        path="/${appName}"
        war="file:${appName.war}"
        update="true"/>

<undeploy url="${manager.url}"
          username="${manager.user}"
          password="${manager.password}"
          path="/${appName}"/>
```

Let's decide which of these attributes you need to use. In the case of `<deploy>`, the filename is the only piece of information a user has to specify. You can set default values for everything else, as shown in Table 12-1.

Table 12-1. *The Default Values for the Command-Line Deploy Task*

Attribute	Default
`password`	Blank
`path`	Built from the name of the WAR file
`update`	`true`
`url`	`localhost:8080/manager`
`username`	Blank

Actually, you won't even let the user decide the value of the `update` attribute, so you won't offer it at the command line. This decision gives you one required command-line option (the filename) and four optional command-line options (`password`, `path`, `url`, and `username`).

The `<undeploy>` task requires only the `path` attribute. The other three attributes will be optional command-line options. For this example, you'll ignore any WAR filename that the user supplies if they run the undeploy version.

The final consideration is how to let the deployer class know which action, deploy or undeploy, the user wants to perform. You already have a required command-line option for each function, so you'll add the action setting alongside these options. This means the user must specify a filename and an instruction to deploy when deploying, and a path and an instruction to undeploy when undeploying.

With all this in mind, Listing 12-2 shows the beginnings of the deployer class. The attributes set at the top of the class definition are the defaults you will supply if the user does not.

Listing 12-2. *The Default Options of the Deployer Class*

```
package org.mwrm.ant.api;

import java.io.File;

import org.apache.tools.ant.Project;
import org.apache.tools.ant.BuildException;

import org.apache.catalina.ant.DeployTask;
import org.apache.catalina.ant.UndeployTask;

public class Deployer {

    // The default URL for the manager application
    private static String managerUrl = "localhost:8080/manager";
```

```
    // The path
    // We'll build the default path below
    private static String path = "";

    // The username
    private static String username = "";

    // The password
    private static String password = "";

    // The filename of the WAR
    private static String filename;

    // The user's desired action
    private static String action = "";

    public static void main(String[] args) {
        ...
    }
}
```

Writing a Usage Check

You've now chosen which attributes to support, so you can write a usage check. Here's the error message that the user will see if they get something wrong:

```
Usage information:
Deployer action [options]
Action:
-a, -action <deploy filename.war [-path <path>] | undeploy -path <path>>
Options:
-url <url>
-u, -username <username>
-p, -password <password>
```

You'll implement two methods that display usage information. The first takes no arguments and prints the previous message, and the second takes a string argument and will display that string as well as the previous message. Listing 12-3 shows these overloaded methods.

Listing 12-3. *The Overloaded usage() Method*

```
    // Display usage information
    private static void usage() {
        System.out.println("Usage information:");
        System.out.println("Deployer action [options]");
        System.out.println("Action:");
        String actionMsg = "-a, -action <deploy filename.war [-path <path>] "
```

```
            + "| undeploy -path <path>>";
        System.out.println(actionMsg);
        System.out.println("Options:");
        System.out.println("-url <url>");
        System.out.println("-u, -username <username>");
        System.out.println("-p, -password <password>");

        System.exit(-1);
    }

    // Display a custom message, then usage information
    private static void usage(String message) {
        System.out.println(message);
        usage();
    }
```

Before you call either of these methods, you need to check the command-line arguments provided by the user. To do so, you'll use a series of `if...else if` statements. If you recognize an argument switch, you must follow it immediately with the value in which you are interested. Therefore, you set the appropriate variable and increase the count to indicate you've processed the next argument as well.

You will set a flag called `action` to keep track of the action the user wants to perform. You'll use this later to instantiate the correct type of task. Listing 12-4 shows the `main()` method.

Listing 12-4. *The `main()` Method Begins by Checking the Arguments*

```
    public static void main(String[] args) {

        try {
            // We'll go through the command-line arguments
            for (int i = 0; i < args.length; i++) {
                String arg = args[i];

                // Check to see whether the user has specified an action
                if (arg.equals("-a") || arg.equals("-action")) {
                    // If it's "undeploy", we'll remember that
                    if (args[i+1].equals("undeploy")) {
                        action = "undeploy";
                        i++;
                    // If it's "deploy", we'll remember that
                    } else if (args[i+1].equals("deploy")) {
                        action = "deploy";
                        i++;
                    // If it's not "undeploy" or "deploy", it's incorrect
                    } else {
                        usage();
                    }
```

```
        // Check for the path
        } else if (arg.equals("-path")) {
            path = args[i+1];
            i++;
        // Check for the URL
        } else if (arg.equals("-url")) {
            managerUrl = args[i+1];
            i++;
        // Check for the username
        } else if (arg.equals("-u") || arg.equals("-username")) {
            username = args[i+1];
            i++;
        // Check for the password
        } else if (arg.equals("-p") || arg.equals("-password")) {
            password = args[i+1];
            i++;
        // If the user has specified any other argument, it's incorrect
        } else if (arg.startsWith("-")) {
            String msg = "Unknown argument: " + arg;
            usage(msg);
        // If there's no prefix, it's our WAR file
        // We check for it only if we're deploying
        } else if (action.equals("deploy")) {
            // This must be our WAR file
            filename = arg;

            // Create a file object
            File warFile = new File(filename);

            // Check whether this file actually exists
            if (warFile.exists() == false) {
                String msg = "File " + arg + " does not exist.";
                System.out.println(msg);
                System.exit(-1);
            }

            // We should set the path if the user did not
            // The path must begin with a '/'
            if (path.equals("")) {
                // If the WAR file is not in the current directory,
                // there will be a slash
                int begin = filename.lastIndexOf("/");
                // We'll add a slash or not depending on where the WAR is
                String slash = "";
```

```
                    // If there is no slash, the index will be -1
                    if (begin == -1) {
                        // Therefore, we need to take the whole filename
                        begin = 0;
                        // and add a slash to the path
                        slash = "/";
                    }
                    // Build the path by removing the .war extension
                    path = slash +
                         filename.substring(begin,
                                          filename.lastIndexOf(".war"));
                }
            }
        }
    // If a command-line option is not followed by another argument
    // the previous checks will throw a ArrayIndexOutOfBoundsException
    } catch (ArrayIndexOutOfBoundsException aioobe) {
        usage();
    }

    // A final set of checks
    if (action.equals("undeploy") && path.equals("")) {
        usage("You must specify a path when undeploying.");
    } else if (action.equals("deploy") && filename == null) {
        usage("You must specify a file when deploying.");
    } else if (action.equals("")) {
        usage("You must specify an action with -a or -action.");
    }
    ...
} // end of main()
```

When the deploy task tries to deploy or undeploy a web application, it uses a web application path that must begin with a /. When you build the default filename, you use the existing / if the WAR file is in a directory; however, if the file is in the current directory, you add a / to the filename. The final step is to strip away the `.war` extension.

Using a Task

The final part of your command-line deployer creates the relevant task, sets its attributes, and uses it to deploy or undeploy the WAR file. The most important point to remember when using the Ant API is that all tasks need a project. As you saw in Chapters 10 and 11, a task's project object is integral to its ability to function. During its life cycle, an Ant task will try to use some of its project's methods, the most common of which is `log()`. If you don't assign your task to a project object and run it, you'll get a `NullPointerException` when the task calls `getProject().log()` to log its progress.

For now you will do the bare minimum and add only your task to a project and no more. (You'll add loggers and listeners in the "Adding Loggers and Listeners" section.) This is sufficient to use the task, and you can trap any exceptions with a `try...catch` block. Once you're at this stage, the only exceptions will be thrown in the event of problems connecting to the server or problems on the server. Displaying the results of a `Exception.getMessage()` call will be enough to inform the user of the problem with the server. Listing 12-5 shows the final section of your class.

Listing 12-5. *Instantiating and Using the Task*

```
public static void main(String[] args) {

    ...

    // Our tasks will need a project
    Project project = new Project();

    // Check what we want to do
    if (action.equals("deploy")) {
        // The deployer that will deploy the WAR file
        DeployTask deployer = new DeployTask();

        // The task needs the project's logger
        deployer.setProject(project);

        // Call init() as good practice
        deployer.init();

        // The next few methods set the attributes of the task
        deployer.setUsername(username);
        deployer.setPassword(password);
        deployer.setUrl("http://" + managerUrl);
        deployer.setWar("file:" + filename);
        deployer.setPath(path);
        deployer.setUpdate(true);

        try {
            // Run the task
            deployer.execute();
            System.out.println("Deployed " + filename + " to " + path + ".");
        } catch (BuildException be) {
            System.out.println(be.getMessage());
        }
    } else {
        // The undeployer that will undeploy the application
        UndeployTask undeployer = new UndeployTask();
```

```
            // The task needs the project's logger
            undeployer.setProject(project);

            // Call init() as good practice
            undeployer.init();

            // The next few methods set the attributes of the task
            undeployer.setUsername(username);
            undeployer.setPassword(password);
            undeployer.setUrl("http://" + managerUrl);
            undeployer.setPath(path);

            try {
                // Run the task
                undeployer.execute();
                System.out.println("Undeployed " + path + ".");
            } catch (BuildException be) {
                System.out.println(be.getMessage());
            }
        }
    } // end of main()
```

Here you check for the action the user wants to perform and instantiate a DeployTask object if they are deploying or an UndeployTask if they are undeploying. From then on, you treat both classes in a similar way by adding them to the project, calling their init() methods, and setting the attributes you have collected from the command line or that you provided as defaults. Notice how the number of setXXX() calls corresponds to the number of attributes you used in the original build file.

The final step in each case is to run the execute() method of the task. This mimics the final stage in the task's life cycle, as described in Chapter 10. The task will run, and if there's a problem, it will throw a BuildException. You catch this and display its message to the user. If the task was successful, you tell the user because the task has no way to display output. You'll use a logger and listener to display both success and failure in the next section.

By calling the execute() method of each task, you are using that task's functionality without knowing any of the implementation details. This is fine because the whole point of using the Ant API is to harness the complex functionality of its tasks and use this functionality in a simple, easy way. You have no need to write the code to connect to the server, send the password, and deploy or undeploy the application. The beauty of the Ant API is that it does most of the work for you. You simply supply the information and validate it to provide a user-friendly experience to your users. Relying on an Ant BuildException in every case does not leave you in control of the output from the command-line task.

Adding Loggers and Listeners

If you want to incorporate a logger or listener into your application, it's a fairly simple matter. At the moment, your deployment class uses System.out.println() calls to display information to the user. This has the advantage that it is simple, but it doesn't save the messages or give you any real flexibility with the output format. The arguments against System.out.println are the same in this chapter as they were in the previous chapter. As you saw then, Ant provides loggers and listeners that can solve the problem.

Another disadvantage of `System.out.println()` when using the Ant API is that messages from a task are swallowed by the project object because there is no logger to display them, which forced you to confirm the success of a task in the previous section. Here are some examples of task messages that are lost when you don't use a logger or a listener:

```
[javadoc] Generating Javadoc
[zip] Building zip: C:\JavaStuff\AntBook\ch12\dist\antBook-docs.zip
[exec] A secret key is required to make a signature.
[copy] Copying 1 file to C:\JavaStuff\AntBook\ch12\build\docs
```

You're using the Ant API in this chapter, so you can quite easily incorporate Ant's logging system into the application. Actually, Ant's logging system may be a useful addition to any class, never mind if it uses an Ant task. Once you see how easy it is to use Ant's loggers, and the Log4j logger in particular, you will see that most of the work is again done by the Ant API.

Ant has two layers of logging: project-level logging and task-level logging. The one that Ant uses depends on where the `log()` method is called, and that's the same whether you use Ant as a build tool or you use the Ant API. This distinction matters only if the loggers and listeners you use discriminate on the grounds of message originator. For example, the default logger prints the name of the task that logged a message before it displays that message but does not prefix a project-level log message. If you use the Log4j listener, you can configure it to differentiate between the two layers if you want.

Let's start by giving the user two more options for logging. You'll use the default logger (`org.apache.tools.ant.DefaultLogger`) to display messages to `System.out`, unless the user specifies a log file with the `-l`/`-logfile` option. Not everyone will want to use the Log4j listener (`org.apache.tools.ant.listener.Log4jListener`) for logging because it requires external libraries, so you'll turn it off by default. If the user wants to use it, they can specify the `-log4j` option. Here's the revised usage information:

```
Usage information:
Deployer action [options]
Action:
-a, -action <deploy filename.war [-path <path>] | undeploy -path <path>>
Options:
-url <url>
-u, -username <username>
-p, -password <password>
-l, -logfile <logfile>
-log4j
```

You'll need some more classes for your new implementation. Listing 12-6 shows the required classes.

Listing 12-6. *The New Imports for the Logging Implementation*

```
import java.io.PrintStream;
import java.io.FileOutputStream;
import java.io.FileNotFoundException;

import org.apache.tools.ant.DefaultLogger;

import org.apache.tools.ant.listener.Log4jListener;
```

I won't show the new `usage()` method because there's nothing exciting there. However, you'll need three new variables to deal with the new information. Listing 12-7 shows these member variables.

Listing 12-7. *The New Variables to Deal with Logging*

```
    // Sets whether the default logger will use the log file or System.out
    private static boolean useLogFile = false;

    // The log file for the default logger
    private static String logFile;

    // Sets whether we use the Log4j listener
    private static boolean useLog4j = false;
```

These new command-line options and variables require some more checks in the `main()` method. You need only two because by setting a log filename, the user has signaled they would like to use a file and not `System.out`. Listing 12-8 shows these new checks.

Listing 12-8. *Determining a User's Views on Logging*

```
            ...
            // Check whether the user wants to use a log file
            } else if (arg.equals("-l") || arg.equals("-logfile")) {
                logFile = args[i+1];
                useLogFile = true;
                i++;
                // Check whether the user wants to use Log4j
            } else if (arg.equals("-log4j")) {
                useLog4j = true;
                // If the user has specified any other argument, it's incorrect
            } else if (arg.startsWith("-")) { ...
```

Each logger and listener belongs to the project and not a task. I've already discussed how each task needs access to the project because that's where the loggers are, so you need to add your logger and listener to the project. Listing 12-9 shows the process of adding a logger and a listener. The `getLogger()` method prepares an instance of the default logger, as shown in Listing 12-10.

Listing 12-9. *Adding a Logger and a Listener*

```
// Our tasks will need a project
Project project = new Project();

// Add the logger
// getLogger() is described next
project.addBuildListener(getLogger());

// Does the user want to use Log4j?
if (useLog4j == true) {
    // The listener is configured with the log4j.properties file
    Log4jListener listener = new Log4jListener();
    project.addBuildListener(listener);
}
```

The `Project.addBuildListener()` adds a logger or a listener to a project and makes it available to any tasks associated with the project. You add the listener only if the user wanted to, though this shows how easy it is to use Log4j through the Ant API. You've just imported the `Log4jListener` class and added it to a `Project` object. From now on, you can log by calling `project.log()`.

Listing 12-10. *The `getLogger()` Method Returns an Instance of the Default Logger*

```
// Return the default logger for the project
private static DefaultLogger getLogger() {
    // The logger for this class
    DefaultLogger logger = new DefaultLogger();

    // The default logger needs somewhere to write to
    PrintStream out = null;

    // Does the user want to write to a file?
    if (useLogFile == true) {
        try {
            // We'll log to the file the user specified
            // "true" here means "append to the file"
            out = new PrintStream(new FileOutputStream(logFile, true));
        } catch (FileNotFoundException fnfe) {
            // We can't use the log just yet
            System.out.println(fnfe.getMessage());
            // We'll fall back to System.out
            System.out.println("Using the console.");
            out = System.out;
        }
    } else {
```

```
            // The default is to print to System.out
            out = System.out;
        }

        // Set the output streams for the logger
        logger.setOutputPrintStream(out);
        logger.setErrorPrintStream(out);

        // Set the message threshold for this logger
        logger.setMessageOutputLevel(Project.MSG_INFO);

        return logger;
    }
```

The most important lines are those that set the output stream, error stream, and message threshold. The rest of the method just prepares the logger before you return it and add it to the project. The final changes to your class are some slight modifications to the end of the `main()` method, as shown in Listing 12-11.

Listing 12-11. *Enabling Logging in the `main()` Method*

```
        // Our tasks will need a project
        Project project = new Project();

        // Add the logger
        project.addBuildListener(getLogger());

        // Does the user want to use Log4j?
        if (useLog4j == true) {
            // The listener is configured with the log4j.properties file
            Log4jListener listener = new Log4jListener();
            project.addBuildListener(listener);
        }

        // The deployer that will deploy the WAR file
        DeployTask deployer = new DeployTask();
        // The undeployer that will undeploy the application
        UndeployTask undeployer = new UndeployTask();

        // Check what we want to do
        if (action.equals("deploy")) {
            // The task needs the project's logger
            deployer.setProject(project);

            // The name of this task
            deployer.setTaskName("deployer");
```

```
            // The next few methods set the attributes of the task
            deployer.setUsername(username);
            deployer.setPassword(password);
            deployer.setUrl("http://" + managerUrl);
            deployer.setWar("file:" + filename);
            deployer.setPath(path);
            deployer.setUpdate(true);

            try {
                // Run the task
                deployer.execute();
            } catch (BuildException be) {
                // The three ways to log with a task
                //System.out.println(be.getMessage());
                //project.log(be.getMessage());
                if (!(be.getMessage().indexOf("FAIL") > -1)) {
                    deployer.log(be.getMessage());
                }
            }
        } else {
            // The task needs the project's logger
            undeployer.setProject(project);

            // The name of this task
            undeployer.setTaskName("undeployer");

            // The next few methods set the attributes of the task
            undeployer.setUsername(username);
            undeployer.setPassword(password);
            undeployer.setUrl("http://" + managerUrl);
            undeployer.setPath(path);

            try {
                // Run the task
                undeployer.execute();
            } catch (BuildException be) {
                // The three ways to log with a task
                //System.out.println(be.getMessage());
                //project.log(be.getMessage());
                if (!(be.getMessage().indexOf("FAIL") > -1)) {
                    undeployer.log(be.getMessage());
                }
            }
        }
    } // end of main()
```

The most interesting pieces here are the `if` blocks around the `log()` calls. As is common with most tasks, in some circumstances the deployment tasks display an error message before throwing a `BuildException`. For example, if the undeploy task tries to undeploy an application that does not exist, it will display the following before throwing a `BuildException`:

```
FAIL - No context exists for path /antBook
```

In this case, you don't want to display the same message again with a `log()` call in the `catch` block. If you did, users would think there's more wrong than there actually is.

You'll run into other occasions where these tasks do not display a message along with a `BuildException`, such as when Tomcat is unavailable. In these cases, you'll want to display the message to the user. The difference between the two situations is that in the first example there was a problem with the command that you sent and Tomcat has rejected it, and in the second example there was a problem before you could execute the command. A similar thing could happen if you did not provide proper user credentials to Tomcat.

These two tasks signal the distinction between an error with the command and a problem executing the command by prefixing the former with `FAIL`. You've taken advantage of this and filtered out your logging so that the task's internal logging messages are the only ones displayed in the event of a failure on the server.

Once you have compiled this class, you need to run it with the following command or add the JAR files to your classpath:

```
> java -classpath dist/antBook-api.jar;%ANT_HOME%/lib/catalina-ant.jar;
%ANT_HOME%/lib/ant.jar org.mwrm.ant.api.Deployer ...options...
```

Let's assume these are in the classpath and run a simpler version to test the default logger:

```
> java Deployer -a deploy dist/antBook.war -u antBook -p antB00k
```

```
 [deployer] OK - Deployed application at context path /antBook
```

Now that you are using a logger, the task can display its own messages, and you don't have to worry about it. The next step is to check that the task logs to a log file. Run the following:

```
> java Deployer -a undeploy -path /antBook -u antBook -p antB00k -l deploy.log
```

The file `deploy.log` will contain the results of this run:

```
[undeployer] OK - Undeployed application at context path /antBook
```

You are sure that the default logger is working as planned, so it's time to test the Log4j logger. As you saw in the previous chapter, Log4j uses a configuration file called `log4j.properties`, so let's write one for your deployment example, as shown in Listing 12-12.

Listing 12-12. *The* `log4j.properties` *File for Log4j Logging*

```
# Set the root logger for Ant API logging
log4j.rootLogger=INFO, AntLogger

# Log to a pattern file
log4j.appender.AntLogger=org.apache.log4j.FileAppender
log4j.appender.AntLogger.File=C:/TEMP/antBook/logs/deploy.log

# Use a pattern layout
log4j.appender.AntLogger.layout=org.apache.log4j.PatternLayout
log4j.appender.AntLogger.layout.ConversionPattern=%d{ISO8601} - %p - %c{1}: %m %n
```

You have to make sure this file is in the classpath so the logger can read it. Also, a few more classes are required in the classpath and are shown in the following command:

```
> java -classpath .;dist/antBook-api.jar;%ANT_HOME%/lib/catalina-ant.jar;
%ANT_HOME%/lib/ant.jar;%ANT_HOME%/lib/ant-apache-log4j.jar;
C:\log4j\dist\lib\log4j.jar org.mwrm.ant.api.Deployer
```

This time you need the current directory (`.`) for the `log4j.properties` file; the deployer class (`antBook-api.jar`); the deployer and undeployer tasks (`catalina-ant.jar`); Ant API classes, such as `BuildException` and `Project` (`ant.jar`); the Log4j logger (`ant-apache-log4j.jar`); and the Log4j classes for the logger to use (`log4j.jar`). Make sure the paths to your versions of these files are correct. Again, let's assume these are all in the classpath and test the Log4j logger:

```
> java Deployer -a deploy dist/antBook.war -u antBook -p antB00k -log4j
```

If Tomcat is running and the command is successful, the default logger will log to `System.out`, and the Log4j logger will log to the `deploy.log` file specified in Listing 12-12. Here's the result:

```
2005-09-17 14:20:51,524 - INFO - DeployTask:
OK - Deployed application at context path /antBook
```

You can use the default logger and the Log4j logger to write to files at the same time with the following:

```
> java Deploy -a undeploy -path /antBook -u antBook -p antB00k -log4j
  -l deploy.txt
```

Writing a Batch Copy Class

As a final example, I'll show how to use some other parts of the Ant API. One particular feature of Ant is its ability to work with batches of files in file sets and pattern sets. You can take advantage of these components in stand-alone classes just as you can take advantage of other parts of the Ant API. For example, in a build you can use the `<copy>` task to copy batches of files that match a certain pattern. You can do the same in a stand-alone class.

I won't go into the details of command-line options as I did for the deployer class because the important concept here is how to use a file set in a stand-alone class. What you do have to consider is the required attributes of a `<fileset>` element. As described in Chapter 4, you must set either the file attribute or the dir attribute of a <fileset> element; the file attribute is shorthand for a file set that contains only one file.

With this in mind, you'll set the dir attribute of the file set. To do so, you need a file set object (org.apache.tools.ant.types.FileSet), and then you need to call the setDir() file with a File object as an argument. As with a build file, you need to build a file set with includes and excludes, which you do with the setIncludes() and setExcludes() methods:

```
public void setIncludes(String includes)
public void setExcludes(String excludes)
```

The parameter in each case is a comma-separated list of patterns to include or exclude, though you can call each method more than once to add patterns to the list of patterns held by a particular file set.

Once you have a file set, you add it to the copy task (org.apache.tools.ant.taskdefs.Copy) with the addFileset() method. The other important method is the copy task's addToDir() method, which sets the destination for the copy operation. Listing 12-13 shows the Copyer class.

Listing 12-13. *The Copyer Class Uses the Ant Copy Task*

```
package org.mwrm.ant.api;

import java.io.File;
import java.io.PrintStream;

import org.apache.tools.ant.Project;
import org.apache.tools.ant.DefaultLogger;

import org.apache.tools.ant.taskdefs.Copy;

import org.apache.tools.ant.types.FileSet;

public class Copyer {

    public static void main(String[] args) {
        // Your tasks will need a project
        Project project = new Project();

        // Add the logger
        project.addBuildListener(getLogger());

        // Instantiate the copy task
        Copy copyTask = new Copy();

        // Build the file set
        FileSet fileset = new FileSet();
        fileset.setIncludes("*.xml");
        fileset.setIncludes("*.xsl");
        fileset.setDir(new File("."));
```

```
            // Add the file set to the copy task
            copyTask.addFileset(fileset);
            // Set the destination for the files
            copyTask.setTodir(new File("copydir"));

            // The name of this task
            copyTask.setTaskName("copyer");

            // Add the copy task to the project
            copyTask.setProject(project);

            // Call init() as good practice
            copyTask.init();

            // Copy the files
            copyTask.execute();
        }

        // Return the default logger for the project
        private static DefaultLogger getLogger() {
            // The logger for this class
            DefaultLogger logger = new DefaultLogger();

            // The default logger needs somewhere to write to
            PrintStream out = System.out;

            // Set the output streams for the logger
            logger.setOutputPrintStream(out);
            logger.setErrorPrintStream(out);

            // Set the message threshold for this logger
            logger.setMessageOutputLevel(Project.MSG_INFO);

            return logger;
        }
    }
```

You set two patterns here (`*.xml` and `*.xsl`), which you want to copy to the `copydir` directory. The rest of the class is straightforward and again demonstrates how easy it is to use the Ant API in complex situations such as this. The Ant tasks do all the work of matching patterns and copying the files.

Summary

This chapter introduced the concept of using the Ant API in normal Java programs. The Ant API contains many powerful classes that do a lot of complex processing for you. You simply have to gather enough information for your chosen task to do its job. This information does not necessarily need to come from the command line, and you can use Ant classes from any kind of Java class if you need its abilities. The first example was a command-line deployment/undeployment task that worked with Tomcat's manager application. You extended this by adding loggers and listeners from the Ant API.

The chapter ended with an example of how to use file sets and the <copy> task in a stand-alone Java class. By doing so, you gained access to Ant's pattern-matching and batch-copying abilities without having to write any complicated code of your own.

Index

Numbers and Symbols

A

B

D

E

F

G

N

O

P

T

U

V

W

X

Z